Santa Cruz Island
A History of Conflict and Diversity

Surveying Santa Cruz Island, 1923-1924
Photo taken by F.F. Flournoy survey team; Pier Gherini family collection

Santa Cruz Island
A History of Conflict and Diversity

by John Gherini

The Arthur H. Clark Company
Spokane, Washington, 1997

Arthur H. Clark Company
P.O. Box 14707
Spokane, WA 99214

LIBRARY OF CONGRESS CATALOG CARD NUMBER 97-904
ISBN-0-87062-264-1

Library of Congress Cataloging-in-Publication Data

Gherini, John.
    Santa Cruz Island: a history of conflict and diversity / by John
Gherini.
        p. 272   cm.
    Includes bibliographical references and index.
    ISBN 0-87062-264-1 (alk. paper)
        1. Law—California—Santa Cruz Island—History.   2. Land titles-
-California—Santa Cruz Island—History.   3. Santa Cruz Island
(Calif.)—History.   4. Santa Cruz Island (Calif.)—Economic
conditions.   I. Title.
KFC1199.S26G47   1997   97-904
979.4'71—dc21   CIP

Table of Contents

Illustrations

8

THIS BOOK IS DEDICATED TO MY FATHER
PIER GHERINI
(1912-1989)

"I wasn't raised on the island, but I might as well have been. I spent almost all my spare time there."

Foreword

The Channel Islands have long held a special fascination for both the amateur and professional scholar. One has to look no further than Adelaide L. Doran's *Pieces of Eight Channel Islands: A Bibliographical Guide and Source Book,* published in 1980, to find ample testimony to that very fact. But of all the Channel Islands, one in particular has commanded the most attention, Santa Cruz Island.

The history of that island, its flora and fauna, archeology and geology, geography and economy—to mention only a few subject-oriented highlights that have received research consideration—have commanded the talents of numerous lay persons and scholars alike. One readily turns to Marla Daily's *California Channel Islands–1001 Questions Answered,* published in 1987, to grasp the extent of detailed information spurred by research on the Santa Cruz Island story. In more recent years, due to the endeavors of the Santa Cruz Island Foundation, a series of splendid *Occasional Papers*—seven to date—have appeared, capably edited by Marla Daily. Concurrent with these Foundation-sponsored publications, two recent books have added new dimensions to the Santa Cruz Island story. In 1993 Helen Caire, whose family was an integral part of island history, published her memoirs, *Santa Cruz Island: A History and Recollections of an Old California Rancho,* while a long neglected aspect of the island's multifaceted history was marvelously detailed in Thomas Pinney's 1994 book, *The Wine of Santa Cruz Island,* a handsome and informative work, issued in a fine-press limited edition.

12   To this select but august group of Santa Cruz Island titles, one must now include John Gherini's impressive book, *Santa Cruz Island: A History of Conflict and Diversity.* His unique contribution to Santa Cruz Islandiana is that for the first time the *legal* history of the island is detailed. To achieve this, the author, a lawyer by profession, brought his special legal skills to bear in what can only be called an impressive research undertaking. Ranging far and wide, he laboriously ferreted out all the court cases and poured over city, county, state, and national documents with extraordinary perseverance. In addition to his yeoman legal research, he had available to him a hithertofore untapped primary resource, the personal papers of his distinguished lawyer father, Pier Gherini, which greatly enhances and enriches the island's legal history. One need only review the book's bibliography to ascertain the wide scope and depth of the author's research in writing this new history of the island.

Happily for the reader, the author has simplified the legal aspects he elucidates by writing a narrative that never fails to hold one's attention. But he has done more. He has placed the island's complicated and thorny legal entanglements within the framework of chronological development, commencing with prehistoric times down to the present.

As one reads this important and valuable study, the reader will readily discover that the author's motivation no doubt was both personal and professional for his family was intimately associated with much of Santa Cruz Island history in this century. However, the author's family heritage in no way colors his bold and capsulated narrative. He eschews any appearance of partisanship or bias: the evidence, based on solid fact, speaks for itself, and eloquently so.

This book deserves to be placed along the aforementioned works as essential reading for those attracted to the never ending lure of California's Channel Islands, especially the one named Santa Cruz.

DOYCE B. NUNIS, JR.
Professor Emeritus of History
University of Southern California

Acknowledgments

Many individuals and organizations assisted me in the research and writing of this book. At the top of the list are my brother Tom who doggedly tracked down information and gave valuable comments on many of the drafts; Dr. Doyce B. Nunis, Jr., Professor Emeritus of History of the University of Southern California, whose invaluable direction kept the book on track; Marla Daily, President of the Santa Cruz Island Foundation, who provided a constant flow of information and feedback; and my secretary Catherine Conley who edited and commented on numerous drafts. Many other individuals also helped with proof reading, editing and providing general comments including my aunt Marie Ringrose, my publisher, Robert A. Clark, Dr. Dolores Pollock of Marymount Academy, Dr. John Johnson of the Santa Barbara Museum of Natural History, Mrs. Geraldine Sahyun, Trustee of Santa Barbara Archive Library, Bob Hanson, formerly of The Nature Conservancy, William Ehorn, Superintendent of Channel Islands National Park (1974-1989), Diane Elfstrom Devine of The Nature Conservancy, Dr. Thomas Pinney of Pomona College, Mack Shaver, Superintendent of Channel Islands National Park (1989-1996), acting Superintendent of Channel Islands National Park, Tim Setnicka, Geraldine Lausch, Margaret Olson who began working for my father in 1949 and is still working for me, my aunt Ilda Gherini McGinness, who along with her sister Marie, provided family photos and William B. Dewey who helped with the selection of the photographs. Dave and Debbie Welborn of The Nature Conservancy graciously provided a much needed tour of

14 that portion of the island I grew up never having visited. I am also grateful to many of those individuals who either assisted in obtaining needed information on selected topics or who related their island experiences to me. Last but not least, my wife, Mary Ann, not only made useful suggestions but also endured the mess of documents, drafts and books scattered throughout the den for well over four years.

In this day and age of the impersonal information highways, I found the personal touch and assistance of the staffs of the following organizations and institutions most helpful: Santa Barbara Museum of Natural History, Santa Barbara Historical Society, Santa Barbara Mission Archive Library, Santa Cruz Island Foundation, Channel Island National Park Archive Library, Santa Barbara Public Library, the library at the University of California at Santa Barbara, Bancroft Library at the University of California, Berkeley, the library at the University of California at San Diego, the San Francisco Pioneer Society, The California Historical Society, and the State Archive Library.

Introduction

Santa Cruz Island is the largest of eight islands located off the coast of southern California. It is about 96 square miles in size, 23.5 miles long, and from 2 to 7.5 miles wide. To put this enormity into perspective, Santa Cruz Island is four times larger than New York's Manhattan Island, whose population exceeds a million people. Santa Cruz Island's population numbers peaked with its prehistoric inhabitants, the Chumash Indians and their predecessors. They are known to have occupied the island over a period of at least seven thousand years, with maximum populations numbering in the few thousands.

Since the Indian era, Santa Cruz Island has fallen under the ownership of three countries (Spain, Mexico and the United States) and two dominant families (Caires and Stantons). Spain (1769–1821) first laid claim to the island as a result of the 1769 expedition of Portolá. Mexico (1821–1848) gained ownership as a result of its independence from Spain in 1821, and the United States took domain as a result of the Treaty of Guadalupe Hidalgo in 1848. Subsequently, 128 years of Santa Cruz Island's history was dominated by the Caire and Stanton families, 1869–1997 and 1937–1987 respectively.

In 1869, the island was purchased from its second private owner since California statehood in 1850 by ten men, one of whom was Frenchman Justinian Caire. Together they formed the Santa Cruz Island Company as equal shareholders in the largest privately owned island in the continental United States.

In 1873 the Company reincorporated and shares were redis-

16

tributed. By 1880, Justinian Caire had acquired all or substantially all of the stock in the corporation, a pivotal point for the island's future. Justinian Caire became the mastermind behind the development of Santa Cruz Island.

In 1880, eleven years after his initial investment, Justinian Caire paid his first visit to Santa Cruz Island to survey his holdings and to pursue the planning of what was to become one of the most prosperous and well-managed operations in California. For the next seventeen years under Caire's direction, a variety of agricultural and ranching endeavors suitable to the island's climate and terrain were implemented, including the development of a large winery, and the raising of sheep and cattle. Ten out-ranches of varying importance augmented the operations of the Main Ranch located in the island's Central Valley. Buildings including ranch houses, bunk houses, barns, wineries, blacksmith and saddle shops, a mess-hall and a chapel were constructed. The 60-foot schooner *Santa Cruz* was built for the Company in 1893. Under Justinian Caire's careful eye and masterful guidance, a very efficient and mostly self-contained island venture grew and thrived.

The publication of *Santa Cruz Island: A History of Conflict and Diversity* marks the centennial anniversary of Justinian Caire's death on December 10, 1897. The extensive family litigation which followed resulted in the island's division into seven parcels in 1925. Of the seven legal parcels created by court action, the western five were purchased by the Stanton family in 1937. The Stantons, in turn, created their own 50 years of Santa Cruz Island history. In 1987, the Stanton land passed to The Nature Conservancy.

The eastern two parcels of the island, however, remained in the hands of the Gherini family, descendants of Justinian Caire. In 1980, Congress created Channel Islands National Park which included the eastern two parcels of Santa Cruz Island. Funds were allocated in 1990 for partial acquisition of this land after one of Caire's great grandchildren, Pier Gherini, died in 1989. In 1992, Caire's two great granddaughters also sold their island interests.

Author John Gherini is the son of Pier Gherini and the great great grandson of Justinian Caire. Like his father and grandfather before him, he is an attorney. Unlike them, his generation is the first to relinquish island ownership to the National Park Service. He is also the first person to openly discuss what has heretofore been considered extremely private family business. For the first time, family issues, conflicts and diversities are discussed in light of their historical context. John Gherini has provided for posterity a factual analysis of the events which have shaped the history of Santa Cruz Island.

MARLA DAILY
Santa Cruz Island Foundation
1997

Aerial view from Chinese Harbor at Santa Cruz Island looking toward the east. Anacapa Island is east of Santa Cruz Island, and the Santa Monica Mountains on the mainland are in the background. *Photo Wm. B. Dewey.*

Aerial view of the east end of Santa Cruz Island looking west. Santa Rosa and San Miguel Islands are in the background. *Photo by Bob Wheeler; Pier Gherini family collection.*

Prologue

Santa Cruz Island, the largest of the California Channel Islands, is located 22 miles off the coast of Santa Barbara and Ventura counties. It is situated almost east and west in the Santa Barbara Channel and is about 23.5 miles long; near its center Santa Cruz Island is approximately 7.5 miles wide. It has a circumference of 70 miles and a land area of 96 square miles or 60,741.74 acres. It is the most rugged and topographically diverse of the Northern Channel Islands group that includes from east to west: Anacapa, Santa Cruz, Santa Rosa and San Miguel. Santa Cruz's geological, topographical and ecological make-up gives some hint of its diversity and its uniqueness.[1]

An east-west fault called the Santa Cruz Island Fault divides the island into two distinct geologic parts.[2] Opinions differ concerning how the division occurred. One theory suggests that cataclysmic earth movement divided the island as early as the Pliocene Period (12 million years ago). Others theorize that two land masses merged. They suggest the southern half of Santa Cruz Island land mass moved from a location near San Diego to its present location against the northern volcanic land part of the island between middle and late Miocene time (24 to 20 million years ago).[3] About 17,000 to 18,000 years ago when ocean levels were at their lowest ebb (-300 feet), it is also speculated that the

---

[1]Referee's Report in Partition of Santa Cruz Island, pp. 4-5; Junak et al., *A Flora of Santa Cruz Island*, pp. 2-3. Santa Cruz Island is in the Second Supervisorial District of Santa Barbara County.

[2]Weaver, *Geology of the Northern Channel Islands*, p. 9. See also Bremner, *Geology of Santa Cruz Island*, pp. 29-30. The island is of igneous origin.

[3]Wenner and Johnson, "Land Vertebrates on the California Channel Island," p. 506.

20 Northern Channel Islands group comprised a single super island called "Santarosae" which would have been 78 miles long and 20 miles wide.[4]

The topography of Santa Cruz Island exhibits rugged, barren, volcanic mountains with the highest peak, Picacho del Diablo, rising to 2,470 feet; sweeping marine terraces on both the east and west ends; rolling hills colored with the annual grasses; chalky white diatomaceous outcroppings; jagged canyons; soft, serene valleys; expansive white beaches; majestic Caribbean-

[4]Orr, *Prehistory of Santa Rosa Island,* pp. 18, 27. Vedder and Howell, "Topographic Evolution of the Southern California Borderland," pp. 21-22.

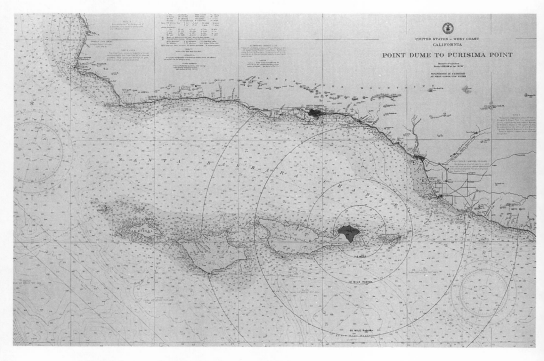

Nautical map showing Santa Cruz Island in relation to mainland. The Gherini Ranch, now owned by the National Park Service, is highlighted on the east end of the island. *Pier Gherini family collection.*

like sea coves; meandering creeks; thick closed-cone pine forests in the head waters of Cañada Cebada; massive cylindrical eucalyptus trees in the Central Valley and along the majority of the coastline, steep volcanic cliffs rising vertically from the water.[5] Over one hundred remarkable sea caves dot the volcanic walls of the island.[6]

Santa Cruz Island contains an interesting array of flora and fauna which enjoy its Mediterranean climate and its cool prevailing northwest winds. Today, vascular plants, including 480 natives, have been identified on the island.[7] Numerous stands of the rare island oak *(Quercus tomentella),* the island ceanothus *(Ceanothus arboreus)* and Santa Cruz ironwood *(Lynonothamnus floribundus asplenifolius)* are among the rare island plants.[8] Unique native fauna also abound. For example, the island Scrub Jay *(Aphelocoma coerulescens insularis),* a subspecies of its mainland counterpart, is a deeper blue color and larger.[9] The small Island Fox *(Urocyon littoralis),* an endangered species, is the diminutive relative of the mainland Gray Fox *(Urocyon cinereoargenteus).*[10]

The island has a special magnetism that lures people to it like the Sirens of Greek mythology. Margaret Holden Eaton personally experienced the lure of the island, spending almost 30 years (1908-1937) living at various locations on Santa Cruz Island with her sea captain husband, Ira. Her diary, kept while on the island, was published in 1980: *Diary of a Sea Captain's Wife: Tales of Santa Cruz Island.* When Eaton was making her first trip to the island in 1908, Captain Colís Vasquez, a veteran mariner of the Santa Barbara Channel, remarked to her: "Yes, once you go over to those islands, you will never be satisfied away from them. . ."[11]

---

[5]Bremner, *Geology of Santa Cruz Island,* pp. 6-12.

[6]Bunnell, *Sea Caves,* p. 1.

[7]Junak et al, *A Flora of Santa Cruz Island,* p. 46. See also *Checklist of Vascular Plants.* And Schuyler, "Control of Feral Sheep," p. 443.

[8]Junak et al, *A Flora of Santa Cruz Island,* pp. 193, 246, 250. See also, Pavlick, *Oaks of California,* pp. 34, 158.

[9]Atwood, "Breeding Biology of the Santa Cruz Island Scrub Jay," pp. 675-688.

[10]Laughrin, "Populations and Status of the Island Fox," pp. 745-756.

[11]Eaton, *Diary of a Sea Captain's Wife,* p. 39.

22   The human occupation of Santa Cruz Island did not take place until about 10,000 years ago.[12] The island then was probably much the way it is today, except it probably had more water. The attraction of the island, however, routinely led people into conflict, wrapping it in a shroud like its morning fog. The modern history of the island would witness the passion to own it, to protect it, to use it and to fight over it.

[12]Glassow, "Recent Developments," p. 79-99. There is well documented evidence of occupation on Santa Cruz Island around 7100 B.P., but recent radiocarbon-dated testing may push the sequence back another 1500 to 3000 years. Arnold,"Craft Specialization," p. 6.

Chapter 1

Early Island Conflict

NATIVE AMERICAN CULTURE ON SANTA CRUZ ISLAND

Any history of Santa Cruz Island would not be complete without a glimpse of the sophisticated Native American traditions that were present there as far back as 8000 B.C. At the time of first European contact (1769) by the Spanish, the Chumash lived along the central California coastline from San Luis Obispo to Malibu. The name Chumash as it is now used refers to all of the Indians who spoke related languages in south central California. There were at least six Chumash languages spoken in this group, including the island language which was not mutually intelligible with languages spoken on the mainland. The two-hundred mile coastline area consisted of 7,000 square miles. Santa Barbara, which the Chumash called *Syuxtun,* was about mid-point. The Island Chumash inhabited the four Northern Channel Islands: Anacapa *('Anyapakh),* Santa Cruz *(Limuw),* Santa Rosa *(Wimal),* and San Miguel *(Tuqan).*[1]

Santa Barbara Channel Islands cultural history is said to be broken down into three distinct prehistoric periods. The Early Period (10,000 B.C. to 1400 B.C.) included the Oak Grove People and most of the Hunting People described by anthropologists.[2] The

---

[1]Arnold, "Craft Specialization," p. 6. For a concise summary of the Chumash people see Grant, "Chumash: Introduction," and "Eastern Coastal Chumash," 8: 505-519, and Kroeber, *Handbook,* pp. 550-568.

[2]Rogers, *Prehistoric Man,* pp. 342-355, and King, *Evolution,* p. 29.

24 Middle Period extended from 1400 B.C. to ca. 1150 A.D., and the Late Period encompassed the period from 1150 A.D. to the beginning of the Historic Period in 1785 A.D. In the Early Period, the Indians had already occupied the Channel Islands with permanent settlements. During the Middle Period, the Chumash populations shifted to predominantly coastal locations and developed a sophisticated marine resource procurement technology. They built a multi-planked canoe called *tomol* which was unique to North America and which represented a technological achievement that impressed the early Spanish explorers.[3] In the Late Period, an intensive cross channel economic exchange system took place as the Chumash shell bead money became the medium of exchange for the Central Coast. Numerous resources and products, including beads, fish, and sea mammal meat from the islands, and baskets, seeds, acorns, animal skins, and deer bone tools from the mainland, moved in the Chumash commerce system.[4] Over the years, the Chumash established a divergent culture with their own music, art, astronomy and mythology.[5]

The mainstay of the Chumash diet was fish, and to a lesser extent shellfish. The island Indians ate sardines, octopi, red fish and other varieties of rock fish.[6] From the *tomol* the Chumash harpooned swordfish *(Xiphias gladius)* which figured prominently both as a source of food and as a religious symbol.[7] Supplementing their fish diet, the Chumash ate vegetable foods, prickly pears, roots resembling sweet potatoes, seeds, acorns and bulbs from wild onions.[8]

---

[3]Kroeber, *Handbook,* pp. 558-559. See also Miller, *Chumash,* pp. 77-81 and Engelhardt, *Santa Barbara Mission,* p. 439.

[4]King, "Chumash Inter-village Economic Exchange," pp. 288-318. See also, Arnold, "Craft Specialization," pp. xiii-xvi, 4-12, and Orr, *Archaeology of Mescalitan Island,* p. 9. Orr uses earlier terminology to describe the evolution of the Chumash culture.

[5]Kroeber, *Handbook,* Chapter 37. See also Miller, *Chumash,* pp. 14-15, and Engelhardt, *Santa Barbara Mission,* pp. 436-443. Engelhardt published the observations of Fr. Pedro Font, O.F.M., who was chaplain and chronicler on one of the Spanish expeditions in 1775-1776. In his *Diary,* Fr. Font provided insight into the life of various Indian tribes along the Santa Barbara Coast.

[6]Johnson, "An Ethnohistoric Study," unpublished thesis, p. 45.

[7]Davenport, "The Chumash and the Swordfish," pp. 257-272.

[8]Johnson, "An Ethnohistoric Study," p. 44.

During the beginning of the California Mission Period (1772-1834) approximately 2,000-3,000 Chumash inhabited the three largest islands of the Northern Channel Islands group (Santa Cruz, Santa Rosa and San Miguel). Twenty-one village sites have been identified on these islands. The site density on these islands was quite high in comparison with the adjacent mainland. This density suggests a high degree of mobility from site to site.[9] On Santa Cruz Island at the time of the first Spanish contact, the Indians occupied at least ten villages, sometimes called *rancherias*. *Swaxil* (Scorpion Ranch) was the largest village with approximately 180-210 Indians. *Kaxas* or *Cajats* (Prisoners' Harbor) was the second largest village and was inhabited by approximately 95-160 Chumash.[10] The island Indians lived in other village sites such as *Liyam* or *Liam* (Coches Prietos), *Lu'upsh* (overlooking Chinese Harbor) and *Nanawani* (Smugglers' Ranch).[11]

In their villages, the Chumash built dome shaped sweathouses and hemispherical homes where they slept on the ground.[12] A village had its own workshop areas, cemetery, and refuse location. They used baskets for collection of roots, bulbs and other foodstuffs, and for storing food and other items. Interestingly, the Chumash used asphaltum not only to caulk their boats but also to line the insides of some of their baskets in order to make them watertight.[13]

On the islands, many stone implements have been found. The Chumash made metates, manos, mortars, bowls and pestles. The Indians used the mortars and pestles to crush vegetables, seeds, and sometimes meat. The mortars were the round bowls and the pestles were the grinding implements. They used other stones such as chert, flint and obsidian to make sharp instruments like knives, scrapers, drills and projectiles.[14]

---

[9]Glassow, *The Status of Archaeological Research*, pp. 14-17.

[10]Johnson, "An Ethnohistoric Study," p. 96, figure 2. Johnson notes that the names of villages are confusing because consistent spellings were not used in the mission records (pp. 87-93).

[11]Kitsepawit, *The Eye of the Flute*.

[12]Kroeber, *Handbook*, p. 558. See also Miller, *Chumash*, pp. 101-102.

[13]Kroeber, *Handbook*, pp. 560-562. See also Miller, *Chumash*, pp. 49-52.

[14]Ibid., pp. 562-564. See also Miller, *Chumash*, p. 61.

The Ventura Chumash called the Santa Cruz Island Indians *michumash* which was derived from the word Chumash. According to linguists, *michumash* may mean something like "the place of those who make shell bead money." In a real sense, Santa Cruz Island was the mint because of its key role in the manufacture of the disk-shaped *Olivella* shell bead money which the Spanish called "abalorios." The remains of the shells can still be seen at various locations on the island where bead money was made.[15] The mainlanders exchanged food and products for the beads which they used as money.[16] A single village located near the eastern portion of the Island near Chinese Harbor produced the highest density of microblade drills found anywhere in North America. Another impressive chert quarry is located above Coches Point. These sites demonstrate that the Santa Cruz Island Chumash mined extensively for chert from which they made the chert microblade drills. These drills were the essential tool used to make the shell bead money. Both quarry sites are located near the contact zone between the Monterey Formation and the Santa Cruz Island Volcanics. At the entrance to Scorpion Bay on the side of the hill, more evidence of chert flakes can be seen. These findings suggest widespread manufacturing of the important microblade tools on the eastern portion of the island.[17]

The Chumash used bead money not only as a medium of exchange but also as offerings at shrines and as payment for the dancers at festival time.[18] For about 900 years before the early Mission Period (1772-1834), island Chumash played an important role in the regional economic system of the Chumash. The introduction of Venetian glass beads by the Spanish (1769-1821) undermined the shell bead currency and contributed to the collapse of the island Chumash economy.[19]

---

[15]The Chumash name for 'bead money' is *anchum* which is the origin of the name *Chumash.*

[16]Johnson, "An Ethnohistoric Study," p. 78.

[17]Johnson interview by author on an island field trip, August 2-5, 1994.

[18]Arnold, "Craft Specialization," pp. 1-6, and Miller, *Chumash,* pp. 111-112.

[19]Johnson interview.

CONFLICT AMONG THE ISLAND CHUMASH

According to Chumash folklore, the Indians fought the first battle for Santa Cruz Island. *Sulwasunaitset,* whose name was said to mean "very respected bear," governed Santa Cruz Island.[20] *Sulwasunaitset* was the first big chief (called *paqwot*) of the island. When his wife was pregnant, the island priest said the child would become ruler of the four Channel Islands. His wife gave birth to a baby girl, proclaimed to be princess of the northern four islands. Civil war broke out on the island because many opposed a female ruler. According to legend, "the seat of this war was at the *ranchería* of *Liyam* [Coches Prietos]. War began upon the meeting of opposing parties; their weapons were rocks and clubs. One fierce battle was fought on the east end of the island, where only Santa Cruz Island people fought each other."[21] The high priest (*'alaqlapsh*) told both sides: "What are you doing? What do you want? Remember that this island has cost our people a great deal of suffering and trouble."[22]

The civil war on the island ended when the leaders heeded the high priest's advice. Neither side won. The woman whose name was *Luhui* (meaning native) was named princess of the island. The high priest's sage advice, however, would be ignored by subsequent owners who many years later took their battles into the courtrooms.

Folklore aside, anthropologist Phil C. Orr states that there is a mistaken impression that the Chumash Channel Indians were peaceful. The fact that the Indians normally did not resist Spanish and Mexican settlers, except for the 1824 uprising, gave rise to this false notion.[23] Combat among tribes and within villages has

---

[20]Anthropologist John P. Harrington (1884-1961) recorded and published Fernando Librado Kitsepawit's recollections in 1977. These recollections provided the basis for the folklore.

[21]Kitsepawit, *The Eye of the Flute,* p. 15.

[22]Ibid.

[23]According to Grant, the Chumash in 1824 made a desperate attempt to escape their Mexican masters. The neophyte Indians revolted at Santa Barbara, Santa Ynez and La Purisima. Grant, "Chumash: Introduction," p. 507.

28 been proven by archeological finds.[24] In many of the ancient cemeteries where numerous skeletons have been found, the remains reveal arrowheads embedded in bones as well as skulls and bones crushed before burial.[25]

Chumash villages seem to have been organized into loose federations under a *paqwot* (big chief). Two such island federations may have existed: one consisting of the villages on Santa Cruz Island and the other uniting villages on Santa Rosa and San Miguel Island.[26] According to Travis Hudson, authority on Chumash culture, internal conflicts or "civil wars" demonstrated the independent nature of each Chumash province.[27]

DISPUTES OVER ISLAND ARTIFACTS

After the last of the Chumash left the Channel Islands, a different type of discord arose over the materials they left behind. In the 1870s, because of widespread interest in their culture, there were numerous excavations to unearth their buried artifacts. Many of the relics unearthed from Santa Cruz Island were placed not only in major American museums but also in such places as Moscow, Madrid, in Paris at the Musée de L'Homme, and London at the British Museum.[28]

Paul Schumacher, while working under the auspices of the Smithsonian Institution in 1875, spent a month on Santa Cruz Island. His work was the first documented archaeological investigation of the island. During his study of the island, he collected over 323 artifacts which are now housed in the Smithsonian Institution. The specific location of his excavations remains unknown.[29]

A French expedition headed by Alphonse Pinart also undertook some of the early island excavations. Leon de Cessac, a scientist who worked for Alphonse Pinart, became Schumacher's main

---

[24]Orr, "Archaeology of Mescalitan Island," pp. 51-52.

[25]Glasgow, *Archaeology on the Northern Channel Islands*, p. 10.

[26]Hudson and Underhay, *Crystals in the Sky*, p. 28.

[27]Ibid., pp. 28-29.

[28]Reichlen and Heizer, "The Scientific Expedition," pp. 9-23.

[29]Glasgow, *The Status of Archaeological Research*, pp. 50-52.

competitor. Cessac, who spent four months on Santa Cruz Island in 1877 making botanical, zoological and archaeological collections, was the first observer to recognize the voluminous debris of the microblade industry on the island.[30] The rivalry between Cessac and Schumacher was intense. Schumacher unsuccessfully attempted to assert political pressure and threatened Cessac with legal action.[31] Despite these obstacles and even though the funding for his work ceased, the defiant Cessac continued his digging for about a year on the Channel Islands and in the Santa Barbara area. He amassed a significant collection of over 4,000 artifacts that were taken to Paris and are now housed in the Musée de l'Homme.[32]

Other prominent archaeologists conducted limited surveys on Santa Cruz Island during the early twentieth century. Like their predecessors, disputes seemed to follow them. Despite a jealous protest by John P. Harrington, Leonard Outhwaite of the University of California undertook in 1918 the first large scale archaeological survey of the island. The significance of the Outhwaite survey, of which there is little published information, was that it demonstrated the high density of some of the island's archaeological sites. In the spring of 1927, David Banks Rogers of the Santa Barbara Museum of Natural History began his limited investigations of the island. He was assisted in the summer of 1927 by two experienced graduate students at the University of California, Ronald Olson and Willard Hill. This cooperative effort soon soured because of a financial misunderstanding between Olson and the Museum of Natural History. After they parted company and became adversaries, Rogers, working under the auspices of the Santa Barbara Museum of Natural History and Olson, of the University of California, conducted separate expeditions.[33] In 1928, Olson returned to the island for more excavations. Some of the artifacts collected by Olson are now housed at the P.A. Hearst

---

[30]Arnold, "Craft Specialization," p. 12.
[31]Reichlen and Heizer, "The Scientific Expedition of Leon de Cessac," pp. 9-23.
[32]Ibid.
[33]Glassow, *The Status of Archaeological Research,* pp. 54-62.

30   Museum of Anthropology (formerly known as the Lowie Museum) at the University of California, Berkeley.[34]

Over time, excavations of Native American artifacts and human remains fell into disfavor because of the violation of their rights. Today, state law prohibits any person from removing Native American artifacts or human remains from a Native American grave or cairn. Any person who violates this law is guilty of a felony which is punishable by imprisonment.[35] Today, Santa Cruz Island remains a significant cultural resource since some 80 percent of its land area remains unsurveyed.[36]

CONFUSION OVER THE ISLAND'S NAME

Juan Rodríguez Cabrillo, a Spaniard, discovered the Channel Islands and its inhabitants on October 15, 1542.[37] This discovery occurred as his ships, *San Salvador* and *Victoria,* flying the Spanish flag, plied the California coast.[38] On this voyage of discovery, Cabrillo encountered many native canoes *(tomols)* in the Santa Barbara Channel. Using canoes the Indians visited the ships and pointed out their villages to the foreigners. Although details of the voyage are scarce, Juan León, a notary of the royal *audiencia* of Mexico, prepared a summary report in 1543 that stated: "The Indians of the island are very poor. They are fishermen and eat

---

[34]Ibid., pp. 61-62.

[35]California Public Resources Code Section 5097.99. It is also a misdemeanor for "every person, not the owner thereof, who willfully injures, disfigures, defaces, or destroys any object or thing of archeological or historical interest or value, whether situated on private lands or within any public park or place." California Penal Code section 622½. See also Public Resources Code Section 5097.991 requiring the return and repatriation of Native American remains and grave artifacts.

[36]Arnold, "Craft Specialization," p. 6; Glassow, *The Status of Archaeological Research,*" p. 50. Glassow estimates that only slightly less than 80 days of field work have actually been undertaken over 100 years.

[37]There is a historical debate as to whether Cabrillo was Spanish or Portuguese. For centuries the prevailing opinion was that Cabrillo was Portuguese. Historian Harry Kelsey, in his book entitled *Cabrillo,* points out that current American historical thought is that Cabrillo was Spanish. The name Cabrillo is not a Portuguese name, and neither Cabrillo nor his family nor relatives mentioned the fact that Cabrillo was Portuguese. Kelsey, *Cabrillo,* pp. 4-21.

[38]Wagner, *Cabrillo,* pp. 35, 65.

nothing but fish. They do not sleep. All their business and occupation is to fish. In each house they say there are fifty souls, who live very filthily, going naked."[39]

The nomenclature of the Channel Islands ostensibly began with Cabrillo (1542) and ended with Vancouver (1793). The designation of names was confusing and often inconsistent. For instance, some historians believe that Cabrillo first used the phrase "Las Islas de San Lucas" to identify the two islands of Santa Rosa and San Miguel that he thought were one island.[40] Others believe he named the entire chain of Channel Islands (from San Clemente and San Nicolas to San Miguel) "Las Islas de San Lucas" because he took possession of the islands on the feast of St. Luke.[41] Cabrillo later used Indian names to identify the islands and called Santa Cruz Island *Limu,* but the name *Limu* may have become confused in the summary of his voyage with the native name for Santa Catalina Island, *Pimu.* He also called Santa Cruz Island "San Lucas" and Santa Rosa Island "Nicalque."[42]

Historical dispute surrounded the death and burial of Cabrillo. It was long thought that Cabrillo, due to a compound fracture of his upper arm (some say he broke his leg), died during the expedition on January 3, 1543, and was buried on one of the Channel Islands, most likely San Miguel. Some have written that he was

---

[39]Ibid., p. 56. Wagner wrote that Juan Paéz de Castro, the royal chronicler of Charles V, authored the summary report. Historian Kelsey provides new information that the author of the summary report was Juan León. Kelsey, *Cabrillo,* pp. 113-122. The description of the Indian living conditions may be a reference to the Indians living on Santa Catalina Island because of the confusion of island names and Indian villages reported by Cabrillo. The Indians on Santa Catalina were Gabrielino, that is, Shoshonean and not Chumash. Kroeber, *Handbook,* p. 554.

[40]Ibid., p. 50. See also, Tompkins, "Channel Islands Nomenclature," p. 9.

[41]Kelsey, *Cabrillo,* p. 147. According to Kelsey, Cabrillo used the names "San Salvador," "Capitana," "Juan Rodríguez," and "La Posesión" to identify the island of Santa Catalina. Ibid., pp. 144-150. To add to the confusion by using multiple names, Cabrillo apparently named San Miguel Island "La Posesión" which is one of the names used to describe Santa Catalina. The Shoshonean name for Santa Catalina was *Pimu* which could easily be confused with *Limu.* Kroeber, *Handbook,* p. 554.

[42]Ibid., p. 157. See also, Kroeber, *Handbook,* pp. 552-556.

32 injured on Santa Rosa Island and buried on Santa Cruz.[43] Another suggests that he was buried on Santa Rosa.[44] More recent research theorizes that he died and was buried on the island of Santa Catalina.[45] After Cabrillo's death, Bartolomé Ferrer, the chief pilot who had earlier been appointed by Cabrillo, assumed command.[46] Shortly thereafter on January 19, 1543, he named Santa Cruz Island, "San Sebastían."[47]

Explorations of the California coast continued. Sebastían Rodríguez Cermeño in 1595 sailed along the south side of Santa Cruz Island but did not name it.[48] Sebastían Vizcaíno's expedition took place in 1602. Vizcaíno, who named the channel "Santa Barbara," added to the confusion about the names of the islands by ignoring the identifications assigned by Cabrillo and assigning his own.[49] For instance, he named Santa Cruz Island *Isla de Gente Barbudo* because it was reported that bearded men had been seen by one of his men on the island.[50] George Vancouver explored the California coast with his two ships *Chatham* and *Discovery,* and sailed around the Channel Islands in November 1793.[51] Vancouver realized the discrepancy in the nomenclature of the Channel Islands on the different Spanish charts. The names he finally used from the Spanish maps for his own charts became the names still used today, thus ending the confusion.[52]

The island's present name reportedly originated at the time of

---

[43]Kinsell, "The Santa Barbara Islands," p. 619, and Ellison, "History of Santa Cruz," p. 271. Kinsell speculates that a more plausible legend was that Cabrillo was buried in one of the beautiful caves on Santa Cruz Island which was supposed to be his favorite island. Ellison asserts he may have been buried at Prisoners' Harbor.

[44]Kroeber, *Handbook,* p. 555. Kroeber points out that the names of the islands and identification of Indian villages on the islands was confused and contradictory. He feels that since nothing certain can be made of the native names that the location of Cabrillo's burial is a problem for the geographer rather than the ethnologist.

[45]Kelsey, *Cabrillo,* p. 159.

[46]Bartolome Ferrer is sometimes referred to as "Ferrelo." See Wagner, *Cabrillo,* pp. 27, 55.

[47]Ibid., p. 28.

[48]Wagner, *The Cartography,"* 2:414. See also Wagner, "The Voyage to California," p. 8.

[49]Wagner, *Cabrillo,* p. 30.

[50]Wagner, *The Cartography,"* 2: 414. See also Tompkins, "Channel Islands Nomenclature," p.11.

[51]Wagner, *The Cartography,* 1:245. See also Holder, *The Channel Islands,* Chap. II.

Captain Gaspar de Portolá's expedition to Alta California in 1769. Juan Pérez commanded the *San Antonio,* one of the expedition's ships. Don Miguel Pino, the pilot, wrote an account in 1772, and Fr. Juan Vizcaíno, one of two Franciscan priests aboard the vessel, penned a diary of the voyage. Fray Francisco Palóu, a contemporary historian of the times, described the event in his *Noticias de Nueve California,* the first general history ever written of the founding of Alta California. According to Palóu, in April 1769 a party from the *San Antonio* debarked and went ashore to the Chumash village of *Kaxas* at Prisoners' Harbor.[53] After exchanging gifts with the Indians, the party returned to the ship only to learn that they had forgotten one of the missionary staffs which had a metal cross on top of it. The next day Indians paddled a *tomol* out to the ship to return the unique staff. The island was thereupon named *La Isla de la Santa Cruz:* "The Island of The Holy Cross."[54] Miguel Costansó, Portolá's chief engineer, officially recorded the name of the presentday island of Santa Cruz on the *Costansó's Carta Reducida* of 1770.[55]

CONFLICT IN THE SPANISH AND MEXICAN ERAS (1769–1848)

As a result of Portolá's 1769 expedition, Spain laid claim to all of California, including the off-shore islands. As exploration and conquest along the coast continued, conflict between Indians and the new settlers developed.[56] The Chumash Indians continued to live on the island under Spain's reign, but their numbers decreased rapidly due to diseases such as measles, tuberculosis,

---

[52]Wagner, *The Cartography,* 2:360.

[53]Johnson, "An Ethnohistoric Study," p. 37.

[54]Palou, *Historical Memoirs,* vol. 2, pp. 17-18. See also, Woodward (translator), *The Sea Diary of Fr. Juan Vizcaino,* xxxi-xxxv.

[55]Wagner, *Cartography,* 1:165 and 2: 414 . Wagner points out that there was confusion as to which of the islands was named "Santa Cruz." After the voyage returned to San Blas, the name "Santa Cruz" was assigned to the island which was westernmost of the group. Wagner notes that Storace may have misunderstood the information given to him.

[56]Fr. Font observed in 1775-1776 that the Indians would be difficult to convert ". . . because . . . they are disgusted with the Spaniards for what they did to the Indians, now taking away the fishes and other food in order to provide themselves with provisions when they passed along the channel and then stealing the Indian women and abusing them. . ." Engelhardt, *Santa Barbara Mission,* p. 441.

34

diphtheria, and syphilis and to migration to the mainland communities.[57]

In the late eighteenth century, the missionaries contemplated the establishment of a mission on Santa Cruz Island.[58] Father Estevan Tapis had been chosen to succeed Father Fermín Francisco de Lasuén as *presidente* of the missions in 1803. Although he had never visited the islands, he urged the establishment of a mission on the island near the Chumash village of *Kaxas* at Prisoners' Harbor.[59] He wrote that there was sufficient population for the establishment of a mission and that the Indians expressed a desire for one so that they did not have to leave the island.

Furthermore, Father Tapis argued that an island mission with a strong guard would provide some protection against the violent and illegal sea otter traders, known as *contrabandista*. There was significant contraband sea otter trade along the California coast and around the Channel Islands during both the Mexican and Spanish and Mexican years (1769-1848).[60] Undoubtedly, the extensive smuggling around the Channel Islands, including Santa Cruz, was the genesis of the name for Smugglers' Harbor located at the southeastern end of Santa Cruz Island. When Santa Cruz Island was surveyed by William M. Johnson in 1855 as part of the Coast Survey, he gave the cove that name.[61]

---

[57]Johnson, "An Ethnohistoric Study," p. 50. The general decrease is consistent with the general decline of the mission populations which became evident by 1780 and continued from then on. Meighan, "Indians and California Missions," pp. 188-190. See also Geiger and Meighan, *As the Padres Saw Them,* p. 8.

[58]Engelhardt, *The California Missions,* 2: 612.

[59]Johnson, "An Ethnohistoric Study," p. 63. See also Engelhardt, *The California Missions,* 2: 618-619.

[60]Ogden, *The California Sea Otter Trade,* p. 41; Engelhardt, *The California Missions,* 2: 619.

[61]Gudde, *California Place Names,* p. 314. After California became a part of the United States, the government realized the importance of having the entire west coast surveyed. The two men who were primarily responsible for the Coast Survey were George Davidson and James Alden. Johnson probably worked under their supervision. Wagner, "George Davidson," pp. 299-301. In all likelihood, Johnson also named "Chinese Harbor" after the numerous Chinese fishing vessels which frequented the Channel Islands in the nineteenth century. The Chinese fishermen introduced abalone to the local fish markets. Bookspan, *Santa Barbara By the Sea,* p. 149. The surveyors also lent their names to geographic locations. For example, Johnson's Lee is named after Johnson and Forney's Cove is named after S. Forney who surveyed the island in 1875.

The establishment of an island mission, however, was never realized. Father Tapis in 1807 admitted the matter would have to be thoroughly investigated since the island Indian population was declining rapidly. He wrote in 1807 that more than 200 Indians had died on Santa Cruz and Santa Rosa Islands during a measles epidemic the preceding year, which would have been perhaps a 15 to 20 percent loss in the number of Chumash Islanders.[62]

The last of the Chumash are reported to have left Santa Cruz Island in 1822.[63] The years 1814 through 1816 witnessed many conversions of Island Chumash Indians. Missions San Buenaventura and Santa Barbara received most of the Indians from Santa Cruz Island. Drought, severe El Niño conditions in 1815-1816, diseases, and the disruption of the Chumash mercantile exchange system combined to cause this large migration of the islanders to the mainland in the middle of the second decade of the nineteenth century.[64] There is no evidence, however, of a forced migration of the Indians from the Channel Islands.[65]

The political conflict that had developed between Spain and Mexico on September 13, 1810, eventually led to Mexican independence in 1821.[66] In May 1822, Agustín Iturbide mounted the throne as Agustín I, emperor of the newly formed Mexican empire. Some weeks later, the Mexican imperial tri-colored flag was raised in California.[67] Mexico now owned the province and its offshore islands.

During Mexican rule (1821-1848), use of Santa Cruz Island was limited but controversial. In 1829, the Mexican government urged the sentencing of criminals to California presidios instead of to Vera Cruz. This edict met with resistance and led to the only recorded use of the island as a penal colony in 1830.[68] In March of

---

[62]Engelhardt, *The California Missions,* 2: 620; Nunis, "Medicine in Hispanic California," p. 42.

[63]Timbrook, "Island Chumash Ethnobotany," p. 47.

[64]Johnson, "Cruzeño Chumash Social Geography" p. 20. See also Johnson, "An Ethnohistoric Study," p. 114.

[65]Ibid., p. 77.

[66]Hittell, *History of California,* 1: 628.

[67]Ibid., pp. 664-667.

[68]Ord, *Occurrences in Hispanic California,* p. 75-76.

36 that year, Captain Andrew Christian Holmes in command of the *Maria Ester,* and with about eighty prisoners on board, sailed to Santa Barbara after being refused entry into San Diego. Not surprisingly, the citizens of Santa Barbara did not want the prisoners either. After a month, on April 23, Captain Holmes decided that thirty-one of the worst convicts would be taken to Santa Cruz Island and left there. *Maria Ester,* with prisoners and a supply of cattle, grain, fish-hooks, tools and other supplies, set sail. At the island, the prisoners were left with their supplies. The harbor where they landed is the island's main harbor and was subsequently called "Prisoners' Harbor." Shortly thereafter, a fire destroyed everything. The prisoners purportedly built rafts and sailed from Santa Cruz Island across the channel to present day Carpinteria.[69]

[69]Bancroft, *History of California* 3: 47-48, See also Mason, *History of Santa Barbara County,* p. 256, and Hillinger, *The California Islands,* pp. 94-95. Accounts differ as to whether the prisoners survived the legendary escape from the island and trip across the channel.

Chapter 2

The Santa Cruz Island Land Grant and the Ensuing Conflict Over Title

D uring Spanish and Mexican rule in California, land grants were a method of settling the new territory. By 1769 Spain had established a colonization scheme that included the *presidio* as the focal point of development. It was hoped that the *pueblos* would eventually be established as people occupied the territory. Even though the Spanish governor could grant land, few grants were made before 1800.[1] Ownership of all California land was assumed by the Crown under the *Laws of Indies.* Enacted in 1680 during the reign of Carlos II, the *Laws of Indies* set guidelines for the ecclesiastical, military and civil administration in America.[2] The laws recognized the rights of Native Americans to use the land as they needed for homes, "tillage" and "pasturage," but it did not recognize any right of ownership.[3]

Spain encouraged the establishment of Franciscan missions to aid in colonizing Upper California.[4] The padres' objective was to

---

[1]Bancroft, *History of California,* VI: 530. Bancroft says "no such grants were made before 1800, though fifteen or twenty farms were occupied under provisional licenses." Ibid., p. 530. Contemporary historians report that there were about 20 private rancho land grants during the Spanish regime and about 500 during the Mexican period. Bean and Rawls, *California,* p. 51.

[2]Engstrand, "The Legal Heritage," 75:209.

[3]Dana and Krueger, *California Lands,* p. 35.

[4]Forbes in his 1832 book entitled *California: A History of Upper and Lower California* at p.

38 educate the Native Americans in religion and prepare them to assume citizenship. The missions then would be the nuclei of the future *pueblos*. The plan did not succeed, and secularization of the missions started in 1834 leading to the eventual decline of the mission system.[5]

Under the Mexican colonization law of 1824 and under the *Reglamento* of 1828, the number of land grants escalated. Under Mexican law, any citizen might select a tract of unoccupied land and apply to the governor for a grant. Formalities in making the grants were not always adhered to.[6] Under the Mexican regime, private ownership of land was greatly expanded.[7]

ANDRÉS CASTILLERO'S ISLAND OWNERSHIP: 1839-1857

Mexican rule in California was not without its problems. A brief look at the internal rift which plagued California sets the stage for Andrés Castillero becoming the first private owner of Santa Cruz Island.

In 1836 Alta or Upper California was in a state of siege. Early that year, President Antonio Lopez de Santa Anna converted Mexico's federal system into a despotic centralized government depriving Upper California a voice in how its affairs were run.[8] In November of that year, José Castro and Juan Bautista Alvarado, leading a group of volunteers, took possession of Monterey, the capital of Alta California. They proclaimed the province to be a

---

xxx, explained the terminology of Upper and Lower California: "The name of California was for nearly two hundred years exclusively applied to the great Peninsula which is now termed Old or Lower California, and which is arbitrarily bounded on the north by a line drawn from the top of the Gulf of California to the shore of the Pacific, considerably to the southward of the port of San Diego. After the discovery and settlement by the Spaniards of the country to the north of this peninsula, and which was also named California, as being part of the same tract of coast and inhabited by the same race of people, the distinctive appellations of Upper and Lower, or New and Old California became necessary, and have since been universally applied . . ." Alexander Forbes is not to be confused with James Alexander Forbes, a native of Scotland, who was a British Vice-Consul for California from 1843 to 1851. (p. xiv)

[5]Cowan, *Ranchos*, pp. 2-3.
[6]Bancroft, *History of California*, 6:529-532.
[7]Dana and Krueger, *California Lands*, p. 36.
[8]Tays, "Castillero," 14: 230.

free and sovereign state. Underlying causes for what is termed the Alvarado Revolt included the desire by some for the rich California lands and the hatred of *Californios* toward Mexico.[9]

Alvarado became the new governor of Alta California, and the territorial government was reorganized. Alvarado and Castro eventually moved the government to Santa Barbara.[10] Soon the leaders in Los Angeles and San Diego formulated plans to overthrow the revolutionary government. When initial attempts to negotiate a peaceful settlement proved unsuccessful, Alvarado proceeded from Santa Barbara to capture the mission at San Gabriel and to subdue Los Angeles. Nicolas Gutíerrez, appointed in early 1836 as interim governor, was deported to Lower California. One of the men who accompanied Gutíerrez was Captain Andrés Castillero. He was soon appointed secretary to the commandant general of Lower California, Don José Caballero. In this capacity, Castillero became the principal negotiator in an attempt to broker a settlement with Alvarado.[11]

In the meantime, the situation in Upper California deteriorated. There were plots and counterplots and different factions attempting to seize power from Alvarado. The central government of Mexico did not have the resources to fight a civil war in California. A peaceful resolution was important to the government, and Captain Castillero was commissioned to travel into the frontier and resolve the crisis. In June of 1837, Castillero met with Alvarado in San Buenaventura to negotiate a settlement. In this meeting, Castillero was able to persuade Alvarado to abandon the revolution and to take an oath to the new constitution. It is likely that he promised Alvarado his support to be the new governor.[12]

In July 1837, Alvarado, his officers and the citizens of Santa Barbara took the promised oath to the new constitution.[13] How-

---

[9]Ibid., p. 231.
[10]Ibid., p. 232.
[11]Ibid., p. 235.
[12]Ibid., p. 241.
[13]Ibid., p. 244.

40 ever, Castillero's peace efforts were criticized, particularly by Captain Don Santiago Arguello who did not trust Alvarado. Castillero argued for Alvarado's appointment as governor. Because Alvarado had little support, particularly from Los Angeles and San Diego, the Mexican government appointed as governor Don Carlos Carrillo who was thought to be more sympathetic to the factions in southern California.[14] The appointment of Carrillo in 1837 led to more unrest in 1838 since Alvarado would not surrender control. In the summer of 1838, Alvarado defeated the Carrillo faction. When hearing of the new clash, the government in Mexico heeded Castillero's advice and appointed Alvarado governor of the Department of California in June 1838.[15] In short, Castillero negotiated two settlements for peace in California.

For his patient work in negotiating a peaceful resolution of the Alvarado Revolt in California, Castillero was given a land grant and allowed to select one of the California Channel Islands as his reward. On July 20, 1838, the Minister of Interior, by the order of the Mexican President, addressed a communication to Governor Juan Bautista Alvarado, governor of California, regarding the selection of land by Andrés Castillero. The terms of the communication directed that Castillero, in consideration for his services to the nation, would be allowed to select one of the California Channel Islands near where he ought to reside with the troops under his command.[16]

Castillero's first choice was the island of Santa Catalina. On March 17, 1839, José Antonio Aguirre, who had Castillero's power of attorney, presented another selection and asked that Santa Cruz Island be granted to Castillero because the island of Santa Catalina "is wholly unfit either for agricultural improvements or the raising of stock."[17] The request of Castillero was

---

[14]Ibid., p. 261.

[15]Ibid., p. 264.

[16]*United States v. Castillero* (1860), 64 U.S. (23 How.) 464.

[17]Ibid. See also the transcripts of the proceedings in *Andrés Castillero v United States,* Case No. 340, transcript no. 176. The transcript is hereinafter referred to as Castillero transcript.

acceded to, and on May 22, 1839, Juan Bautista Alvarado, acting on behalf of the Mexican government and its president, granted Santa Cruz Island to Andrés Castillero, who became the first private owner of the island.

After settling the Alvarado revolt, Castillero was elected a congressman from California. He was later appointed as paymaster general for California in Mexico. He remained in Mexico until 1845 when he returned to California.[18] The purpose of his return visit to California was to negotiate the purchase of Sutter's Fort.[19]

Upon returning to California in 1845, Castillero stopped at the Santa Clara Mission near San José. There he investigated an ancient cave which contained a heavy red ore. After conducting some tests, Castillero determined that the ore was quicksilver (mercury), an essential ingredient in a process to recover gold and silver from mineral ores.[20] The mine was soon to be known as the New Almaden Mine after the great Almaden quicksilver mines in Spain.[21] Castillero quickly filed formal claims (or denouncements) to the mine and the surrounding land. By the end of 1845, Castillero had divided the mining interest into twenty-four barras, or shares, and formed a partnership to operate the mine while keeping fifty percent for himself.[22] The following year, Castillero traveled to Tepíc, Mexico, and met Alexander Forbes, one of the principals of Barron, Forbes & Co. which had interests in Mexican silver mines. During the next several years, Barron, Forbes & Co., as a result of wheeling and dealing, acquired the entire ownership of the San Jose mine. The principal participants

---

[18]Ibid.

[19]K. Johnson, *The New Almaden Quicksilver Mine,* p. 14.

[20]St. Clair, "New Almaden," p. 279.

[21]K. Johnson, *The New Almaden Quicksilver Mine,* pp. 14-19. The red ore was used by the Indians to make a paint which was used to paint the Mission church at Santa Clara. It was observed that "Castillero had located a veritable mountain of cinnabar" that would surpass the quicksilver mines in Spain. Dana, "The French Consúlate," p. 58.

[22]K. Johnson notes that "as provided in the *Ordenanzas de Mineria* there was a formal writing constituting a partnership of twenty-four shares; twelve were retained by Castillero, four were held by General Jose Castro, four by Secundino and Teodoro Robles and four by Padre Real. Castillero thus wisely brought in the military, the church and local rancheros." K. Johnson, *The New Almaden Quicksilver Mine,* p. 20.

42

in the New Almaden Mine Company were Alexander Forbes, Eustace Barron, William Forbes, Eustace W. Barron, Isidoro de la Torre, Juan B. Jecker, Martin La Peidra, Francisco Maria Ortez, James A. Forbes, Robert Walkinshaw and John Parrott. Castillero's contacts and relationships with these individuals led to a complicated web of dealings that eventually involved Santa Cruz Island.[23] One local historian erroneously wrote that Castillero received the island land grant as a reward for the quicksilver discovery.[24] Castillero received an island grant in 1839 and did not discover the New Almaden Mine until 1845.

Little development of Santa Cruz Island occurred during Andrés Castillero's ownership (1839-1857). Since Castillero spent most of his time in Mexico, it is unlikely that he personally used the island. On February 18, 1850, Castillero entered into an agreement with William Forbes, a businessman in the City of Tepíc, Mexico, and Isidoro de la Torre, a businessman in Mazatlán, Mexico. The agreement ceded one half of the island facing the Santa Barbara Channel on condition that "both señores pledge to protect the island in the best way possible to them and as they are most conveniently able."[25] Both Forbes and Isidoro de la Torre agreed not to sell the island, and each was given a right of first refusal to purchase each other's interest in case of death. The parties never recorded the agreement. Forbes and Isidoro de la Torre were the same individuals involved in the New Almaden Quicksilver Mine.

The actual construction of the island's first ranch facilities probably took place during 1852-1853. According to a recorded deed of sale dated November 12, 1852, Thomas Jeffreys sold for

[23]Ibid., pp. 14-25. Alexander Forbes, the British consul at Tepíc and one of the owners of Barron, Forbes & Company, acquired half of the twenty-four shares. Alexander Forbes had the right to work the mine for eighteen or twenty years in consideration of paying one-third of the net profits to the other investors. Dane, "The French Consúlate," p, 61.

[24]Mason, *History of Santa Barbara County,* p. 256. Mason stated that the island of Santa Cruz ". . . next came into possession of Castillero, the discoverer of quicksilver at New Almaden. The Mexican Government, in reward for the discovery, gave him Santa Rosa, but afterwards substituted the neighboring isle, confirming the grant by special act."

[25]Written agreement, dated February 18, 1850, between Andrés Castillero and William Forbes and Isidoro de la Torre.

$10 to Judge Charles Fernald a frame house located at Prisoners' Harbor, the area that was supposed to belong to Forbes and Isidoro de la Torre.[26] It is unknown how Jeffreys acquired the house or what use Fernald made of it.[27] Either Andrés Castillero or Barron, Forbes & Co. hired Dr. James Barron Shaw, a Santa Barbara resident, to manage the island. When Dr. Shaw arrived on the island in 1853, James Box, who lived in a little shanty on the island, was raising pigs there. Box had been on the island from December of 1852 to October of 1853. At that time, Dr. Shaw instructed him to leave. The structure in which Box was living may have been the same one sold by Jeffreys to Judge Fernald the previous month.[28] The first known permanent ranch house was built in the Central Valley and was probably the one depicted in an 1855 water color by James Madison Alden, an artist working for the Pacific Coast Survey team in 1853-1857.[29]

In all likelihood, Eustace Barron and other agents of Barron, Forbes & Co., rather than Castillero, supervised the first development of the island. At this time, Barron reportedly went to Spain to purchase the finest breeds of Spanish sheep and to England to purchase Lancastershires.[30] He may have introduced pigs to the island at this time, but their origin really is unknown. It is also plausible that Box introduced the pigs in the early 1850s.[31] Con-

---

[26]Thomas Jeffreys deed to Fernald, November 12, 1852.

[27]Rogers, *A County Judge*, pp. 26-30.

[28]Ibid., p. 58. See also the Castillero transcript, p. 50. Dr. Shaw testified in the Castillero confirmation proceedings in 1857.

[29]Stanton and Daily, "Santa Cruz Island: Spanish Period to the Present," pp 60-61; See also Neuerburg, "Important Mission Paintings in the Archive-Library," p. 5.

[30]Holdredge, *Mammy Pleasant's Partner*, pp. 113-114. Holdredge also wrote that Eustace had recently bought the island of Santa Cruz from Castillero and that he now had another claim to present to the Land Commission (p.106). This meant that he would prepare and probably finance the processing of the claims to the New Almaden Mine and to Santa Cruz Island. The claims in both situations were filed in the name of Castillero. Holdredge indicated that this information was obtained from Eustace Barron's correspondence at the time.

[31]Box was sued by Thomas Wallace More in 1857 for fraud in the Santa Barbara District Court, 2nd Judicial District. More claimed and the court found that Box borrowed money from More and pledged the island pigs which were represented as "valuable property in good keeping" as security. When Box defaulted, More attempted to get possession of the pigs but found out that Box had neglected the pigs which had withdrawn to the mountains and could not be caught. The Court entered judgment in favor of More.

44 ceivably, the Mexican authorities could have provided pigs among the supplies for the convicts in 1830 when they were marooned at Prisoners' Harbor.[32]

It is interesting that the first private owner of Santa Cruz Island would be a man who was skilled in the diplomacy of resolving conflicts. Ironically, Castillero's claim to the island and his claim to the New Almaden Quicksilver Mine would enmesh him in years of litigation. Subsequently, his claim to the island would be successful in 1860, but his claim to the New Almaden Quicksilver Mine would fail in 1863.[33] After 1861, the details of Castillero's life are obscure. In all likelihood he returned to Mexico.[34]

PROCEEDINGS TO CONFIRM CASTILLERO'S TITLE

The Mexican-American War (1846-1848) had a significant effect on the title of Santa Cruz Island. The Treaty of Guadalupe Hidalgo, signed in 1848 by the United States and the Republic of Mexico, ended the war. The treaty ceded New Mexico, Utah, Nevada, Arizona and California, including the coastal islands, to the United States. This raised immediate concern as to the validity of the land grants. By the terms of the treaty, the United States attempted to protect the private property rights of former Mexican citizens residing in the territories ceded to the United States.

The treaty, however, raised new problems. California land was cheap and plentiful. It attracted many Americans and foreigners, particularly after the discovery of gold. The new immigrants

---

[32]Caire, "Hunting Wild Hogs," p. 121.

[33]In 1863, the United States Supreme Court rejected Castillero's claim to New Almaden. During the period of the litigation, the value of the mine was estimated to be as high as twenty five million dollars. *United States v. Castillero,* 67 U.S. (2 Black) 17. See also K. Johnson, *The New Almaden Quicksilver Mine,* pp. 72-73. There is a suggestion that the Barron, Forbes & Co. and the individual investors suspected that Castillero did not technically comply with Mexican law at the time of his claim to the land and the mine. Holdredge observes: "The right to the mine had to be established before the treaty of peace between the United States and Mexico had been signed and while the mine was still under the jurisdiction of Mexican law. The property was now subject to the laws of the United States and the only way that Forbes and his partners could make Castillero's claim intact was to gain access to Mexican records and doctor them to fit their needs." Holdredge, *Mammy Pleasant's Partner,* pp. 48-49.

[34]Tays, "Captain Andres Castillero," p. 266.

found that vast amounts of land had already been granted by Mexico to Mexican grantees, most of whom were *Californios,* Mexican-heritage citizens of pre-conquest Upper California.[35] The settlers' distrust of the Mexican grants resulted in "squatters riots" in 1850. Congress attempted to solve the land crisis, and after much negotiation it enacted a law called the Act of March 3, 1851. The purpose of the act was to establish procedures in order to fairly and conclusively settle any claims concerning title to California land. This process involved the tedious effort of exposing fraudulent land claims.[36]

The Act of 1851 set up a Land Commission consisting of three commissioners with a secretary and a law agent skilled in Spanish. The terms of the commissioners were for three years. The board was authorized to administer oaths and take evidence. The courts limited the use of oral testimony and gave little weight to it. The courts stressed the importance of public documents located in the Mexican archives.[37] Any person who claimed any interest in land in California under a Spanish or Mexican title was required to file a claim with the necessary documents and other evidence with the board within two years for adjudication, or thereafter be barred. The review process allowed an appeal to the United States District Court that could take additional evidence, and ultimately to the United States Supreme Court. All lands for which there were rejected claims remained in the public domain. All confirmed claims would be surveyed by the surveyor-general; on the presentment of the claimant's certificate and plat, a patent would be issued. The patent would be conclusive against the United States but would not affect the rights of third parties.[38]

On April 13, 1852, Castillero filed a petition with the United States Land Commission to confirm his Mexican land grant to

[35]Bastian, "I Heartily Regret That I Ever Touched a Title in California," 72: 311-323.

[36]Field, "Attorney-General Black, and the California Land Claims," 4: 236-238. Field noted that the value of the forged titles amounted to $150,000,000. He pointed out that by 1862, 813 claims were filed. The Land Commission settled 264; 450 were finally decided by the District Court, and United States Supreme Court decided 99.

[37]*Peralta v. United States.*

[38]Bancroft, *History of California,* 6:540-541.

46 Santa Cruz Island. The commissioners who heard his case were Peter Lott, R. A. Thompson and S. B. Farwell. Castillero filed his petition despite his 1850 agreement with William Forbes and Isidoro de la Torre. Forbes and Torre did not enter any claim of ownership interest. William E. Barron, who eventually purchased the island from Castillero, represented to the commission in 1854 that he was Castillero's agent and attorney in fact. Other individuals, however, did oppose Castillero's claim of ownership. José Antonio Aguirre, who described himself as a merchant of the port of Santa Barbara and an agent for Castillero, claimed an interest in the island. In support of Aguirre's claim, Governor Alvarado, who was appointed to that post on the recommendation of Castillero, testified against Castillero before the commission on September 25, 1854. Alvarado swore that Castillero had told him that he promised Aguirre should have one half of the island for taking care of it.[39] He stated that Castillero told him this in 1838 and that Castillero had not returned to the area from Mexico after 1847.[40]

In addition to Aguirre, James R. Bolton of San Francisco also claimed an ownership interest in Santa Cruz Island. Bolton was a close friend and business associate of William E. Barron, who testified as an agent of Castillero. Bolton was not averse to land manipulations, particularly if he could acquire land cheaply.[41] He testified that he purchased his one-half interest in June 1851 for

---

[39]Castillero transcript, p. 31.

[40]Ibid., pp. 29-36.

[41]James R. Bolton had claimed a large amount of acreage in San Francisco but that claim was eventually dismissed in 1860 by the United States Supreme Court. *United States v. Bolton,* 64 U.S. (23 How.) 435. In that case, the claim consisted of 10,186 acres known as lands belonging to Mission Dolores in the County of San Francisco. Padre Jose Prudencia Santillan, a secular priest, sold the acreage to Bolton for $200,000 in April 1850. The property had an estimated value of over two million dollars. Bolton presented the claim to the Land Commission in March 1852. The claim was confirmed by the commission in 1855 and by the District Court in 1857. The Supreme Court reversed these decisions and denied the claim. Bolton reportedly only paid $18,000 to Santillan and never paid the balance. The land was allegedly resold for $13,000,000. Bolton's land scheme to acquire the Mission Dolores lands was described by Helen Holdredge in her book, *Mammy Pleasant's Partner,* pp. 129-131, 163, 178. Holdredge described Bolton's scheme as "fraudulent" and that Bolton had acquired "some stigma of infamy." (p. 163)

the sum of $130 from Francisco de la Guerra who had allegedly acquired the southeastern half of the island for $26 at a tax sale held on November 20, 1850.[42] Dr. James B. Shaw testified on January 7, 1857, on behalf of Castillero and said that as his agent he paid the taxes for the year 1851 which amounted to $45.[43] Dr. Shaw also related that he had given his "personal attention to the island as the local agent, both of the original owners, and of the commercial agents of the claimants, who are Bolton, Bar[r]on & Co. of San Francisco."[44]

On July 3, 1855, the land commissioners confirmed Castillero's title and rejected the claims of Aguirre and Bolton.[45] The United States government, arguing that Castillero's claim was invalid, appealed the decision. The government claimed that the island belonged to the United States by virtue of the Treaty of Guadalupe Hidalgo entered into between Mexico and the United States on February 2, 1848.[46]

The Federal District Court for the Southern District of California affirmed the Land Commissions' decision on January 14, 1857. Ultimately, the United States Supreme Court also upheld the decision in April 1860.[47] The *Sacramento Daily Union*, in reporting the decision, noted that the island "contains no special soil, minerals, grass, timber but so large a body of land, it must possess value for many purposes."[48] Supreme Court Justice

---

[42]Castillero transcript, pp. 22-23. Antonio Maria de la Guerra indenture to Francisco de la Guerra was recorded in Book B, page 10 of Official Records of Santa Barbara County. The Bolton indenture was recorded in Book B, page 43 of the Official Records of Santa Barbara County.

[43]Castillero transcript, p. 50.   [44]Ibid., p. 49.

[45]Caire, *Santa Cruz Island*, p. 35. Ms. Caire states: "His [Castillero] claim to the island was confirmed by patent from the Mexican government in 1843. It was not until April 13, 1867, that the U.S. Land Commission officially recognized his claim." The Castillero transcripts and other source materials show that the dates cited by Ms. Caire and her description of the confirmation process in her book are incorrect. Castillero transcript, p. 38.

[46]Castillero transcript, pp. 44-45.

[47]*United States v. Castíllero*, 64 U. S. (23 How.) 464. See also Hoffman, *Reports of Land Cases*, p. 25. The Castillero Santa Cruz Island case was heard by the United States District Court for the Southern District of California. His New Almaden case was heard by Judge Hoffman of the United States District Court for Northern California.

[48]*Sacramento Daily Union*, June 2, 1860, p. 2.

48   Nathan Clifford, who would later rule against Castillero in the
New Almaden Quicksilver Mine case, delivered the court's opinion. In its review, the Supreme Court determined, among other
issues, that the 1839 grant to Castillero was valid under Mexican
law. In addition, the court noted that the documentary evidence
presented in support of the Castillero claim was credible in that
the documents were found in the Mexican archives, and the signa-
tures of the documents were identified.[49] The legal proceedings
involving the confirmation of the island title were only the beginning of legal entanglements that would long plague Santa Cruz
Island.

After the confirmation of Castillero's title, a survey was made
and a patent was issued to him on March 25, 1867, by the United
States government.[50] The patent, signed by President Andrew
Johnson, stated that the island has as "its boundaries the water's
edge." The patent also reserved to the United States the right to
select one hundred acres for lighthouse purposes at such point or
points as may thereafter be designated with the right of way to
and from the same across the island.[51] This reservation of right
would later be raised as an issue in the island partition litigation.

The intent of the Treaty of Guadalupe Hidalgo was to protect
land titles in California acquired under Mexican rule. In explain-
ing the purpose of the treaty, the United States Supreme Court
observed that the West was new and rich in mineral wealth, particularly gold. This wealth produced an unparalleled state of pros-
perity and increased property values. The treaty was designed to
ascertain and settle all land claims.[52]

OTHER CLAIMS OF TITLE TO SANTA CRUZ ISLAND

Despite the salutary purposes of the Treaty of Guadalupe
Hidalgo and the implementing Act of March 3, 1851, the discus-

---

[49]*United States v. Castillero,* 64 U.S.(23 How.) 464.

[50]The patent was issued to Castillero rather than Barron who was the owner at the time
the patent was issued because it was the Mexican land grant that was being confirmed.

[51]Patent from United States of America to Andres Castillero was recorded February 22,
1869.

[52]*Peralta v. United States.*

sion of who owned the island still persisted. Over the years, there was publicity stating that Mexico was still claiming the island as its territory.[53] Since 1915 the question of the sovereignty of the off-shore islands of California has been unofficially broached at least four times. The primary impetus for the question was the fact that the Treaty of Guadalupe Hidalgo did not mention the offshore islands.

Historian J. N. Bowman examined the question of sovereignty in 1962.[54] Bowman concluded that the offshore islands were included in the treaty. Clearly, the islands passed from Spain to Mexico since the Spanish-Mexican Treaty of 1836, ratified by Mexico on February 28, 1838, referred to the islands. One of the reasons that Mexico made the land grants of the islands, includ-ing Santa Cruz Island to Andrés Castillero, was to facilitate the control of the use, occupation and smuggling by American and European traders around the islands. Bowman pointed out that undoubtedly Mexico considered the channel islands part of its national territory because it made the land grants to settle the uninhabited islands. One of the purposes of the Treaty of Guadalupe Hidalgo was to provide protection for the Mexican land grants. Bowman explained that in the ninety years of litiga-tion of the private land grants none of the parties raised the ques-tion of sovereignty over the offshore islands. In 1849, the territorial consequences of the Treaty were well understood as demonstrated by the language of the California Constitution which specifically referred to the offshore islands. When Califor-nia was admitted into the Union in 1850, the channel islands were included, and Mexico never took exception. The treaty makers were intent on defining the general boundary of Upper and Lower California rather than taking inventory of the property that would be ceded to the United States. Clearly, the contracting governments had a mutual understanding of the land that was to be ceded.

---

[53]For example, *Los Angeles Herald-Examiner,* "California Islands Claimed by Mexico," March 25, 1970, A-8.

[54]Bowman, "The Question of Sovereignty," 31: 291-300.

Because of continued speculation, the United States Department of State investigated the issue of the sovereignty and found no basis for the assertions that the offshore islands still belonged to Mexico. On April 1, 1970, the Mexican Secretary of Foreign Relations, Antonio Carrillo Flores, pointed out that a thorough study made in 1947 found that the Mexican government was not making any such claim to any of the California Channel Islands.[55]

The Chumash Indians also challenged the title to the island in a lawsuit filed in June of 1984—one hundred and twenty-four years after Castillero had his title confirmed by the United States Supreme Court. In their suit, the Chumash sought declaratory relief, damages for trespass and conversion, injunctive relief and attorneys' fees. The Chumash argued that they did not have to follow the claim procedures established by the Act of March 3, 1851, because they based their claim on "aboriginal title" which entitled the tribes to full use and enjoyment of the surface and mineral rights of the land. This claim was novel since the United States Supreme Court at the turn of the century stated that mission Indians were required to file a claim.[56] The Chumash also renewed an old argument that the Treaty of Guadalupe Hidalgo did not specifically mention Santa Cruz Island.

The Chumash claim was not successful. The Federal District Court in Los Angeles dismissed the case on November 29, 1984, but the Chumash appealed. The Ninth Circuit Court of Appeals affirmed the decision by noting that even though the Mexican government's grant did not extinguish their aboriginal title, they lost all rights when they failed to present their claims pursuant to the Treaty of Guadalupe Hidalgo and the Act of March 3, 1851.[57] The Ninth Circuit Court relied on Bowman's analysis of the Treaty by stating that "the absence of any reference to the island in the Treaty of Guadalupe Hidalgo is explained by the fact the treaty drafters were primarily concerned with the latitudinal

---

[55]Letter from J. Brian Atwood to Honorable Robert J. Lagomarsino, July 26, 1979.

[56]*Barker v. Harvey.* See also *United States v. Title Insurance and Trust Co.*

[57]*United States of America ex re. Chunie v. Ringrose et al.*

boundary between the two countries."[58] The court also observed that the treaty had two maps attached to it: the 1847 Disturnell Map which includes the islands and the 1782 Pantoja Map which does not. The maps, however, were not conclusive on the issue of whether the islands were part of the treaty since the United States Supreme Court had already decided that the treaty included the islands. The failure of the Chumash to file their claims under the claims procedures established in 1851 was fatal to their case. The Court also pointed out the admitted historical fact that the Chumash had abandoned the lands prior to cession. Having done so, they relinquished their right of occupancy and this also supported the conclusion that their claim had no merit.[59]

---

[58]Ibid., p. 643.

[59]Ibid., pp. 643-645. Some Indians actually received a few land grants, some of which were documented in the United States Commission Case No. 387, Federal Court, Southern District. Johnson, "The Chumash Indians After Secularization," pp. 144-145.

William E. Barron (1822–1871)
Barron purchased Santa Cruz Island in 1857 and sold it to
ten investors including Justinian Caire in 1869.
Photo courtesy of California Historical Society.

Chapter 3

The Barron Era (1857-1869)

CASTILLERO SELLS THE ISLAND

Andrés Castillero, having received a favorable decision from the United States District Court on January 14, 1857, promptly sold his interest in the island on June 23, 1857, to William E. Barron.[1] The sale took place even though the proceedings confirming the title were not over and would not be concluded until the 1860 Supreme Court decision. William E. Barron, born in Calese, Spain, was a close personal friend of James R. Bolton, who also worked for Jecker, Torre & Co.[2] Together they opened a commission business at 92 Merchant Street in San Francisco in the early 1850s and advertised their business as "Bolton, Barron and Co., agents for the New Almaden Quicksilver Mine" which was owned by Barron, Forbes & Co. of Tepíc, Mexico.[3] As noted in the previous chapter, Bolton had opposed Castillero's confirmation of the island title by claiming he owned half of the island. Dr. James Barron Shaw, who was then managing the island, had testified that Bolton, Barron and Co. of San Francisco were also Castillero's commercial agents. It appears that Bolton, by presenting a claim before the Land Commission, was trying to undermine Castillero's title. It is unknown what role, if any, William E.

---

[1]Castillero to Barron indenture, June 23, 1857. Helen Caire erroneously wrote that the date of the transfer was May 22, 1859. Caire, *Santa Cruz Island,* p. 36.

[2]Holdredge, *Mammy Pleasant's Partner,* pp. 16-17.

[3]Frank River, *San Francisco Directory for 1854,* p. 27.

54 Barron had in this scheme and whether this had anything to do with him eventually getting title to the island. Barron, following a family political tradition, also served as Mexican Vice-Consul for several years.[4]

The Barron Era, however, was not without confusion concerning title to the island even though record title was clear. An unrecorded 1850 agreement, located at Bancroft Library, University of California, Berkeley, together with other historical reports and rumors of ownership raised questions, some of which are still unresolved, as to who actually owned the island. According to the 1850 agreement, Castillero sold a half interest in the island to William Forbes and Isadoro de la Torre. Torre, a Spaniard, was a principal of Jecker, Torre & Co. which competed with Barron, Forbes & Co. Nevertheless, some of the principals like Torre were business associates not only in the New Almaden Quicksilver Mine but also in Santa Cruz Island as evidenced by the 1850 agreement. Torre was described as a "remarkable man, clever, quick tempered, farseeing."[5] He was known to be the best friend of William E. Barron's uncle, Eustace Barron.[6] William Forbes, also a party to the 1850 agreement, was an active member of Barron, Forbes & Co. which was owned by Eustace Barron and William Forbes' uncle, Alexander Forbes.[7]

Some historians wrote that the island was actually owned by Eustace Barron. For example, Eustace Barron wrote Thomas Bell, an employee of Barron, Forbes & Co., that he had recently purchased Santa Cruz Island from Castillero and had to present the case to the Land Commission to confirm Castillero's title.[8] Other historians state that in 1852 Castillero transferred his interest in the island to Barron, Forbes & Co., and Jecker, Torre & Co.[9] If

[4]San Francisco directories, 1853-59.
[5]Holdredge, *Mammy Pleasant's Partner*, p. 52.
[6]Ibid., p. 53.
[7]Forbes, *California,* introduction by Priestley, p. xiii.
[8]Holdredge, *Mammy Pleasant's Partner,* p. 106. Thomas Bell became involved in a number of business dealings with Alexander Forbes and Eustace Barron.
[9]In O'Neill's *History of Santa Barbara County,* he reported that Castillero "made no endeavor to develop it [Santa Cruz Island], and in 1852 his rights were transferred to Jecker, Torre & Company and Barron, Forbes, & Company. The latter obtained the major

there is any validity to the 1850 agreement and to other reports of ownership, then in a sense the Barron Era really started in the early 1850s. To add to the confusion, for some reason Castillero transferred the island's title to Eustace's nephew, William E. Barron, a resident of San Francisco. This may well have been the result of other unrecorded agreements among the investors of Barron, Forbes & Co. or simply because Eustace, a resident of Tepíc, Mexico, and perhaps in poor health, wanted title held by a California resident. It is also plausible the transfer had something to do with the New Almaden Mine which was originally discovered by Castillero and later acquired by Barron, Forbes & Co.

Less than a year after Castillero's sale to William E. Barron, Eustace Barron died in April 1858,[10] and Barron, Forbes & Co. reportedly advertised in the *Daily Alta California* on May 25, 1858, that Santa Cruz Island was for sale.[11] The company represented that there were only fifty sheep on the island. After the initial attempts to sell the island failed, Barron decided to establish an extensive sheep ranch under the management of Dr. Shaw. By this time, the New Almaden litigation was in full swing; the quicksilver mine had been shut down because of a court injunction.[12]

---

portion of the island. They were a British firm of Tepíc, Mexico. They immediately stocked the island with sheep and sent Dr. J.B. Shaw to Santa Barbara as manager." O'Neill and Meier, *History of Santa Barbara County*, p. 366.

[10]Holdredge, *Mammy Pleasant's Partner*, p. 164. William E. Barron's uncle was not only named Eustace, but so was his brother. This is verified by William's will which was printed in the *Daily Alta* on November 11, 1871. This information is consistent with an article which stated that Eustace and William Barron, as brothers and principal shareholders in the New Almaden Company wrote an article in the *San Francisco Bulletin* on July 23, 1863. This obviously can't be the same Eustace who died in 1858. See Ascher, "Lincoln's Administration," p. 49, fn. 34.

[11]Doran, *Pieces of Eight*, pp. 161-162. The advertisements in the *Daily Alta* did not identify who placed the ads nor did the ads specifically refer to Santa Cruz Island. There is no question, however, that the ads concerned the island as one ad read as follows:

> For Sale–an island containing about 60,000 acres of land well watered and abounding in small valleys of the best pasturages for sheep. There are no wild animals on it which would interfere with the stock. There is a good harbor and safe anchorage. The Owner is now in this City and if a party should desire to place stock on it, an arrangement may be made to do so by putting the island, to a certain extent against the stock furnished. There are about fifty sheep now on the island. Apply at 119 Sansom Street."

The ads ran for a period of weeks.

[12]Holdredge, *Mammy Pleasant's Partner*, p. 165.

56 Undoubtedly, the lengthy court proceedings involving the New Almaden Mine taxed the resolve of the Barrons and the other investors to hold Santa Cruz Island. William E. Barron, however, did not sell the island until 1869.

BARRON, FORBES & CO.

Because of various reports that the island was either owned by Eustace Barron or by his company, Barron, Forbes & Co., some background is important. The company, founded in 1834 by Alexander Forbes and Eustace Barron, operated mines, cotton mills, distilleries and other commercial ventures from its main office in Tepíc which is located near the important sea port of San Blas on the western coast of Mexico. Both men had been prominent merchants in Tepíc since 1824.[13] Forbes, a rugged Scotsman, was well known as he authored *California: A History of Upper and Lower California,* the first book in English relating wholly to California.[14] Barron, a blue eyed Irishman born in Spain and a veteran of the wars against Napoleon in Spain, served several stints as the British Vice-Consul and Consul in Tepíc beginning as early as 1824.[15] Forbes also served in that capacity for a two-year term.[16] Both men advocated a strong British presence in California.[17]

The politically powerful firm, however, left a tainted history of unsavory business dealings. In 1846, the company and its principals knew that Andrés Castillero's mining claim to the lucrative New Almaden Mine in Santa Clara, California, was invalid but nevertheless purchased shares in it. Thereafter, the company and its agents, including Alexander Forbes, "connived . . . in securing fraud, forgeries, interpolations, and antedating of documents . . ." in order to validate Castillero's mining claim.[18] The United States Supreme Court saw through the scam and nullified Castillero's claim to the mine.[19] Between 1846 and 1853 the company also

---

[13]Jackson, "Two Pro-British Plots," p. 136.
[14]Forbes, *California,* with introduction by Priestley, p. xix-xx.
[15]Jackson, "Two Pro British Plots," p. 136, fn. 9.
[16]Forbes, *California,* with introduction by Priestley, p. xiii.
[17]Jackson, "The British and California Dream," p. 253.
[18]Forbes, *California,* with introduction by Priestley, p. xv.
[19]*Castillero v. United States,* (1863) 67 U.S. 17.

"controlled the port of San Blas by corrupting the customs employees" in order to stifle competition.[20] Some of its principals like Eustace Barron and Alexander Forbes' nephew, William Forbes, who acquired a half interest in the island in 1850, earned a reputation as notorious money lenders.[21]

The company also appeared to engage in smuggling activities which led in 1847 to the famous seizure of the schooner *William* owned by William Forbes and used by Barron, Forbes, & Co. The vessel, flying the British flag, was destined, according to the manifest, for the Sandwich Islands. The vessel, however, stopped in Monterey to unload its entire cargo, including money for the New Almaden Mine venture. The United States, at war with Mexico at the time, seized the vessel because it was in enemy territory. The company vigorously protested the seizure and eventually appealed to the United States Congress but to no avail. The Committee on Foreign Affairs, which heard the petition, viewed with suspicion the disposal of the entire cargo in Monterey which left the vessel to proceed to the Sandwich Islands, its main destination, without cargo.[22] The United States auctioned the vessel and its cargo; the successful bidder was an agent for Barron, Forbes & Co. and the *William* was soon back in business.[23] Undaunted, the company involved itself in another incident in 1859, when it smuggled large quantities of silver through the small port of Santa Cruz on Mexico's west coast to avoid customs. This time they used their diplomatic clout to avoid payment of the customs.[24]

MANAGEMENT OF THE ISLAND DURING PART OF THE CASTILLERO ERA AND ALL OF THE BARRON ERA

Dr. James Barron Shaw (1813-1902) managed the island from 1853 to 1869. Shaw, whose father was Scottish and his mother English, may have been related to the Barrons as his middle name suggests, but there is no direct evidence of this. Barron, Forbes &

---

[20]Gulick, *Nayarit, Mexico*, p.44.
[21]Meyer, *De Canton de Tepic*, pp. 26-29; 50-67.
[22]House of Representatives, Report No. 16, 31st Cong., 1st Sess., 1850.
[23]Johnson, "The Judges Colton," p. 354.
[24]Gulick, *Nayarit, Mexico*, p. 104.

58   Co. was well known, and Shaw never mentioned that he was
related to any of its principals either in his interview about his life
or in his testimony before the Land Commission.[25]

Dr. Shaw, who managed Santa Cruz Island for sixteen years, had
a fascinating background. He was born in London, England, on
November 4, 1813. Although he wanted to be a sailor in the navy,
he was urged to enter the medical profession by his mother. He
later studied at the Royal College of Surgeons in London and
obtained his medical degree at the University of Glasgow in April
1836. He returned to London and became a member of the Royal
College of Surgeons in August of the same year. Subsequently, he
traveled extensively around the world and eventually was lured to
California because of the gold rush. He arrived in San Francisco
July 3, 1849, and immediately set out in search of gold. His efforts
were not particularly successful, so he opened a medical office in
the gold country. This did not last too long, and after hearing
about Santa Barbara, he travelled to the little southland village on
January 6, 1850.[26]

Unimpressed with Santa Barbara, Dr. Shaw decided to travel to
Mazatlán, Mexico. From there he traveled to Tepíc to visit Barron,
Forbes & Co. and then proceeded to Mexico City. At this time he
first became acquainted with Andrés Castillero, the owner of
Santa Cruz Island, who lived in Mexico. During his stay in Tepíc,
Mexico, Dr. Shaw stated that he "made arrangements with Bar-
ron, Forbes & Co. of Mexico with whom I agreed to return to Cal-
ifornia to take an interest in the management of their island of
Santa Cruz . . ."[27] Castillero had already entered into an agreement in 1850 with William Forbes of Tepíc, and Isidoro de la
Torre whereby they would receive one half of the island. Obviously, Dr. Shaw viewed Barron, Forbes & Co. as one of the owners
of Santa Cruz Island. In May 1853, Dr. Shaw returned to Santa
Barbara and began his sixteen-year tenure in managing the

---

[25]Storke does relate that Shaw traveled to Mexico "where he had friends and relatives
residing." Storke, *A Memorial*, pp. 633-634.

[26]Storke, *A Memorial*, pp. 633-636.

[27]Shaw transcript.

[28]Storke, *A Memorial*, p. 636.

island.[28] In the meantime, he represented to the district court that he was Castillero's agent.[29]

Dr. Shaw played a prominent role in establishing a large, quality sheep operation on Santa Cruz Island. He probably was given extensive management powers in view of the fact that Eustace Barron and his other business associates were involved in the complicated New Almaden Quicksilver case. Dr. Shaw purchased 200 ewes from Alphonso Thompson, who at the time owned half of Santa Rosa Island and was selling the island's livestock.[30] With this purchase, the history of the island sheep ranching began. The first yield of wool was inferior, and in 1854 Dr. Shaw purchased 1,000 head of sheep in Los Angeles, herded them to Santa Barbara and then transported them to the island by schooner. In 1857, the *Daily Alta California* reported that two hundred acres of land were under cultivation; this was the first attempt of any extended plan to test the agricultural resources of the island.[31] In this year the Santa Barbara County assessor's records reveal that the reported value of the personal property nearly doubled from the year 1855. The importation of livestock, particularly sheep, obviously caused the increase in the assessed value. If the advertisements offering the island for sale were accurate, then most of the sheep were sold in 1858 since the ads represented that there were only fifty sheep on the island.

The ads, however, attracted no buyers. The island owners must have opted for a larger sheep operation. This may have been due in part to the Civil War fever sweeping the nation and its effect on the wool market. In 1860, the assessor's records show a substantial increase in the value of personal property, including a reported 12,375 sheep, 116 rodeo cattle, 3 bulls, 72 cow calves, 2 oxen, 42 mares, 11 lame horses, 53 colts and 2 stallions.[32] The following year, Dr. Shaw, as manager of the island, imported a number of valuable jacks (costing $1500 each) and sheep from the Balearic Islands and from England. The sheep were Spanish and Merino

[29]Castillero transcript, p. 48.
[30]Vail and Daily, "Santa Rosa Island," p. 100.
[31]*Daily Alta California,* April 27, 1857, p. 1.
[32]County of Santa Barbara Assessment Roll for year 1860.

60   bucks and Leicester bucks and ewes.[33] By 1864, 24,371 sheep roamed the island.[34] One can conclude that the island sheep operation expanded significantly between 1858 and 1864, particularly with the Civil War wool demand for uniforms, blankets, etc.

By 1869 Shaw had established a well known sheep ranch on the island. A number of wooden framed buildings were built and kept in good repair, and, of course, there were corrals and shearing sheds.[35] One of the early island photographs taken in 1869 shows a substantial wharf at Prisoners' Harbor. This historically important structure was the first large wharf built in Santa Barbara County and was the artery through which essential goods and supplies have flowed to and from the island ever since.[36] The building of the wharf probably coincided with the expansion of the island sheep operation in the early 1860s.

By the end of Dr. Shaw's tenure in 1869, local historian Yda Addis Storke wrote that there were 54,000 head of sheep on the island in addition to a large number of cattle and horses. The sheep census seems to be consistently exaggerated since the county assessor records for 1869 show 23,819 sheep. In Shaw's last year, the gross proceeds from the island operation were reportedly $50,000. Dr. Shaw was known to be the first to ship sheep to San Francisco by steamer. Some of the finer animals were sold for as much as $30 a head. After leaving the island, Dr. Shaw continued ranching at the ranchos of La Laguna de San Francisco and Los Alamos, both of which he stocked with sheep from the island.[37] Island workers gave Dr. Shaw high praise for transforming the island "wilderness" into a quality

---

[33]An article "The Early Life of the Late Dr. Shaw " appeared in the *Santa Barbara Morning Press* on February 9, 1902 and was reprinted by the *Santa Barbara News Press* on August 28, 1945.

[34]County of Santa Barbara Assessment Roll for the year 1864.

[35]Ellison, "History of the Santa Cruz Island Grant," p. 278. See also *Santa Barbara Post,* March 3, 1869. Too little credit has been given to Dr. Shaw for establishing the large sheep ranch on Santa Cruz Island.

[36]Lima, "Historic Study," p. 9.

[37]Storke, *A Memorial,* p. 637.

sheep ranch.[38] Dr. Shaw died in Santa Barbara on January 7, 1902.[39]

THE END OF THE BARRON ERA

Barron's ownership of Santa Cruz Island lasted for twelve years (1857-1869). On February 16, 1869, he sold the island to a group of ten San Francisco investors for $150,000 or $1.86 per acre.[40] The ten investors who purchased the island were: Gustave Mahé, Camilo Martin, Alexander Weill, T. Lemmen Meyer, Nicholas Larco, Adrien Gensoul, Giovanni Battista Cerruti, Justinian Caire, Thomas J. Gallagher, and Pablo Baca. Caire would later control the entire island through his ownership of all the stock of the Santa Cruz Island Company which the investors formed on February 20, 1869. Some authors have stated that Justinian Caire managed the island as early as 1865, four years before the formation of the Santa Cruz Island Company.[41] This statement is not historically accurate since Caire first went to the island in 1880, and it is well documented that prior to 1869, James Barron Shaw managed the island.[42]

The investors were not buying a desolate uninhabited island and starting from scratch, since a substantial sheep operation had

---

[38]*Santa Barbara Post*, March 3, 1869.

[39]*The Santa Barbara Morning Press,* February 9, 1902. The article notes the many accomplishments of Dr. Shaw in Santa Barbara County. It states that he was one of the builders of the town of Los Alamos; he built the first Episcopal church on Gutierrez Street in Santa Barbara; he was involved with the building of the first wharf at the foot of Chapala Street. The article incorrectly states that he was manager for the Santa Cruz Island Company which was formed after he left the island.

[40]The indenture from William E. Barron to Gustave Mahé, February 16, 1869 was recorded in Book F, p. 792-799 of County of Santa Barbara Official Records. The Santa Cruz Island Company took title from the ten investors on March 29, 1869. The 1869 assessor record shows personal property valued at $37,018. This would leave a land value of $112,982 for 60,741.74 acres.

[41]Towne and Wentworth, *Shepherd's Empire,* p. 209 and Wentworth, *America's Sheep Trails,* p. 204.

[42]There is no evidence that Caire ever managed the island for Barron, Forbes & Co., as reported by Warren, "The Agriculture of Santa Cruz Island," p. 27. At the time, Caire was busy running the Justinian Caire Co. in San Francisco, and it is unlikely that he would be involved with or working for Barron, Forbes & Co. of Tepíc, Mexico.

62 already been established. What they saw was a business opportunity. The sale was reported by the *Santa Barbara Post* on February 17, 1869: ". . .the purchasers have certainly secured a great bargain, for the island is one of the largest and most fertile on the California Coast."[43] The new owners wasted no time in getting started; the local paper wrote, they purchased the schooner *T.G. Sanborn* which had recently arrived in the Port of Santa Barbara from San Francisco "with a load of piles for the wharf at Santa Cruz Island."[44]

On October 25, 1871, William E. Barron died at the age of forty-nine.[45] His era will be remembered for the establishment of the first serious development of the island as an island rancho. His associations, however, with the infamous James R. Bolton and with the notorious Barron, Forbes & Co., raise questions as to how he acquired the island.

---

[43]*Santa Barbara Post,* February 17, 1869.

[44]Ibid., May 5, 1869.

[45]*Daily Alta California,* October 26, 1871, p.1. See also Holdredge, *Mammy Pleasant's Partner,* p. 212. It is interesting that on November 14, 1871, the *Daily Alta* published William E. Barron's entire will. The will, signed in San Francisco the day before he died, indicates that he left an estate of approximately $605,000. His friends, Thomas Bell, Darius O. Mills, and William G. Ralston, were named executors. Barron was survived by brothers Eustace, Phillip, and Joseph and his sister Katalina Avil de Barron. James Barron Shaw was one of the witnesses to the will.

Chapter 4

Justinian Caire,
His Family and Businesses

The second half of the nineteenth century witnessed the transformation of an uninhabited isle into a successful and diversified enterprise. The success of this transformation would eventually lead to conflict in the Caire family and the ultimate breakup of the Santa Cruz Island Company and the division of the Caire family.

JUSTINIAN CAIRE AND HIS FAMILY

Justinian Caire was born in 1827 in Briançon in the French Hautes-Alpes. He spoke several languages, including English, Italian, French, and Spanish and was responsible for many of the Spanish names on the island.[1] When he was nineteen years of age he went to Genoa, Italy, where he learned Italian and met Albina Cristina Sara Molfino, his future bride.[2] In the commercial city of Genoa, Justinian learned the hardware business and became successful enough to build up some capital. He decided to go to San Francisco to establish a business.

A wide spectrum of French society traveled to California. A large portion of the French emigrants to California came from the provinces, small towns, and villages and included all profes-

---

[1]M. Gherini, "Santa Cruz Island," in *Anthology,* pp. 67.

[2]Her full name was Maria Christina Sara Candida Molfino Caire. Helen Caire, *Santa Cruz Island,* p. 58. On their mariage record, Justinian's name was spelled "Guistiniano."

64

Justinian Caire
(1827-1897).
*Pier Gherini
family collection.*

sions and occupations.[3] The French emigration was not as great
as other European countries such as England and Germany.[4] *Auri
sacra fame* (the gold fever) was not the sole cause for the French
influx into California during the gold rush (1848-1850). Economic difficulties, civil strife, and political revolts motivated
many to leave France.[5] The French government encouraged emigration to California as a way to relieve economic pressures in the
country. Promoters of gold companies, some scrupulous and others dishonest, urged their investors to make a trip to California in
order to realize huge profits.[6] Against this background Justinian
Caire journeyed to California.

[3]Chinard, "When the French Came, " p. 307

[4]Ibid., p. 313. Two or three hundred Frenchmen would make the journey to California
on a monthly basis as opposed to thousands leaving monthly from the British Isles and
Germany.

[5]Ibid, p. 291.   [6]Ibid. p.295.

Caire boarded the *Aurelie* in Le Havre, France, in the fall of 1850 and traveled with seven other passengers around Cape Horn. One hundred and fifty-two days after leaving France, he arrived in San Francisco on March 29, 1851.[7] Claude Long, Justinian's long-time friend, traveled with him. The cargo of the *Aurelie* consisted of a case of watches, 1,000 packages of champagne, 2,557 cases of wine, oil, vinegar, sardines, fruit, 5 barrels of pork, and 452 packages of merchandise.[8] Prior to 1851, tens of thousands of passengers came to California by way of Cape Horn. After 1850, however, the preferred route to California was either by the Isthmus of Panama or through Nicaragua.[9]

The experience of rounding Cape Horn must have left a lasting impression on Caire. Passengers who voyaged around Cape Horn had many similar experiences. There was ". . . stress of continual personal contact in a cramped, filthy ship. . .Quarrels, fights, and sexual promiscuity were features of some stressed-filled voyages."[10] It took courage for anyone, even the most seasoned sailor, to make the voyage. The seas were heavy and violent; the ships were small by modern standards; the winds blasted both man and ship with chilling sleet and rain. The violent reputation of the Cape was widespread.[11] One can only imagine what Caire must have thought of the passage around the Cape while he was under the watchful eye of the Southern Cross.

At San Francisco a different experience awaited Caire, like others who traveled to California. He immediately saw "a forest of ships in rows two or three deep" as vessels of all sizes and descriptions choked the bay.[12] From the waterfront where nine wharves bustled with activity, Caire could hear, see and smell the chaotic vibrations of San Francisco. Rats and criminals swarmed the city

---

[7]Jean Caire, "In Memoriam," 29 pp. 81-83.

[8]Rasmussen, *San Francisco Passenger Lists.* Justinian was described on the passenger list as "J. Cayre." The captain of the ship was Gouin. Other passengers in addition to Caire were Long and his wife, C. Gouffroy, F. Bau, V. Bigot, and E. Martin.

[9]Delgado, *To California by Sea*, p. 26.

[10]Ibid., p. 27.

[11]*Santa Barbara Daily Independent,* May 11, 1899.

[12]Garrett, "San Francisco in 1851," p. 253.

66 streets. Caire, however, was consoled by the fact that San Francisco had a large French population and some sections of the city were completely French in appearance.[13] In March 1851, when he arrived, the state's immigration explosion was in full swing. People from around the world flocked to California, particularly San Francisco, which "was a clarion of opportunity, of possibility, of new beginnings and great expectations."[14] California entered the Union in 1850, and San Francisco with over 100,000 people was its largest city. Wooden structures hastily built to accommodate the rapid expansion fueled by the gold rush covered the hillsides. Speculation was rampant. Merchants profited because "scarce items sometimes rose in value two or three hundred times their market price in the East, and nearly everything that was sold went at prices far above those in any other market."[15]

Richard Henry Dana, who chronicled his maritime travels in *Two Years Before The Mast,* personally witnessed the explosive transformation of San Francisco. He recalled that in 1835 there was "one board shanty." The discovery of gold in 1848 drastically changed San Francisco. Law and order were difficult to maintain as the city attracted "many of the worst spirits of Christendom."[16] Fires became a way of life in San Francisco. Five devastating fires wasted portions of the City between 1849 and 1851.[17] Fires and violence became so prevalent that in 1851 citizens formed a Committee of Vigilance "to become the judge, jury, courts and law of San Francisco . . . to induce undesirables to leave this port [meaning California] by whatever means necessary."[18]

By the early 1850s, reports received in France about the living conditions in San Francisco were not always favorable. As a result, extreme caution probably guided Justinian and his fellow Frenchmen in making their decision to come to California.[19] Caire obvi-

---

[13]Ibid., pp. 254-268.
[14]Watkins, *California,* p. 102.
[15]Ibid., p. 106.
[16]Dana, *Two Years Before The Mast,* p. 409.
[17]Watkins, *California,* p. 107.
[18]Ibid., p. 110.
[19]Chinard, "When the French Came to California," p. 293.

ously saw the opportunity for merchandising mining supplies and fine luxury items made in Europe. It appears that he carefully planned his relocation to California since he opened his hardware business soon after his arrival. The discovery of mineral wealth also interested Caire. This is evident by his involvement with the Buena Ventura Company, a mining enterprise, and also his purchase of mineral land located in Chili Gulch Mining District, Calaveras County.[20]

Caire traveled back to Genoa, Italy, in 1854 and married twenty-three-year-old Albina Christina Sara Molfino on December 13th of that year. After their marriage, they sailed across the Atlantic to Nicaragua, which had become a popular route for California-bound travelers. They crossed Nicaragua by land to the Pacific Ocean where they boarded a steamship for the twenty-day trip to San Francisco.[21] At first, Albina was disillusioned with the rough-and-tumble life of early San Francisco; hence she refused to learn English. When she saw there was no possibility of permanently returning to her home country, she finally learned the language.[22] Justinian and Albina Caire had nine children. Six children survived to adulthood: Delphine A. Caire (1856-1949), Arthur J. Caire (1859-1942), Amelie Caire Rossi (1862-1917), Aglae Caire Capuccio (1864-1943), Frederic F. Caire (1865-1950), and Helene Caire (1867-1929). Three children died in early childhood: Adrien M. A. Caire (1858-1858), Albert A. Caire (1862-1875), and Marie C. Caire (1871-1873).[23]

Delphine Adelaide Caire, the oldest child, was born in San

---

[20]See Inventory and Appraisement and Decree of Final Distribution in the *Estate of Justinian Caire.*

[21]Delgado, *To California by Sea,* pp. 55-59. To avoid the trip around Cape Horn, two alternate routes were developed: 1) the Panama route, and 2) the Nicaragua route which was thought to be easier than the Panama route. The heyday of the Nicaragua route was 1851-1855. In 1855, the Panama Railroad was completed across the isthmus making travel considerably easier across land. After 1855, the Nicaragua route fell into disfavor because of poor travel conditions and several steamer disasters. By 1856, only 8,053 passengers crossed Nicaragua as opposed to 30,335 who used the route through Panama.

[22]M. Gherini, "Santa Cruz Island," in *Anthology,* p. 64 .

[23]Dates of births and deaths and spellings of the family names were taken from death certificates.

68 Francisco on May 6, 1856. Her name described her roots. She was named for the snowy heights of Dauphine, France. Her middle name was the name of her paternal grandmother, Maria Adelaide Arduin Caire. After receiving a private Catholic education in San Francisco, she went to Paris at the age of twelve where she was educated at the convent of the Trinitarian Ladies. During the Franco-Prussian War she spent a year in Briancon, the birthplace of her father. She was a linguist and reading was her favorite pastime. One of her avocations was gardening. She loved trees, and during her many visits to Santa Cruz Island, she planted many of them.[24] For instance, at the east end of Santa Cruz Island she planted an Italian cypress grove high above the Scorpion Valley in the middle of a field where there is no water. The little montecito became known as "Delphine's Grove." Never having married, Delphine died on December 29, 1949, the year of the only recorded snowstorm on the island.

Arthur Joshua Caire was born in San Francisco on July 17, 1859. As the older of the two Caire sons, he became the spokesperson for both the Santa Cruz Island Company and the Justinian Caire Company. Arthur and his brother Fred married sisters. Arthur Caire married Mary Suich. According to Arthur Caire's niece, Helen Caire, he "studied chemistry and physics at the University of Santa Clara where he made a brilliant record; but he had also taken up surveying in one of his engineering courses at the University of California."[25] One of his avocations was photography, and he took many of the early photographs of the island. He developed the photographs on glass plates, and over the years he amassed a collection of historically invaluable photographs of the early days of island life. For many years Arthur served as president of the Justinian Caire Company and as secretary of the Santa Cruz Island Company. He died just short of his eighty-fourth birthday on June 29, 1942.[26]

---

[24]Caire, "In Memoriam," pp. 81-83.

[25]Caire, *Santa Cruz Island*, p. 70.

[26]*In the Matter of the Estate of Arthur J. Caire.* At the date of his death the inventoried probate estate was valued at $108,612. Arthur's 20 shares of the Santa Cruz Island Co. stock were valued at $96,000 and the 113.8 shares of the Justinian Caire Company were valued at zero.

Justinian Caire family (probably around 1908)
shortly before the legal battle that split the family:
Back row: Helene Caire, Esther Rossi, Ambrose Gherini, Fred Caire, Arthur Caire. *Next row:* Marie Rossi Gherini, Delphine Caire, Bob Rossi, Albina Caire (Mrs. Justinian Caire), Justinian Caire II on the lap of his mother Mrs. Arthur Caire. *Next row:* P. C. Rossi, Amelie Caire Rossi, Aimee Rossi. *Next row:* Beatrice Rossi, Olga Rossi, Mrs. Fred Caire, Caire child, Marie "Dini" Gherini, Nori Rossi, Edmund Rossi. *Next row:* Albina Rossi, Caire child, Caire child, Caire child, Carlo Rossi (partially hidden behind Caire child). Not pictured is Aglae Caire Capuccio *Photo courtesy of Marie Gherini Ringrose.*

70   Justinian Caire's next two daughters were Amelie Caire Rossi and Aglae Caire Capuccio. They were the only Caire daughters who married; this fact would later prove to be significant because of the role their husbands would play in the historic litigation over the ownership of Santa Cruz Island.

Amelie Caire Rossi was born on January 22, 1862. As a young lady of eighteen years, she married Pietro Carlo "P.C." Rossi in 1880. At the time of the marriage, Rossi was poor.[27] Justinian Caire introduced Amelie to Rossi, a graduate of the University of Turin, Italy. According to Edmund Rossi, one of their 14 children, his father was a druggist and chemist.[28] The University of California offered him an appointment in the Chemistry Department, but he turned it down to accept a position in 1881 as chief wine-maker of the Italian-Swiss Agricultural Colony located in Asti, California. He later became president of the Italian Swiss Colony, a director of the Italian American Bank, and secretary of the Swiss American Bank of San Francisco. Rossi was a well respected businessman. In 1907, Victor Emmanuel III of Italy conferred on him the title of Cavalier of The Order of the Italian Crown, which is equivalent to knighthood. Rossi met an untimely death on October 8, 1911, when he was thrown from his horse and buggy at Asti. He was fifty-four years of age when he died and was survived by his wife Amelie and ten of their children.[29] Two thousand people attended Rossi's San Francisco funeral. Persons of all walks of life mourned his tragic death. Rossi was known as a "friend of every man who knew him."[30] Six years after the death of her husband, Amelie died in 1917 at the age of 55.

---

[27]Unpublished memo of Ambrose Gherini, 1937, p. 12. Ambrose Gherini actually wrote three memos concerning the litigation which is discussed in this book. One memo was probably written in 1925 before the conclusion of the partition case; the second memo was probably written in 1937 after the Caires sold their interest to Edwin Stanton; and the third memo was written during the litigation and referred to settlement negotiations between Ambrose Gherini and Frank Deering in 1922. The memos, therefore, will be identified as: Unpublished memo of Ambrose Gherini, 1925; Unpublished memo of Ambrose Gherini, 1937; and the Deering memo.

[28]Rossi interview by Teiser, p. 6.

[29]*San Francisco Chronicle,* "Pietro C. Rossi killed in an accident," October 8, 1911, p. 1.

[30]*San Francisco Examiner,* October 12, 1911, p. 1.

Aglae Caire, born in 1864, married Goffredo Capuccio Sr., whom she met on the island, and they had two children, Goffredo, Jr., (1907-1986) and Aglae E. "Cita"(1910-1994). Goffredo Capuccio, Sr., worked for both the Santa Cruz Island Company and the Justinian Caire Company in San Francisco. Beginning in 1891, he periodically spent time as an employee on Santa Cruz Island where he eventually became a superintendent from 1892 to 1894.[31] He was first paid $40 a month, but when he became superintendent, he received $100 monthly. He left the island on June 21, 1894. Capuccio, Sr., also acted as secretary for the Justinian Caire Company and handled duties for the Italian Swiss Colony at Asti. Both Capuccio, Sr., and P.C. Rossi were close friends of their father-in-law, Justinian.[32] Goffredo died after suffering a stroke at Asti on July 2, 1915, at the age of forty-nine. His wife, Aglae, died on February 5, 1943 at the age of 79.

Frederic ("Fred") Caire was born on November 19, 1865. He became president of the Santa Cruz Island Company in 1897 and served in that capacity until the corporation was dissolved in 1946.[33] Fred devoted his life to the ranching operations on the island. Red Craine, who worked on the island from 1930 to 1951 for both the Caires and the Stantons, remembered Fred as a "very strict, very straight laced, but a very fair person."[34] After his brother's death in 1942, Fred carried on as president of the Justinian Caire Company until it was dissolved in 1945. He married Lillian Suich, the sister of his brother Arthur's wife. He was known as a Shakespeare buff. In addition, he entertained celebrities including John Barrymore who was interviewed by the *Santa Barbara Morning Press* in 1930 about his island experience. Barrymore's observations provide an intriguing insight into one of the possible underlying causes of conflict among island owners:

> He said he would like to own an island kingdom like Santa
> Cruz. "I'm going to have an island of my own some day," he

---

[31]Santa Cruz Island employee records.
[32]Cappucio, Sr. unpublished memo.
[33]Crocker-Langley, *San Francisco Directory, 1897*, p. 1505.
[34]Craine interview, p. 7.

said, "It must be great to be king of such a place, I envy Fred Caire more than anyone else I know; Santa Cruz is such a great, fantastic real dream of nature's own. It is one of the most picturesque places I have ever visited."[35]

Fred Caire died at the age of eighty-five on December 22, 1950, realizing that the island kingdom was no Camelot.[36]

Helena ("Helene") Caire, the youngest of the Caire children, was born on July 5, 1867. She never married and was never actively involved in the business of the Santa Cruz Island Company. She was known to have a "fine contralto voice" and would sing at the island chapel.[37] She died on January 19, 1929, at the age of sixty-two. She left no will, and as a result her estate was distributed equally to her brothers and sisters or to their descendants, despite the bitter and lengthy litigation among her siblings.

What type of man was Justinian Caire? He was a remarkable individual and an astute businessman with a very businesslike demeanor.[38] His eldest granddaughter Maria Rossi Gherini gives some insight.[39] Maria, the oldest of the children of P.C. and Amelie Caire Rossi, recalled that her grandfather "was a very kind man, with a keen sense of humor, and, maybe, somewhat formal at times."[40] She remembered him as a robust man with very blue eyes.[41] Maria Rossi Gherini received many notes from Justinian. Perhaps the most cherished was the note dated May 26, 1893, inviting her to see the new schooner *Santa Cruz* that her grandfather had just had built and which was moored at the Italian fisher-

---

[35]Caire, *Santa Cruz Island,* pp. 162-163.

[36]*In the Matter of the Estate of Fred F. Caire.* At the date of his death in 1950, his probate estate was $56,078 but did not include shares of the Santa Cruz Island Company which had been dissolved in 1946.

[37]Caire, *Santa Cruz Island,* p. 182.

[38]Rossi interview by Teiser, p. 12.

[39]According to the baptismal record of Maria, Justinian Caire and his daughter Delphine were her baptismal sponsors.

[40]M.Gherini, "Santa Cruz Island," in *Anthology,* p. 65.

[41]Gherini, unedited notes to Spaulding.

man's wharf in San Francisco. Maria was ten years old at the time. The note read:

May 26, 1893

Miss Maria Rossi—from town

Dear young lady,

If my memory fails me not, I will call for you tomorrow, Saturday at 2 P.M. to show you the new schooner *Santa Cruz,* which is moored at the Italian fisherman's wharf. Give all a good kiss for me. A hearty hug for yourself.

Justinian Caire[42]

In the next month, Maria Rossi Gherini along with others sailed to Santa Barbara to visit Santa Cruz Island.[43]

Because of his wife's fragile health, Justinian was advised by her medical doctors in San Francisco that Albina should return to Genoa. Accompanied by her younger children, she traveled to Italy in 1874 where she was met by her oldest daughter, Delphine, who was completing her education in Paris. The family remained in Genoa for about four years before returning to San Francisco.[44] Albina, despite her health problems, lived another fifty years.

THE JUSTINIAN CAIRE COMPANY

After Justinian Caire arrived in San Francisco at the age of 24, he went into partnership with Claude Long who made the journey around Cape Horn with him in 1851. Long and Caire were long-time friends and traveling companions. They opened a hardware business at 178 Washington Street under the name of Caire and Long Hardware.[45] It was a very successful store specializing in mining equipment, chemicals, assayers' equipment, and imported luxury items from Europe such as Sheffield plates from England, porcelains from France, and dolls from Germany. Later,

---

[42]Ibid.

[43]*Santa Barbara Morning Press,* June 28, 1893.

[44]Gherini unpublished memo, 1925, p. 2; M. Gherini, "Santa Cruz Island," in *Anthology,* p. 65.

[45]Morgan and Company, *San Francisco City Directory, 1852,* p. 16.

74 in 1854, they relocated to 142 Washington Street, San Francisco.[46] The partnership lasted until 1857.[47] In that year Long started his own hardware business at 64 Commercial Street.[48] Justinian then went into partnership with his brother, Adrien, who resided in Paris in order to purchase supplies for the store. The business was known as the Caire Brothers and remained at 142 Washington Street for ten years. Later the business was named the Justinian Caire Company and was located at 530-532 Washington Street until 1880 when Justinian relocated to 521-523 Market Street.[49] The firm was well known along the Pacific Coast.[50] Justinian Caire was president until his death in 1897. Thereafter his son, Arthur, became president, and Frederic served as vice president.[51] A year after Justinian's death, the company advertised its business as "hardware, chemicals, assayers' and chemists' materials, glassware, wire cloth, wine growers' supplies, optical and fancy goods and proprietors Excelsior Wire Works." In 1901, the company moved its business to 565-567 Market Street. In 1906, the San Francisco earthquake destroyed the Caire building, causing the company to relocate to 528 Mission Street where it opened in 1907. The following year, Arthur and Fred Caire moved the business to yet another downtown location at 573-575 Market Street where it remained for many years. The last address of the company was 268 Market Street.[52]

In the early days, Justinian Caire experienced one or two of the historic San Francisco fires that destroyed his business. Because of the fire risk, he dug a deep hole beneath his store which earned him the sobriquet "the crazy Frenchman." Justinian, however, had the last laugh. In a short while, another destructive fire swept

---

[46]Lecount and Strong, *San Francisco Directory, 1854*, p. 5.

[47]Joseph Bagget and Company, San Francisco Directory, 1856, p. 138. This was the last year that the business was advertised as "Caire and Long."

[48]Colville, *Colvilles's San Francisco Directory, 1856-1857*, pp. 30 and 131.

[49]Caire, "In Memoriam," p. 81. See also, Caire, *Santa Cruz Island*, pp. 37-39.

[50]Child, *Tools of a Chemist*, pp. 205-206.

[51]Fred became president of the Santa Cruz Island Company in 1897 and at one point later also served as president of the Justinian Caire Co.

[52]Crocker-Langley, *San Francisco Directory, 1898–1943*.

the town, but Caire had time to store his inventory in his cellar. As soon as the fire was extinguished, Caire was one of the few merchants in town who had an inventory of goods to sell.[53]

The Justinian Caire Company was incorporated on November 15, 1895. At that time the capitalization of the company shown by the Articles of Incorporation was $200,000. Four hundred shares with a par value of $500 were issued. Justinian gave each of his six children ten shares. Justinian held the other 340 shares and later transferred these shares to his wife Albina.[54] The original directors of the corporation were Justinian and four of his six children: Delphine (age 39), Arthur (age 36), Aglae (age 31), and Fred (age 30). The company advertised its business in the San Francisco Directory every year through 1943.[55] When Arthur died in 1942, his estate reported that the value of the company was zero. The Justinian Caire Company was finally dissolved in 1945.[56] There is little known evidence of what happened to this highly successful hardware business established by Justinian Caire. In 1917, the stock was appraised at $750 per share.[57] By 1929, the stock was reported to be worth $650 per share.[58] Between 1929 and 1942, the company's value collapsed, but the reasons for the collapse of the Justinian Caire Company are beyond the scope of this book since there are no source materials available. The company primarily imported specialty items. Certainly Prohibition, the Depression, and the decline in the mining and wine business contributed to its eventual demise.

FORMATION OF THE SANTA CRUZ ISLAND COMPANY

The ten investors who purchased Santa Cruz Island from

---

[53]M. Gherini, "Santa Cruz Island," in *Anthology,* pp. 63-64.

[54]Articles of Incorporation of Justinian Caire Company, November 15, 1895.

[55]Crocker-Langley San Francisco directories for years 1898-1943.

[56]Certificate of Winding Up and Dissolution of Justinian Caire Company, November 13, 1945.

[57]*In the Matter of the Estate of Amelie A. Rossi.* The executor valued the ten shares of the Justinian Caire Company at $7,500 or $750 per share in 1917, and after audit, the Internal Revenue Service accepted the value. As of 1917, the total value of the 400 shares issued would have been $300,000.

[58]*In the Matter of the Estate of Helene Caire.*

76 William E. Barron on February 16, 1869, immediately formed a corporation called the Santa Cruz Island Company. The Certificate of Incorporation declared that the corporation was formed "for the purpose of engaging in, conducting and carrying on the business of raising cattle" and that it "shall exist for fifty years from and including the date of this certificate."[59] On March 29, 1869, the ten investors conveyed their interest in the island to the Santa Cruz Island Company.[60] The company also purchased land, referred to as lot 325, in Santa Barbara on April 9, 1869, from James Barron Shaw who had purchased the lot in September 1858.[61] The vacant lot located on the corner of Bath Street and what is now known as Cabrillo Boulevard measured 300 feet by 200 feet. The lot contained corrals where the island sheep could be kept until there were enough to ship to the various markets.[62] The company probably also used the lot to process animals being shipped to the island.

The ten island investors, Gustave Mahé, Camilo Martin, Alexander Weill, T. Lemmen Meyer, Nicholas Larco, Adrien Gensoul, Giovanni Battista Cerruti, Justinian Caire, Thomas J. Gallagher, and Pablo Baca, were prominent San Franciscan business leaders whose associations with one another pointed to the widespread cooperation between the Italian and French communities in early San Francisco. Camilo Martin was consul for Spain. Giovanni Battista Cerruti of Genoa served in the Italian diplomatic corps. Alexander Weill of Alsace-Lorraine, France, worked for Lazard Fréres & Co., a hardware business he converted to an investment banking firm. Nicola (Nicholas) Larco, born in Genoa, established himself as an import-export commission dealer in groceries, provisions and coffee.[63] Larco owned a fleet of commercial

---

[59]Copy of Certificate of Incorporation, February 20, 1869.

[60]Indenture from Gustave Mahé, et al., to Santa Cruz Island Company, March 29, 1869.

[61]Indenture from James Barron Shaw to Santa Cruz Island Company, April 9, 1869. The company sold the parcel on May 21, 1900 to Edward R. Spaulding. See also indenture from Augustine and María Hinchman to James B. Shaw, September 23, 1858. This information was researched by John Hebda of Equity Title Company.

[62]Storke, *A Memorial,* p. 636.

[63]Baccari and Canepa, "The Italians of San Francisco," pp. 351-353; San Francisco Chronicle, December 11, 1996.

vessels that operated between Mexico and San Francisco and was probably the leading Italian merchant of the Pacific Coast in the 1850-1860s. Gustave Mahé, a banker, was simultaneously president and manager of *La Societé Francaise d'Epargnes et de Prévoyance Mutuelle,* a French Bank founded in 1860.[64] Larco was a founding officer of the bank and remained as its vice-president through 1862. On September 14, 1869, *La Societé Francaise d'Epargnes et de Prévoyance Mutuelle* paid off $50,000 of the Santa Cruz Island mortgage owed to William E. Barron and assumed the balance.[65]

In addition to the island investment venture, some of these men formed the Buena Ventura Company which was established on April 27, 1863. The Articles of Incorporation stated that the purpose of the company was "mining detaching, reducing ores and business appertained to mines. . ." The original capitalization for the company was $150,000.[66] The board of directors elected Justinian Caire as president and Larco as treasurer. The shareholders in this company included, among others, not only Caire, Martin and Larco, but also Domenico Ghiradelli, the famous chocolate manufacturer. The Buena Ventura Company was located at 612 Clay Street in San Francisco and was listed in the *San Francisco Directory* in 1863 and 1864.[67]

The 1870s were traumatic years for California. Prior to "The Terrible Seventies," gold and silver mania fueled speculation. The price of wool, inflated by the Civil War demand, collapsed by

---

[64]Ibid., p. 353. Baccari and Canepa point out that the investment and membership in the French Bank was shared by the French and Italian communities to such an extent that the bank was officially known under both its French and Italian names. Another example of the cooperation between the French and Italian communities is seen by the Italian Mutual Benefit Society sending its members to the French Hospital for major medical care, an arrangement continued after the demise of the Italian Hospital in 1874. (p. 354). See also Giovinco, "Democracy in Banking," 47: 202, and Caire, "A Brief History," p. 31.

[65]*La Societé Francaise d'Epargnes et de Prévoyance Mutuelle* mortgage to Barron, September 14, 1869.

[66]Articles of Incorporation of the Buena Ventura Company.

[67]Langley, *San Francisco Directory, 1863-1864,* pp. 83 and 87. Langley started publishing his directory in 1858. He usually published the directories annually. Prior to his directory there were various other directories which are mentioned in the notes.

78   1872.[68] In bankruptcy proceedings, the United States District Court in December 1872 ordered Nicholas Larco to turn over all his assets to the bankruptcy trustee.[69] On March 31, 1873, the directors of the Santa Cruz Island Company reincorporated to increase the capital stock of the company from $300,000 to $500,000 and to decrease the number of shares from six hundred to one hundred.[70] At this time, Justinian Caire owned one tenth of the outstanding shares. California's leading bank, the Bank of California, failed. The silver market disintegrated, and the drought of 1877 caused crippling losses leading to an economic depression that lasted from 1877 to 1880.[71]

From 1869 to 1880, the Santa Cruz Island Company experienced hard times. In the severe economic climate of the 1870s, the French Bank, which had assumed the mortgage of the Santa Cruz Island Company, also failed, thereby jeopardizing the shareholders' investment in the island company. This probably occurred after 1875 since the French Bank was still listed as being located at 411 Bush Street in San Francisco with Camilo Martin as treasurer and Gustave Mahé as a director.[72] To add to the company's woes, thousands of sheep were slaughtered for their pelts and tallow during the drought of 1876-77.[73] The San Francisco business directory in 1878 listed Gustave Mahé as president of the Santa Cruz Island Company and Marc De Kirwan as secretary.[74] On December 26, 1879, the company filed a certificate to diminish the capital stock with the Office of the Secretary of State. The certificate showed that the capital of the corporation was diminished to $50,000 from $500,000.[75] Gustave Mahé, one of the direc-

---

[68]Cleland, *The Cattle on a Thousand Hills,* pp. 208-209.

[69]Copy of bankruptcy order, dated December 13, 1872.

[70]Articles of Re-Incorporatlon of Santa Cruz Island Company, March 31, 1873.

[71]Bancroft, *History of California,* VII:688-689; Watkins, *California,* pp. 199-204.

[72]Bishop, *San Francisco Directory, 1875,* p. 24A.

[73]Cleland, *The Cattle on a Thousand Hills,* p. 209. Cleland says 70,000 were killed; Mason estimates that 25,000 were slaughtered. Mason, *History of Santa Barbara County,* 256. The County of Santa Barbara Assessors' Record show a flock reduction from 33,000 to 3,200 from 1876 to 1879.

[74]Bishop, *San Francisco Directory, 1878,* p. 755.

[75]Certificate of Diminution of the Capital Stock of the Santa Cruz Island Company, December 26, 1879.

tors, committed suicide, and the other directors could not meet the payments to Barron.[76] Because of the financial difficulties of the corporation, Justinian Caire began acquiring the other shareholders' shares. It is not known when, but Justinian Caire eventually became sole shareholder of the island company sometime in the 1880s or early 1890s, including the 30 percent ownership interest of Alexander P. More, one of the four More brothers who owned Santa Rosa Island at the time.[77] By 1880, Caire, having acquired a considerable number of shares of the Santa Cruz Island Company, first visited the island and decided to develop a diversified island rancho.[78]

---

[76]M.Gherini "Santa Cruz Island," in *Anthology*, pp. 64-65.

[77]Mason, *History of Santa Barbara County*, p. 204. Capuccio, Sr., unpublished memo. Mrs. Ambrose Gherini also refers to More's interest in the island in her interview with Spaulding as does Wentworth in *American Sheep Trails*, p. 204, fn. 42. Wentworth mentions that More owned "an important interest in the eighties and early nineties." There are no source materials such as the original stock certificates or other records of the Santa Cruz Island Company to verify More's ownership interest. The More brothers, however, were well known for their vast land holdings. Storke, *California Editor*, p. 24. It is not unreasonable to assume that the information was correct. The directors of the Santa Cruz Island Company during the 1870s were looking for an infusion of cash to expand operations of the company. It is for this reason that they probably increased the capitalization of the stock in 1873. Later in the 1870s, the company hit upon economic hard times. It was also reported that in 1876, a drought occurred and the wool market collapsed. See O'Neill, *History of Santa Barbara County*, p. 366. Justinian Caire most likely purchased at substantial discounts the interest of the other shareholders who were affected by the economic downturn and wanted or had to sell their shares in the Santa Cruz Island Company.

According to Arthur Caire, the island "has been in the Caire family exclusively since 1888–1889." Transcript on Appeal in *Rossi v. Caire*, S.F. 7101 (174 Cal. 74), p. 65.

[78]Caire, "First Visit to Santa Cruz Island, 1880," unpublished memo. In this unpublished memoir, Delphine states that she visited the island with her father and brother Arthur.

Justinian Caire Family

Justinian Caire and Albina Molfina*
(1827-1897)   (1831-1924)

Delphine A.	Adrien M.A.	Arthur J.	Amelie A.	Albert A.	Aglae S.	Frederick F.	Helene A.	Marie C.
1856-1949	(1858-1858)	(1859-1942)	(1861-1917)	(1862-1875)	(1864-1943)	(1865-1950)	(1867-1929)	(1871-1873)
		m. Mary Suich	m. Pietro Carlo		m. G. Capuccio	m. Lillian Suich		
		(1876-1961)	Rossi		(1866-1915)	(1878-1960)		
			(1855-1911)					

Arthur J. line:

1. Justinian Caire II
   (1906-1986)
   m. M. Bernheim
   Yvonne (b. 1939)
   Jacquiline (b. 1941)
   Justinian III (b. 1948)
2. Olivia Lucille (1909-93)
   m. G. Swortfiguer
   Arthur
   Robert
3. Miriam Frances
   (b. 1912)

Amelie A. line:

1. Albert (1882-1887)
2. Maria (1883-1960)
   m. Ambrose Gherini
   Marie (b. 1907)
   Elena (1908-1908)
   Ilda (b. 1910)
   Rosalia (b. 1949)
   Pier A. (1912-1989)
   Pier A., Jr.(b.1942)
   Elena (b. 1945)
   John F. (b. 1946)
   Thomas R. (b. 1951)
   Joseph (1955-1955)
   Francis (b. 1914)
   Francis Denby (b. 1942)
   Catherine (b. 1944)
   Andrea (b. 1956)
3. Sophia (1885-1891)
4. Luigi (1887-1891)
5. Robert (1888-1961)
   m. N. Mahoney
6. Edmund (1888-1974)
   m. B. Brandt)
7. Esther (1890-1968)
8. Aimee (1892-1985)
9. A. Olga (1893-1983)
10. Beatrice (1896-1989)
    m. J. Torrens
11. Gioberto (1897-1899)
12. Albina (1899-1988)
    m. C. Wall
13. Elenore (1901-1991)
    m. m. V. O'Donnell
14. Pietro Carlo (1902-1992)

Aglae S. line:

1. Goffredo (1907-1986)
   m. I Reidenauer
2. Aglae E. "Cita"
   (1910-1994)
   m. M. McDougald
   Lawrence (b. 1941)
   Catherine (b. 1945)

Frederick F. line:

1. L.A. Jeanne (1902-1978)
2. Marie (b. 1903)
3. Helen (b. 1905)
4. Delphine (b. 1906)
5. F. Vivienne (b. 1910)
   m. J. Chiles
   Mary B.
   Frederic
   James F.
   Catherine
   John G.

*Justinian's father and mother were Giovanni Battista Caire and Maria Anna Adelaide Arduin. Albina's parents were Benedetto Molfino and Brigida Rossi. (Marriage Record of Justinian and Albinia Caire.)

Chapter 5

Caire's Early Island Rancho: 1880-1897

The development of an island rancho presented formidable logistical problems of transporting large quantities of supplies to and from an island located twenty miles off the coast of California. Justinian Caire took on the challenge as the sole shareholder of the Santa Cruz Island Company. Justinian first visited the island in 1880; thereafter, he visited the island to oversee his company on many occasions.[1] Goffredo Capuccio, Sr., who knew and worked for Caire, and who married Caire's daughter, Aglae, described his management style: ". . .Caire was and acted all the time as the absolute owner of the island on which nothing was done, changed or performed in the least detail without his wish by anyone from his wife to the youngest boy."[2] A good example of this attention to detail is a letter Caire personally wrote on November 14, 1892, to the Santa Barbara Tax Collector

---

[1] For instance, some of his visits were noted in island diaries. There are ten diaries referred to in this book, most of them written in Italian by the foremen at Scorpion Ranch located on the east end of Santa Cruz Island. Dr. Bernadette Luciano, a lecturer in Italian at the University of California at Santa Barbara, translated specific entries. In one of the 1887 diaries, notation for January 21 reads "Il signor presidente arriavato" (president arrives). The diary on January 23rd reads: "Il signor presidente in compagnia della signora partitio per main ranch"(president and wife leave for main ranch).

[2] Unpublished memo of Capuccio, Sr.

82   inquiring of the amount of property taxes owed for the company's beach front lot No. 325.[3]

JUSTINIAN CAIRE'S EARLY ISLAND MASTER PLAN

Preliminary planning for an island enterprise began in the late 1870s. On Caire's first visit to the island in 1880, he observed that there was no running water to the buildings or water system. Unchecked streams dictated the course of stream beds as well as roads and caused much erosion. Previous owners, through the direction of Dr. Shaw, erected a number of structures including many of the buildings at the Main Ranch such as the superintendent's house and the house that sheltered the *mayordomo* who oversaw the workers. These and other facilities, like a kitchen, men's mess hall, bunkhouses, corrals, wagon sheds, stables, and shearing sheds at the Central Valley, demonstrated the existence of a major ranch operation established during the Barron era (1857-1869). Living conditions, however, were primitive and much remained to be done.[4]

Planning began in earnest after Justinian Caire bought out the other shareholders of the Santa Cruz Island Company. From 1880 through the 1890s, Justinian set out a master plan for establishing his creative and diverse enterprise on the island. Detailed drawings reveal the meticulous planning made for the entire island. The drawings show the locations of buildings and fields. Some of the drawings were on thin oil cloth sheets while others were on paper.

The aggressive development of an island ranching operation coincided with two significant events on the mainland at Santa Barbara. In 1871, workers completed Stearns Wharf which measured two thousand feet. This wharf replaced the Chapala Street pier built in 1868.[5] In 1887, eighteen years after the completion of the transcontinental railroad, the first Southern Pacific railroad arrived in Santa Barbara from the south.[6] It would take another 14

---

[3]Justinian Caire to Santa Barbara Tax Collector, November 14, 1892.

[4]Caire, "First Visit," unpublished article.

[5]Bookspan, *Santa Barbara By The Sea,* p. 49; Tompkins, *Stearns Wharf,* p.5.

[6]O'Neill and Meier, *History of Santa Barbara County,* pp. 218-225. See also Tompkins, *Stearns Wharf,* p. 26; Bookspan, *Santa Barbara By The Sea,* p. 37.

The last remaining blacksmith shop on Santa Cruz Island,
probably built in the 1880s, is located at Gherini Scorpion Ranch.
Photo by Wm. Girvan, 1960; Pier Gherini family collection.

years to complete the rail link to San Francisco.[7] Improvement to
the city's transportation system and increased competition from
the railroad facilitated the movement of heavy equipment, supplies, and livestock to and from the island.

To some extent, the island operation was self-sufficient; the
Santa Cruz Island Company developed many of its own resources
such as water, feed, meat, and vegetables. Because of the size of

[7]*Santa Barbara News-Press,* January 21, 1996.

84 the operation, the company nevertheless shipped vast amounts of supplies constantly to the island. The island enterprise included the production of wine, wool, tallow, meat, and olives. In the 1880s, workers cultivated extensive vegetable gardens which invoices show grew "red and white beans, red beet, cabbage, carrot, cauliflower, celery, chervil, onion, parsley, pea, sweet pea, chili pepper, Burbank seed potato, salsify, spinach, and turnip."[8] In addition, the ranch hands planted a variety of fruit trees including "the pear, apple, cherry, plum, peach, fig, pomegranate, orange, and lemon."[9] The blacksmiths repaired most of the equipment, fixed and sharpened the tools (plow points, picks, crowbars, etc.), and shoed the horses. They worked in several blacksmith shops which contained anvils, drills, vises, presses, bellows, and forges made with white firebricks manufactured by Tomas Carr & Son (1827–1893).[10]

The island superintendents kept detailed records of the island operation. They usually wrote their records in English, but sometimes they used French and Italian. For instance, the company's early purchase orders, printed in Italian, contained the following instructions: *"Vi occuperete quanto prima, od alla prima opportunita delle cose seguenti, e farete un repporto sopra ognuna delle stesse a questo ufficio"* (You will take care of as soon as possible or at your earliest opportunity the following and you will make a report on each of the same to this office).[11] Other records monitored the island's production capacity as well as all of its personnel. Caire obviously used meticulous record keeping to monitor the operations of this unique nineteenth-century island enterprise.

THE NINETEENTH CENTURY ISLAND WORKERS

The history of the island enterprise is also a history of the workers. Many of the early island workers came to the United States from Italy during the general wave of immigration to America between 1860-1920. The immigrants who came to the United States wanted work. Caire had just the place for them to

---

[8]Junak at al., *A Flora of Santa Cruz Island,* p. 30.

[9]Ibid; Warren, "The Agriculture of Santa Cruz Island," p.33.

[10]Lux Report during visit to Scorpion Ranch on December 9, 1895.

[11]Translation by Luciano.

fulfill their ambition.[12] The names of hundreds of Italian employ-ees filled the payroll registers. For example, the early personnel roster lists Pietro Bossi (laborer), Carlo Conterio (carpenter), Moglia Giacinto (cook), Guiseppe Laferrera (horse shoer), Domisio Monesi (saddler), Antonio Rabboni (mason), Paolo Pianfetti (blacksmith), Steffano Lififu (dairyman), Francesco Battaini (vineyard worker), Urcelli Giovannini (gardener), Battista Frova (painter), F. Mirati (butcher), A. Luricelli (fences), Faustino Fontano (driver), Giacomo Vitale (sailor) and many others.[13] The records reveal that Caire had hired numerous artisans and skilled workers, and his reliance on Italian workers may be explained by the fact that he was a close friend of his son-in-law, P.C. Rossi, who as manager of the Italian Swiss Colony encountered many Italians seeking to come to the United States to work.[14] It is not unreasonable to suppose that Rossi assisted Caire in the hiring of many of these workers. Over time, the work force became more diversified. Many of the vaqueros and shearers were of "Mexican-California stock, often with a dash of Indian."[15] At times the island work force may have exceeded one hundred employees but ususally sixty were employed on a regular basis.[16]

Life on the isolated island was rugged, undoubtedly lonely, and at times dangerous, resulting in occasional accidental deaths. For example, Tomás Sansoni was killed at the age of 28 by a runaway cart. Juan Bautista Pico drowned on July 6, 1891, and the *Santa Barbara Morning Press* reported in 1893 that Willie Raynol died from injuries suffered when he was badly cut by a mowing machine.[17] Angelo Forno died on August 4, 1895, after being thrown by a horse.[18]

Shore excursions to the mainland also could be perilous. In the same year, the *Santa Barbara Morning Press* told of the death of

[12]Graffy, "The Italian Renaissance in Santa Barbara," p. 75-76.
[13]Santa Cruz Island Payroll Records, 1885-1890.
[14]Unpublished notes of Pier Gherini.
[15]Caire, *Santa Cruz Island,* p. 85.
[16]Stanton and Daily, "Santa Cruz Island," p. 63; Pinney, *The Wines of Santa Cruz,* p. 21.
[17]*Santa Barbara Morning Press,* May 23, 1893.
[18]Daily, "Deaths on Santa Cruz Island," pp. 61-62.

one of the island's blacksmiths, Sicilio Ferdinando, who was sixty-four years old. Sicilio had apparently come to Santa Barbara from the island and started celebrating by "walking about town and drinking with his friends." As a result, he fell off the railroad bridge at Rancheria Street.[19]

Island work was hard and strenuous, but the food was excellent. The workers were allowed a quart of "piquette," a watered down wine, with their lunch and evening meals; on Sundays "they were allowed a quart of the best wine."[20] The pay probably was satisfactory. Early records show that the average worker's pay was $20 per month.[21] There was little time for social life, and family life was non-existent since few families lived on the island. Before the turn of the century, the only means of communication with the outside world was provided by the infrequent boat trips ferrying men and supplies back and forth to the mainland.

Fred Lux, who made a nine-day visit to the east end of the island on December 9, 1895, provided a glimpse of working days on the island and expressed his observations in a handwritten report. Lux noted that the men in the field with picks and shovels were leveling the ravines to make them passable. He remarked that the work should be done with "plow and scraper." At the Campo Grande field, which is located west of Scorpion Valley, he examined the fence. Even though the fence was in good condition, Lux felt that it needed some strengthening because of the rusting iron posts.

Lux advised that the water situation was adequate and that the plowing was progressing favorably. He observed that the blacksmith was making the necessary repairs to equipment, shoeing horses, sharpening drills and plow points. The sheep looked better than the feed would indicate, and the horses were in good

---

[19]*Santa Barbara Morning Press,* May 7, 1893.

[20]Eaton, *Diary of a Sea Captain's Wife,* p. 139; McElrath, *On Santa Cruz Island,* p.7; Pinney, *The Wine of Santa Cruz Island,* pp. 74-75. Pinney explains that "piquette" is "obtained by taking the tightly-compacted residue of skins and seeds from the press basket, breaking it up and adding water." The fluid produced by this method is low in alcohol and very likely to turn to vinegar unless sugar is added and additional fermentation allowed.

[21]Santa Cruz Island Company payroll records, 1885-1890.

shape. He saw workers repairing the stable, cutting and hauling the hay to the barn, and cleaning the yard. Lux also inspected the "zacateras" or hay barns and found them "in about the same condition as last year, except that the barn was braced on the inside with heavy poles which makes it firm against the wind."[22]

Because of the island's isolation, and the large number of employees, discipline was a key ingredient to the successful operation of the enterprise. A large sign consisting of eight slats of wood, written in Italian, hung in the dining room at the Main Ranch. The caption on the sign read: "Nella Sala Da Pranzo E Probito DI"(In the dinning room it is forbidden to"). Below the caption the wood slats read: *"Disdegnarella minestra"* (don't scorn your soup); *"Gettare Cibunterra"* (don't throw away nutritious food); *"Sporcare Latavola"* (don't mess up the table); *"Farchiasso a Tavola"* (don't make noise at the table); *"Sprecare il pane"* (don't waste the bread); *Nutrire i Cani"* (don't feed the dogs) and *"Annoiar i compagni* (don't annoy your companion). These phrases reminded workers of the rules of conduct.

As could be expected, not every employee subscribed to the required work ethic, and turnover was high. The company employee records (1885-1892) contained remarks about the worker's job performance. For instance, a notation described one worker as a "blockhead, not to return"; another worker was "discharged for drunkenness," and yet another worker was dismissed "as introducing whiskey on the island." One description characterized a worker as a "good worker but too talkative on the sly." The comments, however, were not all negative. Many of the workers received the notation, "good man," "good worker," "steady worker" or "good man in every respect."[23] These descriptions contradict the erroneous notion that under the patriarchal rule by the Caires, all the employees "were very happy" and "it was rare thing for anybody to leave the island."[24]

---

[22]Lux Report.

[23]Santa Cruz Island Employee Journals, 1885-1892.

[24]Gleason, *Islands of California,* p. 71.

THE SANTA CRUZ ISLAND RANCHES

The Santa Cruz Island Company under the direction of Justinian Caire divided the island into ten ranches/outposts that functioned as an integrated operation: 1) the Main Ranch; 2) Prisoners'; 3) Campo Punta West; 4) Rancho Nuevo; 5) Christy Ranch; 6) Buena Vista; 7) Portezuela; 8) Rancho del Sur; 9) Scorpion; and 10) Smugglers'.[25]

Santa Cruz Island is 23.5 miles long, but the distance by road or trail between the east and the west end of the island was much greater. Because of the widespread locations and the topographical separation of the areas of operation, Justinian Caire established the largest known private telephone system so that there could be communication from the outlying ranches to the Main Ranch.[26] His workers took four years (1885-1888) to build the communication system. The company installed hand crank telephones powered by one and one-half volt batteries at the different ranches.

The Main Ranch located in the Central Valley of the island was the headquarters for the entire operation and contained a number of buildings, including two winery buildings, a concrete reservoir, a dwelling, a mess hall and kitchen, an office, bunk houses, shearing sheds, a red brick stable, saddle shop, and blacksmith shop, as well as carpenter and tool sheds. Corrals, barnyards, gardens, and pastures accented the valley headquarters.[27]

Skilled workers made bricks of island clay. After shaping the bricks, they laid them in rows to dry. They used these bricks to build many of the buildings at the Main Ranch. The red brick walls of the chapel, the large and small stables, the double warehouse (1887) at Prisoners' Harbor and the two expansive winery buildings (1892) including a storage cellar of 151 x 51 feet and a fermenting cellar of 65 x 65 feet at the Main Ranch provide contemporary evidence of the workmanship.[28] Another small wine

[25]Daily and Stanton, "Santa Cruz Island, A brief history of its buildings," unpublished article, 1981.

[26]Caire, *Santa Cruz Island,* p. 68.

[27]Ibid., p. 63.

[28]Ibid., p. 76; Pinney, *The Wine of Santa Cruz,* p. 41.

Aerial view of Central Valley of Santa Cruz Island and Main Ranch complex.
Photo, 1985, by Wm. B. Dewey.

Photo taken around 1924 of Main Ranch complex in the Central Valley of Santa Cruz Island. *Photo taken by F. F. Flournoy survey team; Pier Gherini family collection.*

Winery buildings at Main Ranch in the Central Valley on Santa Cruz Island. The upper building was the crushing and fermenting cellar and the lower building was the storage cellar. *Photo, 1991, by Wm. B. Dewey.*

cellar called *Cantina Vieja* was built in 1890 when the original wooden bee house from the Barron era was raised and the stone cellar was constructed underneath it as the first floor.

Santa Cruz Island is perhaps the best watered of the offshore islands. There are five streams which flow throughout the year: *Cañada del Medio* in the Central Valley, *Cañada del Puerto* flowing to Prisoners' Harbor, *Cañada la Cuesta* and *Los Sauces* in the western part of the island and the *Aguaje* on the eastern end. In the early years of development of the ranch, lack of a water system, however, presented a major problem. At the Main Ranch, workers originally carried the water by wheelbarrow from the spring in the *Cañada del Medio*.[29] This was obviously insufficient for a grow-

[29]D. Caire, "My First Visit," unpublished article.

ing ranch operation, and the company soon developed a water system for the entire island. To improve the situation, particularly on the east end of the island where the water supply was more precarious, workers hand-dug water wells to a depth of 30-35 feet and lined the wells with elaborate circular stonework that can still be seen today. The wells were, in some cases, ten feet or more in diameter, and the wells had stepping stones along the inside so that workers could descend into the wells and clean them. Windmills were erected over the water wells to pump water into reservoirs or water tanks. The company also built two concrete covered reservoirs, capable of holding roughly 26,600 gallons, at the Main Ranch in 1889 and at Scorpion in 1885. Early ranch hands also constructed concrete collecting tanks and rock dams at three springs known as *Pato, Gallina* and *Mission.* From these collection points, water flows by gravity in pipes that lead to the Main Ranch.[30]

Although a mission was never established on the island as Father Tapis originally had recommended in 1803, Justinian Caire in 1891 built a small brick chapel at the Main Ranch. The chapel, located in the middle of the vineyard on the side of a hill overlooking the valley, measured 27 by 18 feet. Workers constructed the chapel from island fired bricks made by an expert Frenchman, island stone cut by able Italian stonemasons, and wrought iron crafted by a Sicilian blacksmith.[31] Years later, Pete Olivari (1886-1961), who came to the island in 1902 and worked on the island for fifty-nine years, took it upon himself to be the official caretaker of the little red-brick church. Every year he made an annual inspection of the chapel at Christmas time.[32] Olivari is buried at the chapel cemetery along with his parents.[33]

The Santa Cruz Island Company continued to use the Prison-

---

[30]Symmes & Associates' Report, pp. 43-48.

[31]D. Caire, "The History of the Holy Chapel," p. 17.

[32]Hillinger, *The California Islands,* pp. 97-98.

[33]Daily, "Cemetery of the Holy Cross," p. 41. The article notes that when Pete Olivari died he was buried on the mainland. Dr. Carey Stanton, who designed the cemetery in the mid 1970s, arranged with the Catholic Church to transfer the graves of Olivari, his parents, and the Stantons to the island.

ers' Harbor Ranch (known as "La Playa") as the central receiving point for all supplies necessary to maintain the extensive island operation. The company improved the large wharf that had been built during the Barron era. The wharf, made of eucalyptus piles, extended 475 feet into 16 feet of water. In 1887, the company constructed the twin red brick warehouses on the shore at Prisoners' and installed a small gauge rail from the end of the wharf to the warehouses. Flat rail cars were then used to transfer the heavy supplies from the wharf to the warehouses. Later, trucks took the supplies from the wharf to the Main Ranch. There were also large corrals for the sheep and cattle.[34] A post office existed for a brief period at Prisoners' Harbor. Arthur, Justinian Caire's older son, was commissioned as postmaster on March 28, 1895, but the small postal operation was discontinued in 1903.[35]

A beautiful two-story 10-room adobe was also built at Prisoners' Harbor in the Barron era, and later Justinian Caire substantially remodeled it in the style of Italian Renaissance in the 1880s. This handsomely proportioned two-story family house with its beautifully designed ironwork graphically highlighted the skill of the island artisans hired by Caire.[36] Unfortunately, this historic structure was dismantled in January 1960 because of severe damage from flooding.

Campo Punta West, adjacent to Forney's Cove, was located on the far west end of Santa Cruz Island, approximately six miles west of Christy. It was isolated, constantly buffeted by winds, and its primary function was to serve the hay fields on the island's west point. Early maps made in 1890 show a ranch house, a reservoir, foreman's quarters, sheep corrals, some hay barns, and other structures. This outpost was discontinued sometime prior to 1919.

Rancho Nuevo was located approximately midpoint between Campo Punta West and the Christy Ranch. The structures located

---

[34]Caire, *Santa Cruz Island,* pp. 61, 68; Symmes & Associates' Report, pp. 5, 50.

[35]Caire, *Santa Cruz Island,* p. 68.

[36]Letter from Robert I. Hoyt to Mr. Edward S. Spaulding, dated July 21, 1959; a copy of the letter was published in an article by Maria Gherini, "Santa Cruz Island," in the *Noticias* (Fall 1958).

Prisoners' Harbor wharf was originally built in the early 1860s.
Pier Gherini family collection.

at Rancho Nuevo were a two-story wood ranch house, a stable, chicken house, barn, and corral. Like Campo Punta West, its use eventually was abandoned.

The Christy Ranch, a well known out ranch located approximately 11 miles west of the Main Ranch, was situated on the western end of the island's Central Valley. The derivation of the name "Christy" is unknown, but a plausible explanation for the Christy name would be that Justinian Caire named it after his wife, Albina Christina, or after the Caire's youngest child, Marie Christian Caire (1871-1873). When Justinian took over the island, the Christy Ranch was known as the West Ranch, as shown on the early island maps prepared in 1890. The first known reference to the name Christy Ranch appeared on the payroll records of December 1891. It was spelled "Christi." Later the Santa Cruz Island Company records of 1894 show "West Ranch Station (Christy)."[37]

The centerpiece of the Christy Ranch was the Casa Vieja (formerly known as Casa La Cruz), a two-story adobe constructed during the Barron era in the early 1860s.[38] Dr. Shaw reportedly

[37]Santa Cruz Island Company Records.
[38]Symmes & Associates' Report, p. 54.

94 used this house as his residence at least during the shearing season at this location.[39] It is unknown when the adobe was built, but there is a significant black and red cross painting on an inside adobe wall (above the former door, now window, in the end bedroom) bearing the date of 1864.[40]

The Christy Ranch also included corrals, sheds, stables, a blacksmith shop, and other buildings necessary for a ranch operation. Since the Christy Ranch was eleven miles from the Main Ranch, it had to be more self-sufficient. Harvesting and shearing were its primary operations. Margaret Eaton, enchanted by the ranch's idyllic setting, commented: ". . .It looked so home-like with its coat of whitewash, nestled among the tall eucalyptus trees. . . I thought that place looked just like the farms back in Quebec, and commented that everything about the farm life was so peaceful. . ."[41]

Traveling east out of the Christy Valley and beyond the Centinela grade, one comes upon Buena Vista ("good view"), once a small wooden cabin built in the 1880s or 1890s, located on the road between the Main Ranch and Christy Ranch. It was not a ranch but only a temporary shelter for the workers and road building crews. Its panoramic view of the desolate Mount Diablo, the highest peak on the island, justified its name.

Just east of Buena Vista and before the descent into the Central Valley, one finds Portezuela, a major permanent outranch like Christy, Scorpion, and Smugglers'. Again, the early maps of 1885 and 1890 show a number of buildings, including an adobe residence, hay barns, corrals, and other ranch buildings. The structures at Portezuela ultimately fell into disrepair and vanished; the

---

[39]Reference to Dr. Shaw's house was made in the transcript in *Capuccio v. Caire*, p. 105. It would also be reasonable to assume that Shaw also had a residence at the Main Ranch which was the hub of ranch activity.

[40]Neuerburg, "The Painted Cross of Santa Cruz," unpublished article dated July, 1987. Neuerburg writes that the most probable candidate for painting the picture would be an elderly Chumash neophyte who had painted similar designs in one of the Indian rancho chapels such as Cieneguitas. This would be consistent with the fact that some of the island Indians returned to the islands to work in the 1860s. Johnson, "An Ethnohistoric Study," p. 76.

[41]Eaton, *Diary of a Sea Captain's Wife*, p. 105.

only standing remnant of the ranch buildings is the adobe two-hole outhouse which featured its own arched opening at the base of the foundation so that the toilet could be easily cleaned and remain well ventilated.

Rancho Sur, though not a major outranch, was located about two and one-half miles east of the Main Ranch in the island's Central Valley. Its wood buildings were constructed in the 1890s.

Scorpion and Smugglers' Ranches: Their Early Significance

Scorpion and Smugglers', located on the east end of Santa Cruz Island, were important permanent out-ranches. Little has been written about the early ranch days of this section of the island. These ranches not only played an important part in the development of Justinian Caire's island enterprise, but also comprise the area that the National Park Service acquired for the Channel Islands National Park. Scorpion and Smugglers', known as the granary, were the bases that supplied many of the food products and hay for the island operation.[42] The east end of the island contained large fields, each of which was numbered on the maps. These fields supported a variety of crops such as wheat, corn, potatoes, beans, barley, and onions, besides hay and alfalfa. The workers raised hogs for meat and chickens for meat and eggs. The foreman maintained a chart to keep track of production of each of the numbered fields; he even inventoried the number of eggs produced by the chickens. The Santa Cruz Island Company transported by ship many of these crops to Prisoners' Harbor. There the workers unloaded and transported the crops to the ranch headquarters by wagon. Sheep, cattle and horses grazed on the east end as well, which was ideal for such purposes because of the expansive mesas.

The early unpublished maps and diaries give a good account of the development of the east end of Santa Cruz Island. This section of the island would later be known as parcels 6 and 7 and consisted of approximately 6,200 acres. The maps contained a greater

---

[42]For example, the 1890 diary shows that in January/February of that year, 190 bales of hay being shipped from Scorpion to Prisoners' Harbor.

96 linguistic diversity than the diaries. Many of the early maps (1870s and early 1880s) contained French legends and described the fields as *champ*. Later maps contained a mixture of Italian, Spanish and English descriptions. The map makers, probably foremen or superintendents, used common Spanish words like *potrero* (a field or pasture for horses), *barranca* (ravine or gorge); *campo* (field); *grande* (great or large); *llano* (a level field or even ground); and *cañada* (ravine or canyon).[43] Some of the foremen working on the east end kept diaries (1885-1900) which described the nature of the ranch work for a given day. They usually wrote the entries in Italian, although some were written in French, with a sprinkling of a Spanish word or phrase.

Scorpion Ranch was the headquarters for the east end island operations, and Smugglers' served as an outpost for laborers who worked in the olive orchard and the vineyards located in Smugglers' Valley. A road connected the two bases of operation. In the 1880s the Santa Cruz Island Company usually employed eight to twelve men to work on the east end. In later years, the work force decreased. Most workers were Italian, although some were of Mexican descent.

The superintendent visited the east end of the island twice a month.[44] He would come from the Main Ranch either by horseback or by boat from Prisoners' Harbor. The horseback ride from the east end to the Main Ranch was about fourteen miles and took several hours. It was common for some of the workers to make the ride once a week.[45] The trail connecting the two ranches was located between the Montañon and Campo Chino. One superintendent observed that the trail was in the area where the "Montañon . . . cuts across the main east and west axis of the island like the arms of a cross."[46]

---

[43]For example, the Spanish name for 'pasture' was one of the most common generic terms in California and appears in the names of more than twenty land grants or claims. Gudde, *California Place Names,* pp. 48, 119, 169 and 255.

[44]Eaton, *Diary of a Sea Captain's Wife,* p. 148.

[45]Pier Gherini unpublished summary of his translation of the diaries.

[46]McElrath, *On Santa Cruz Island,* p. 74. For this reason, McElrath speculated, albeit erroneously, that this might be the origin of the island's name.

The ranches at Scorpion and Smugglers' were in full operation by 1885. Early maps depict many buildings, sheds and other structures at the Scorpion ranch including a residence, wood sheds, a carpenter shop, a blacksmith shop, baking ovens, wool sheds, a bakery, a granary, a general storage building, a *matanza*, a butcher shop, tallow furnaces, a garden store, barns, stables, corrals, a wagon shed, a chicken yard, wells, windmills, a water tank, water troughs, and a concrete reservoir.[47] At Smugglers', the ranch facility consisted of a residence, a separate one-room building for the foreman, a cookery, a bake oven, a tool shed, a supply shed, a stable, a well, a hog corral and water closets.[48] The 1885 maps show that both ranches had vineyards and large vegetables gardens.

During 1885, the company workers built roads, put in fences, enlarged the "old house," continued to build the barns, erected

[47]Map No. 22, 1885.   [48]Map No. 34, 1885.

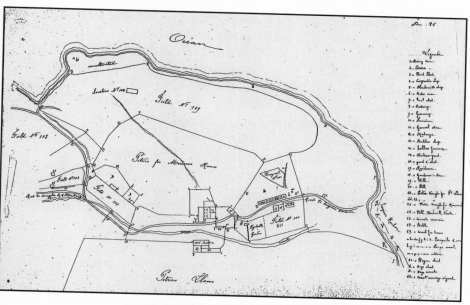

1885 Map of Scorpion Ranch complex.

98

shelters for pigs and sheep, strung a chicken fence, paved the stalls with stones and built a concrete reservoir. The laborers also planted some vineyards, fenced them presumably to keep out the pigs, and planted some corn and beans.[49]

The Santa Cruz Island Company made more improvements in 1886. Company laborers built a stone wall around the new barn, framed another sheep shelter, constructed a fence around the new wheat fields, built a barn in the *Campo Grande* ("large field"), and repaired the roof of the milk cellar. At the same time, workers planted potatoes, corn, and beans. Wool was shorn, sacked and shipped by schooner often referred to in the laborers' diaries in Spanish as *la goleta* (the schooner).[50]

Supplementing the other enterprises on the island, Caire's employees planted an olive grove at Smugglers' on the east end probably around 1887.[51] In 1885, the *Santa Barbara Daily Independent* reported that the olive industry was attracting attention and that California was the only state that had a suitable climate for olives. The newspaper article pointed out that olives did well in dry, rocky soil unusable for other crops or grazing of animals. This helps explain why Caire planted olive trees on the island.[52] The island company probably harvested and produced the fruit and the olive oil for both island consumption and occasional sales. The olive grove, which has been unattended for years, still remains at Smugglers'.[53] The olive orchard demonstrated Caire's intent to make maximum use of the island's resources.[54]

Caire also introduced eucalyptus trees in 1887 at Smugglers' Cove. He had his company field hands plant other trees such as fig, walnut, plum, chestnut, orange, and acacia. In addition, they

[49]Diaries from year 1885.

[50]Diaries from the year 1886.

[51]Unpublished notes of Pier Gherini's translation of work diaries.

[52]*Santa Barbara Daily Independent*, June 26, 1885.

[53]When Symmes & Associates, agricultural engineers, made their inspection in 1922 they observed that "no care or cultivation had been given for a number of years." pp.73-74.

[54]According to Pier Gherini's unpublished notes (probably in 1980s), he had the olives tested by Dr. Melville Sahyun, a prominent and well-respected scientist who developed many medicines. He found that the olives were edible and could be used for producing olive oil.

The Gherini Ranch house, built approximately 1887, at Scorpion, Santa Cruz Island. *Photo by Wm. Girvan, 1960; Pier Gherini family collection.*

planted more vineyards in Scorpion Valley and in Smugglers' Valley. The foreman, in his 1887 diary, reported that the workers continued to install stone floors for the barns, that work on the telephone lines between the Main Ranch and the east end had started, and that more rock work was done in the *potrero llano*.[55]

The company foreman, in an 1887 diary, wrote that there is "work on the attic of the new house."[56] This entry probably referred to the work on the two-story building that still stands in

---

[55]This diary entry could refer to the clearing of the field of rocks which were then piled into large mounds which can still be seen. It may also refer to numerous little rock walls built for trails and soil erosion control.

[56]Diaries from the year 1887. The houses at Scorpion and Smugglers' are often referred to as adobes. While some adobe may have been used, the primary construction materials were cement, limestone and other island rocks.

Scorpion Valley. One of the prominent features of the building is the two-story bread oven located on its west end in a small room. The room was used to store flour, bake bread and to keep the finished bread. Margaret Eaton observed that the large oven was made of white bricks and had a large iron door. With a four-foot long wooden spatula, the cook put the loaves into the piping hot oven which could bake twenty-five loaves at a time.[57]

According to an 1888 diary, workers continued setting up poles and stringing wire for the island telephone system between the Main Ranch and the east end of the island. The foreman noted that the workers "raised the roof" on barns No. 103, 104 and 106, and were constantly planting and harvesting crops, including the laborious task of clearing the fields of non-native mustard.[58] The mustard plant still grows wild and when in bloom provides a spectacular splash of color over large areas of the fields.

Extensive work continued in 1889. The foreman in his diary jotted down that the workers planted more eucalyptus trees, cleared field 107 to prepare for the planting of potatoes, planted more vineyards, reinforced barn 102 with poles, changed the poles at barns 103 and 104, built a fence around the alfalfa field, cracked and split stones to build water wells, and continued the constant planting and harvesting. The company also made a shipment of sheep from Scorpion which meant that the sheep were lightered to the schooner. While the foreman's 1889 diary does not specifically mention work on the house at Smugglers', the building itself bears the date "1889," which is probably when it was completed. Early maps, however, show a residence at the same location as early as 1885.[59] To make better use of the land, workers cleared the fields of rocks; then they piled the huge rocks into cairns which remain today as a monument to their labor. The island company built elaborate rock walls throughout the island particularly on the east end, both for road support and erosion control.[60]

---

[57]Eaton, *Diary of a Sea Captain's Wife*, pp. 146-147.
[58]Diaries from the year 1885-1888.
[59]1885 Maps, Nos. 30 & 34.
[60]Diary from year 1889.

One of many rock cairns on the Gherini Ranch, east end of Santa Cruz Island.
Wm. B. Dewey and wife, Anne, standing on top. *Wm. B. Dewey collection.*

The foreman, in his 1890 diary, scrawled a notation about work on building the "wall"; some of the narrative was in French. He also mentioned that "butter and cheese" were taken to the Main Ranch; early island maps show that the volcanic caves at Scorpion were used as "dairy caves" to store the dairy products.[61] According to the diary, the horses were brought to the Main Ranch, and the workers were burning the cactus.[62] Today, there is very little cactus to be seen.[63]

---

[61]See map No. 22, December 1885.

[62]Diary from the year 1890.

[63]Goeden, "Biological Control of Prickly Pear Cacti," pp. 579-606. Historically, two species of coastal prickly pear infested Santa Cruz Island. Overgrazing by the sheep rapidly spread the cactus. After the sheep denuded the grasslands, the cactus thrived when it came in contact with the soil. The cactus presented a constant problem for the owners over the years because it spread rapidly and rendered vast amounts of rangeland useless. Years later, island owners attempted to eliminate the prickly pear cactus through biological control. A number of insects which fed on the cactus were introduced with mixed results. Finally, in the 1950s and 1960s, the owners worked with the Department of Agriculture and introduced the cochineal insect called *Dactylopius* which was the most successful biological control agent.

The 1892 diary reflected that workers built more retaining walls to control erosion. The foreman described the wall work as *"porta pietre per fare l'impietramento [sic]"* (bring rocks to build wall) and *"fa l'impietramento nel torrente"* (builds wall in the stream).[64] At this time there were as many as four workers engaged on this project. The work presumably involved building the wall in the Scorpion stream bed, which is still evident today. The rock work throughout the island attests to Caire's reputation as a pioneer in soil conservation.[65]

The Santa Cruz Island Company in 1892 decided that a new road from Scorpion to Smugglers' needed to be built. The original dirt road to Smugglers' wound its way up the hills in upper Scorpion Valley but was unsatisfactory because of washouts from the rains. In early June 1892, laborers began work on the new Scorpion road located on the side of the Scorpion Valley hill near the beach. The hill had large outcroppings of volcanic rock. The foreman described the work as *"Lavora alla pietra"* (work at the rock). This work continued until the end of November 1892 and involved as many as thirteen workers a day. Usually the daily work crew consisted of nine to ten workers. The author of the 1892 diary identified some of the Italian laborers working on *"alla Pietra"*: Banduci, Bari, Marini, Benedetti, Mirati, Bottarini, Cantini, Boggio, Viole, Giuchetti, Ghigo, and Seri. Fred Caire arrived at Scorpion on September 17 to inspect the work. Map number 92, dated 1892, indicated for the first time that there was a road at this location leading out of Scorpion Valley to Smugglers'. The rock walls built to support the road were the largest rock walls built on the island. When Margaret Eaton first observed the roadwork in 1909 she quipped, ". . . Some stonemason who knew his business built that road."[66]

Over the years, the east end ranches continued to show their importance as a support base for the island operation. The island's east end, however, was obviously not self sufficient;

---

[64]Diary from the year 1892.

[65]Towne and Wentworth, *Shepard's Empire,* p. 211.

[66]Eaton, *Diary of a Sea Captain's Wife,* p. 136.

accordingly, the company shipped supplies, tools and equipment to Scorpion and to a lesser degree to Smugglers'. As was customary in those days, the company used small boats or lighters to off load supplies when there was no wharf.[67] The freight was unloaded onto a pontoon, and a heavy rope run from the schooner to a deadman on the beach. The crew working on the pontoon would guide it to shore as a team of horses on the beach would pull the lighter ashore.[68] The Santa Cruz Island Company used the "lighting" procedure to unload not only supplies but also heavy equipment. One of the largest pieces of equipment off loaded in the early years at Scorpion was the 6,000 pound two-speed Waterloo Boy kerosene-fueled tractor (Model S/N 12176).[69] The actual purchase and delivery of the Waterloo Boy tractor to the island occurred sometime in 1920.[70]

THE ISLAND'S BOAT TRANSPORTATION

Because of its location, the primary method of transportation to and from the island was by boat. Over the years many boats served the island. This was particularly true before the turn of the century when there were no airplanes to shuttle supplies and workers back and forth from the island.

The Santa Cruz Island Company purchased in 1869 a vessel *T. G. Sanborn* as its first schooner to serve the island.[71] Subsequently, the company bought the *Star of Freedom*, on which Justinian Caire made his first trip to the island and the sloop *Young*

---

[67]Prior to the construction of Stearns Wharf in Santa Barbara, lighters were used to off load supplies from the boats. Tompkins, *Stearns Wharf*, p. 3.

[68]Eaton, *Diary of a Sea Captain's Wife*, p. 144.

[69]Information concerning the 1918 Waterloo Boy tractor was researched by Tim McMahon. Other samples of equipment relics identified by McMahon and still located on the east end are: a horse drawn Van Brunt grain drill (circa 1920s), horse drawn John Deere mover (circa late 1920s); Adriance Platt & Co., horse drawn mower (circa 1920s). Symmes observed in 1922, that "with few exceptions, the equipment was old and insufficient. . ." Symmes & Associates' Report, p. 75.

[70]Santa Cruz Island Company reports, May 9, 1918. Superintendent Swain noted that the Waterloo Boy could be purchased for $1,450 f.o.b. Los Angeles. He suggested borrowing the lighter from the San Miguel Island Company.

[71]*Santa Barbara Post*, May 5, 1869.

104   *America.*[72] Captain Chase reportedly ran the *T. G. Sanborn* in 1869 and then later the *Star of Freedom* in 1874. The 1879 assessor's record show that one of the vessels was valued at $1,000 and this probably was the *Star of Freedom.*[73] The local newspapers often mentioned the sailing of these island boats. For instance, in 1880, the *Santa Barbara Daily Press* reported that the *Star of Freedom* brought from the island "over 180 lambs and 300 old sheep."[74] In 1885, the paper told of the sheep shearers going to the island for shearing on the *Star of Freedom.* In another instance, the newspaper reported in 1893 that the schooner *Star of Freedom*[75] took supplies back and forth to the island while the sloop *Young America* was the mail boat.[76]

Numerous other schooners and steamers transported supplies to the island. From 1849 through the mid-seventies, the Pacific Mail Steamship Company monopolized coastal transport. Service was unsatisfactory and at times unreliable. Another shipping company, Nelson and Perkins, bought the southern coast routes in 1875.[77] During the 1880s and 1890s, company invoices indicate not only the supplies shipped to the island but also the names of the vessels. For example, the records name such ships as the *Eureka, Mexico, Los Angeles, Newsboy, Bonita, Pomona, Alex Duncan, Corona, Coos Bay, Yaquina, Queen, Faralon, St. Paul, City of Pueblo, Homer* and finally the well-known shipping vessel *Santa Rosa* that ran aground and broke up on July 7, 1911, near Honda Creek just north of Point Arguello.[78]

Justinian Caire decided to build his own island schooner which he named *Santa Cruz.* Caire commissioned shipwright Matthew Turner to build the *Santa Cruz* in Benecia, California. "Build her strong!" he told Turner.[79] The vessel was launched on May 9,

[72]Justinian Caire, II interview by Marla Daily, November 14, 1981.
[73]Santa Barbara County Assessor Record, 1879, p. 279.
[74]*Santa Barbara Daily Press,* March 29, 1880.
[75]Ibid., March 21, 1885.
[76]*Santa Barbara Morning Press,* May 5, 18, 1893.
[77]O'Neill and Meier, *History of Santa Barbara County,* p. 226.
[78]*Santa Barbara Daily Independent,* June 21, 1990.
[79]Caire, *Santa Cruz Island,* p. 61.

1893, and underwent a series of trial runs. For sixty-seven years, the schooner battled the often mountainous waves of the Santa Barbara Channel while making its weekly trips to Santa Barbara for mail and supplies. The trip took 3-4 hours each way. The *Santa Cruz* carried 200-250 head of sheep which was a full load and sufficient to fill a double-decker rail car if the destination was other than Santa Barbara. When hauling cattle, the schooner could also carry 15-22 head which was satisfactory for the local market.[80]

The *Santa Cruz* sailed for Santa Barbara on June 25, 1893. The *Santa Barbara Daily Independent* heralded the long awaited arrival:

> . . . The steamer schooner *Santa Cruz* arrived in the harbor Sunday night from San Francisco, which port she left Saturday morning. The *Santa Cruz* is the vessel recently built for Justinian Caire, for the coasting trade between Santa Barbara and Santa Cruz Island, and the island and San Francisco. She is forty-three tons of burden, sixty-four feet in length, eighteen feet in beam, and has a forty-four horse power gasoline engine. Capt. John Revello is in command.[81]

On June 27, 1893, the *Santa Cruz* made its maiden voyage to the island from Santa Barbara. On board for the trip were Justinian Caire, his wife Albina, their children Aglae and Helene and their granddaughter, Maria Rossi Gherini.[82] In 1960, after sixty-seven years of continuous island service, the *Santa Cruz* sank. She broke her mooring lines in a strong northeaster wind and crashed onto the shore at Prisoners' Harbor.[83]

THE ISLAND VINEYARD (1884-1939)

The Santa Cruz Island Company started planting vineyards in various locations on the island as early as 1884. The company planted in the Central Valley an extensive vineyard that eventually expanded to approximately 150 acres. To a lesser extent, it estab-

---

[80]Symmes & Associates' Report, pp. 87-88. The schooner was subsequently modified in the 1930s by its skipper, Red Craine, to carry more cattle. Craine interview.

[81]*Santa Barbara Daily Independent,* June 26, 1893.

[82]*Santa Barbara Morning Press,* June 28, 1893.

[83]Caire, *Santa Cruz Island,* p. 63. Previously, on Sept. 19, 1913, the *Santa Cruz* wrecked at Rincon Point. The company refloated and repaired the schooner. Transcript on Appeal in *Rossi v. Caire,* S.F. 7101 (174 Cal. 74), pp. 124-25.

106   lished vineyards in Scorpion and Smugglers' Valleys on the east end of the island.

In 1881, about the time Justinian was developing the island, Andrea Sbarboro, a Genoese, founded the Italian Swiss Colony winery in Asti, California. He came to California in 1852. Sbarboro, a banker, conceived the idea of forming an agricultural cooperative. It was originally called the Italian Swiss Agricultural Colony. His idea was to provide Italian and Swiss immigrants with work and an opportunity to purchase shares in his cooperative by deducting a small amount of money from their pay check. While the cooperative idea did not succeed, the establishment of a grape growing and wine production operation did.[84] Later, Sbarboro helped to organize the Italian-American Bank that had a variety of prominent businessmen on the board of directors, including P.C. Rossi.[85] Sbarboro, credited with the founding of the Italian Swiss Colony, was not active in its management. Rossi was largely responsible for the successful wine operation. Because of their close relationship, Rossi probably advised his father-in-law, Justinian Caire, concerning the growing of vineyards on Santa Cruz Island.

Historically, it was well-known that there was "Franco-Italian cooperation in early San Francisco, a symbiosis which ranged from journalism, to mutual aid and medical institutions, to business and politics."[86] There is strong evidence that not only was there cooperation in providing work opportunities for Italian immigrants, but also there must have been substantial cooperation among Caire, Sbarboro, Rossi and others in the development of the island enterprise—particularly the vineyards.[87]

There were many similarities between the island wines and growing practices and those of the Italian Swiss Colony in Asti.[88]

---

[84]*History of Italian Swiss Colony,* 1915, pp. 8-10, See also Rossi interview by Teiser, pp. 3-10.

[85]Giovinco, "Democracy in Banking," 47: 203-204.

[86]Baccari and Canepa, "The Italians of San Francisco in 1865," 60: 354.

[87]For example, Adrian Merle worked for Caire and was said to be one of his principal advisors. Merle was also involved with the Italian Swiss Agricultural Colony as a stockholder and director. Unpublished memo of Goffredo Cappucio, Sr., p. 3.

[88]Pinney interview by John Gherini and Marla Daily on April 23, 1993.

Both the types of grapes used and the growing practices were similar and consistent with other California growers. The island vines were probably obtained from California sources.[89] The dominant red grape produced on the island was the Zinfandel. In 1880, the *Santa Barbara Daily* reported that "it is claimed that the Zinfandel is now the most popular grape in California."[90] The second most frequently planted red grape on the island varied, and sometimes included Burgundy, Mataro and Grenache. As for the white grape, Burger dominated until 1912 and then Muscatel took on the role as the leading white wine in the final days.[91]

Once the vines were established, cuttings were propagated from on-site nurseries. The company planted the vineyards so that there was wide spacing between the vines and rows. The workers "head-pruned" the vines to allow them to grow as self supporting bushes instead of being tethered to a support or trellis. The workers plowed and cultivated the vineyards in the spring and summer and harvested the crop in the fall. During the summer months vineyard work was light and easily handled by a few men.[92]

Justinian Caire's decision to go into wine growing and production seemed like a logical business decision and was consistent with other California growers. The early diaries and records suggest that the wine growing operation started in 1884. The California wine industry had been expanding since 1880 as reported by the *Santa Barbara Daily Press* which noted the potential for expansion of California's viniculture industry.[93] This expansion was fueled by the crisis in wine growing in Europe created by the devastation caused by the plant louse called *Phylloxera vastatrix* (devastating dry-leaf creature).[94]

---

[89]Helen Caire stated that selected vine stocks from France were obtained in the 1880s. Caire, *Santa Cruz Island*, p. 73. This is probably not correct. It is unlikely that any European wine stocks were used on the island before the turn of the century since *Phylloxera* was destroying many European vineyards. Pinney, *The Wine of Santa Cruz Island*, p. 27.

[90]*Santa Barbara Daily Press*, February 24, 1880.

[91]Pinney, *The Wine of Santa Cruz*, pp. 46-48.

[92]Ibid., pp. 63-65.

[93]*Santa Barbara Daily Press*, March 4, 1880.

[94]Pinney, *The Wine of Santa Cruz*, pp. 25-27.

108   Justinian Caire probably planned from the start to build a winery instead of just marketing grapes. The logistics of simply shipping the grapes to market would have been difficult, and there was no winery of sufficient size in the Santa Barbara area to handle the island grape crop. As a result of poor demand for California wines, the grape market collapsed in 1886.[95] This event certainly would have changed Caire's mind if his original plan was to market the grapes and not produce wine. Nevertheless, he continued the development of his vineyards, and the diversification of his other island enterprises enabled him to withstand the collapse of the grape market.

According to the Santa Cruz Island Company records, most of the wine produced on the island included various types of red wine. In 1904, 44,000 gallons of wine, red and white, were produced. The company reached its highest production in 1910, almost doubling the figure for 1904, with 83,000 gallons.[96] Red wine predominated over the production of white wine. "The proportion was never less than three to one, and sometimes it was a good deal higher than that: it was almost ten to one, for example in 1912 and 1913, and twelve to one in 1914."[97]

At one point, the Santa Cruz Island Company was the largest wine producer in Santa Barbara County and was one of two to grow grapes other than Zinfandel and Mission. The company shipped most of the island wine in barrels to the mainland, but wine was also bottled on the island. The usual shipment consisted of 50 gallon barrels or 168 gallon puncheons.[98] The island wine production (100-150 acres) was small in comparison with other wine operations such as the Italian Swiss Colony which had over 4,400 acres in production and had different wineries with a storage capacity of 14,650,000 gallons.[99]

Prohibition in 1919 halted the island wine operation with the

---

[95]Ibid., pp. 27,

[96]Ibid., pp. 46, 66. Pinney calculates that one acre produces 3-4 tons of grapes. Each ton yields approximately 150 gallons of wine.

[97]Ibid., p. 47.

[98]Ibid., p. 79.

[99]*History of Italian Swiss Colony.*

last vintage in 1918 producing 63,000 gallons of wine.[100] After the repeal of Prohibition in 1933, the wine operation resumed for a while, but it was not successful. However, Prohibition did not end the use of the island grapes. During Prohibition the island company shipped grapes to Santa Barbara for the Commercial Transfer Co., located at 14 East Cota Street in Santa Barbara and owned by Peter Giorgi and Angelo Miratti.[101] They in turn hired the island crew to pick the grapes. After shipping them to Santa Barbara on the *Santa Cruz*, Giorgi and Miratti sold the grapes to Italian families who made their own "fruit juice."[102] Wine production on the island ended in March 1936. In that year Santa Cruz Island Company produced 25,641 gallons of mostly Zinfandel. The last wine was disposed of in 1939.[103] By this time, Edwin Stanton owned most of the island which he purchased in 1937. Stanton wanted to get out of the wine business which was dormant at the time of his purchase. The wine started to spoil and Stanton decided to drain the vats which contained almost 25,000 gallons of wine. Justinian Caire II, Justinian Caire's grandson, recalled that "the wine drained down the road. . .this was pretty tough on the men."[104] The curtain fell on fifty-five years of island winemaking.

THE ISLAND SHEEP

Justinian Caire, noted as one of the pioneer sheep barons, conducted a consistently profitable sheep business on the island.[105] Much of the credit for establishing a profitable island sheep ranch, however, should be given to William E. Barron who preceded Caire on Santa Cruz Island, and to his superintendent, Dr.

---

[100]Pinney, *The Wine of Santa Cruz Island*, p. 87.

[101]The company was unincorporated, and Giorgi and Miratti advertised their business as "freight hauling and moving of all kinds." *Santa Barbara Directory*, 1932.

[102]The Volstead Act, the law implementing the constitutional amendment, permitted families to produce up to 200 gallons a year of "non-intoxicating fruit juice," a term difficult to define and enforce. Pinney, *The Wine of Santa Cruz Island*, p. 88. See also Craine interview.

[103]Ibid., pp. 93-94.

[104]Justinian Caire II interview by Marla Daily on November 14, 1981.

[105]Towne and Wentworth, *Shepard's Empire*, p. 209.

James Barron Shaw. They had already established a large sheep operation on the island by 1869 when Caire, along with other investors, bought the island and formed the Santa Cruz Island Company. After he became the sole shareholder of the company, Caire improved the sheep operation and introduced the pure bred Rambouillet-Merinos to the flock.[106] Approximately 35,000 to 40,000 sheep roamed the island in the early years. The company sheared the sheep twice a year; in the summer of 1890 the company reportedly herded over 50,000 into the corrals.[107] The island company raised the sheep both for the meat and for the high quality wool, a characteristic of the Rambouillet-Merino stock.

In 1880, when Justinian Caire first went to the island, he saw that a profit could be made not only in wine, but also in the sheep market. In the boom of the 1880s, good quality wool sold for 82 and 85 cents per pound.[108] Caire soon realized that any successful sheep operation would be a daunting task considering the size of the island. The vast acreage and rugged terrain made it impractical to fence many areas of the island, although some 60 miles of fencing enclosed approximately 9,000 acres of *campos* and *potreros*. The island sheep for the most part had the run of the land and grazed on the island's various forage plants.[109]

Cowboys, called *Barbareños* from the Santa Barbara area, undertook the actual sheep roundups called *corridas*. They were usually hired during the time of the roundups and would find other work during the slack season.[110] It took a skillful rider and a trained horse to herd the sheep over steep and dangerous canyons. Clifford McElrath, island superintendent in 1920, observed that "the sheep are like deer in some respects. When they see a rider, instead of heading down hill for the valley or flat land, where they can be driven in a bunch to the corrals, they

---

[106]Caire, *Santa Cruz Island*, p. 71.
[107]Ibid., p. 101. See also Symmes & Associates' Report, p. 60.
[108]*Santa Barbara Daily Press*, March 30, 1880.
[109]McElrath, *On Santa Cruz Island*, p. 98; Symmes & Associates' Report, pp. 40, 58, 77.
[110]Caire, *Santa Cruz Island*, p. 85.

head for the highest and roughest country."[111] At other times the roundup would go smoothly until something spooked the lead sheep, and the flock then would break at a pell-mell speed in all directions. If 10,000 sheep were corralled out of 25,000, McElrath recalled that they thought they had done well.[112]

McElrath stated that the *Barbareños* would one day be riding the range in the roundup and the following day become shearers.[113] While there may have been cowboys doing double duty, it is more likely that the shearers followed the *Barbareños*. The number of shearers who participated in the annual island shearing gives some idea of the scope of the operation. The *Santa Barbara Morning Press* reported in March 1893 that "forty-five shearers left for Santa Cruz Island yesterday on the schooner *Star of Freedom*. The shearing will take six weeks."[114]

The backbreaking work of shearing, referred to as *trasquila*, took place in the hot and dusty shearing sheds which were usually subdivided into smaller pens for the shearers. From a pen, the shearer pulled a sheep which could weigh between 90-200 pounds depending on the age and type of animal (ewe, lamb or ram), wrestled it to the ground, tied the feet and then started shearing. In case the sheep was cut or nicked in the process, a young boy, called *el aceitero* (the oiler), quickly dabbed the cut with a brush dipped in a mixture of pine tar and turpentine. The shearer then took to the tying table the fleece which could tip the scales anywhere from 15 to 25 pounds. There above the table sat the *mayordomo* or *el fichero* who dispensed a *ficha*, a small coin about the size of a penny which had the company initial emblazoned on it. For every sheep shorn, the shearer received one *ficha;* the *mayordomo* awarded the shearer an extra *ficha* for shearing a buck. At the end of the day, the shearers turned in their *fichas;* accordingly, the bookkeeper recorded the number on their account.[115] A strong

[111]McElrath, *On Santa Cruz Island,* p. 27.

[112]Ibid., p. 35.

[113]Ibid., p. 32.

[114]*Santa Barbara Morning Press,* March 26, 1893, and *Santa Barbara Independent,* March 21, 1885.

[115]Caire, *Santa Cruz Island,* p. 112.

112 shearer could shear 70 to 80 sheep a day with hand clippers which had to be sharpened often on a sharpening stone.[116]

The *sacador* (the sacker) packed the shorn wool in six-foot long burlap sacks weighing over 300 (and sometimes over 400) pounds when full. These large sacks were hung from a wooden scaffolding which had a platform on the top. A worker charged with gathering the wool tossed the fleece up to the platform. A sacker on the platform stuffed the fleece into the sack by physically getting into the sack and stomping on the wool to compact it. When the sack was full, the sacker sewed it closed. The workers then removed the heavy sack from the scaffold so that they could weigh and mark it. After this task was completed, the workers moved the cumbersome wool sacks to the side of the shearing shed and started stacking them. They eventually removed the wool sacks from the shearing sheds and stored them in the brick warehouses at Prisoners' Harbor. The storage facilities allowed the company to hold the wool until market conditions dictated a sale. When that happened, the company shipped the wool to the markets.[117]

Once the sheep were shorn, the flock was often separated. The *capadores* then castrated some of the bucks. The cut buck was called a wether. The ranch hands divided the flock into fat lambs, wethers, and sometimes fat ewes, and they herded a number of animals aboard the schooner and transported them to the mainland.[118] Shipments would either be made directly to San Francisco and San Pedro by coastwise steamships or directly to Santa Barbara. Before the building of Stearns Wharf, boat crews lightered ashore the sheep but pushed the cattle overboard to swim ashore. The animals off loaded in Santa Barbara were usually shipped to the Los Angeles stockyards. The fine island wool gained a well known reputation among buyers from Philadelphia, Boston and Chicago.[119]

The island sheep experienced few diseases. Before being

---

[116]McElrath, *On Santa Cruz Island,* pp. 32-33.
[117]Caire, *Santa Cruz Island,* pp. 116-118.
[118]Ibid.
[119]Towne and Wentworth, *Shepard's Empire,* p. 210.

shipped to the island, the company quarantined the flock and dipped, wormed and disinfected the animals. Ranch hands repeated this procedure on the island before the new flock was mixed with the other sheep.[120] Among the few natural predators that the sheep faced were ravens and eagles that usually attacked the small lambs.

Besides the wool and meat, tallow was sometimes produced when the island became overstocked or when in seasons of drought there was not enough feed for the sheep. In that event, the company slaughtered large numbers of sheep at the Main Ranch for their pelts and tallow. The slaughter took place in the *matanza,* a two-story building located in the southwest portion of the Main Ranch yard. The company built a smaller facility in 1885 or earlier at the Scorpion Ranch.[121] The operation consisted of killing and dressing the sheep, putting the carcass in a closed boiler or steamer and subjecting the animal parts to immense heat and pressure. The process forced out the tallow and glue, which were separated for market. The workers then fed the dry residue to the hogs. A local historian reported that 12,000 sheep were processed in the *matanza* in 1875 and another 25,000 slaughtered in 1877.[122]

THE CATTLE OPERATION

The original Articles of Incorporation of the Santa Cruz Island Company, filed on February 20, 1869, stated that the business of the corporation was "raising cattle." The initial investors in Santa Cruz Island obviously had something more than sheep in mind when they bought the island. A cattle operation, started after 1869, was maintained for over a century on the middle of Santa Cruz Island particularly between Chinese Harbor and Prisoners' Harbor and on the east end of the island. Initially, the cattle on the island were not longhorns. The standard island breed was gentle shorthorn cattle. The Island Company allowed the cat-

---

[120]Ibid. See also, Symmes & Associates' Report, p. 60.

[121]The 1885 diaries refer to a "fence built around sheep to be slaughtered." See also map no. 22.

[122]Mason, *History of Santa Barbara County,* p. 256.

114   tle to roam free for the most part. Until 1918, the company never branded the cattle. Then a state law was enacted that established the Bureau of Livestock Identification in 1917. It became necessary to brand the cattle to sell them. Santa Cruz Island Company thereupon established its own brand, S+, and registered it on April 17, 1918.[123]

A large cattle operation was never practical for the rugged terrain of the island. Al Vail, one of the former owners of Santa Rosa Island where there has been a substantial cattle operation since 1902, explained that at least ten acres of good grazing land is needed for every head of cattle.[124] From 1937 to 1987, when nine-tenths of the island was owned by the Stanton family, a small cow and calf operation became the cattle operation on the island. In 1988, the cattle operation was discontinued.[125]

The sheep and cattle operations at times led to armed conflict. The island was so large and the areas where both sheep and cattle roamed so remote that the livestock was perfect prey to poachers. It presented a difficult problem both for the company and law enforcement agencies. One diary notation made in June 1898 stated, "I surprised some individuals shooting at the sheep in the *llano* field. As soon as I arrived on the site, they fled quickly and I was unable to obtain any further information."[126] Eventually, some of the island workers armed themselves. Exchange of gunfire between the workers and rustlers occasionally occurred.[127] Arrests and convictions, however, were rare.[128]

Justinian Caire's granddaughter, Helen Caire, in writing about the rustling situation on the island, observed:

---

[123]Caire, *Santa Cruz Island*, p. 72. See also McElrath, *On Santa Cruz Island*, pp. 53, 75. McElrath's claim that he suggested the brand is probably not correct since it was registered in 1918, and he did not come to work for the island until 1919.

[124]Oral interview with Al Vail by John Gherini on Santa Rosa Island on June 30, 1993. The Symmes' Report estimated that the island's capacity could be "800 head of stock cows and some 2,000 head of all ages." p. 79.

[125]See editors comment in Caire, "The Last Vaqueros," p. 107. During the Stanton era there were generally 2000-3000 head of cattle at any one time.

[126]Diary from the year 1898.

[127]Letter from McElrath to Sheriff James Ross, September 20, 1920. See also McElrath, *On Santa Cruz Island*, pp.41-42.

[128]Caire, *Santa Cruz Island*, pp. 54-55.

... from these accounts it may seem that the islands are places of turbulence and unrest. On the contrary, they lie peacefully under the open sky. From the mainland of California they seem to hover on the horizon like dreams, but they are real.[129]

Reality, however, was that island conflict, in one fashion or another, continued.

---

[129]Ibid., p. 57.

Chapter 6

Conflict Among the Caires: 1897-1932

The Caire family controlled Santa Cruz Island for fifty-seven years (1880-1937) through the Santa Cruz Island Company. Legal proceedings dominated the later Caire era. Justinian Caire wanted his family to enjoy the fruits of his labor and wanted all his children to equally share his fortune. Caire's plan unraveled after his death in 1897. His surviving wife, Albina, made unequal distributions of stock and other assets among her six children. As a result, Justinian's married daughters, Amelie and Aglae, were virtually disinherited but for 14 shares of stock in the Santa Cruz Island Company and 20 shares of stock in the Justinian Caire Company, which were later determined to be worthless.

Little has been written about the twenty years of litigation during the Caire era.[1] The Caire litigants for two decades used the legal system to vindicate their positions. Amelie and Aglae attempted to salvage a small portion of their father's vast estate. Arthur, Frederic, and Delphine navigated the courtrooms to maintain control of the island through the Santa Cruz Island Company. Helene tried to remain out of the family fray. To this

---

[1] While there has never been a comprehensive reporting of the litigation, it is discussed in an article published in 1937. See Ellison, "History of the Santa Cruz Island Grant," pp. 270-283. More recently, see John Gherini, "Santa Cruz Island: Conflict in the Courts," pp. 165-170.

118 day the topic of the Caire family litigation has been studiously avoided by Caire family members through five generations.[2]

JUSTINIAN CAIRE'S WILL AND DEATH

Justinian Caire set forth a simple estate plan in his will which he signed on January 24, 1889. In the will, Caire left all his estate to his wife, Albina, if she survived him and named Albina as executor of his estate. His will stated, "It is my present desire, if the wishes and interests of my said wife and children should unite therein, that the business now conducted by me in this city, should after my death, be continued by them in the same place, with as little change and alteration as possible."[3] There was no specific mention of the Santa Cruz Island Company or the Justinian Caire Company in the will. Presumably, Caire meant "the business" to mean collectively both companies since they were both managed in San Francisco.

Four days later Justinian Caire amended his will to provide that if his wife Albina did not survive him, his estate was to be given to his children to "share and share alike; and should one of them be dead, I leave to his or her children the share which would belong to their father or mother according to the distribution mentioned above." In the event his wife did not survive him, Justinian named his sons, Arthur and Frederic, as executors and stated that they were to become "guardians of their sisters." In other words, Justinian Caire felt that his sons had a fiduciary obligation toward their sisters.[4] In his amended will, Justinian Caire also made a sim-

---

[2]Justinian Caire's granddaughter, Helen Caire, in her 1993 book about the island briefly but incompletely alludes to the litigation: ". . .A long, self-defeating litigation which began in 1912 dragged through the courts for years, ending in 1925 in a partition of the island among the litigants. This partition was based on Christmas gifts by Mrs. Justinian Caire of seven shares of the Santa Cruz Island Company to each of her six children some years previously." Caire, *Santa Cruz Island,* p. 175. The historical evidence indicates that there was more to the litigation than the "Christmas gifts" of stock. As will be explained in this chapter, what caused the underlying problem between the Caires was a desire by some of the Caire children to gain additional stock and therefore the control of the Santa Cruz Island Company.

[3]Justinian Caire's will dated January 24, 1889 was filed in his probate case.

[4]Today, under California law, both the directors and majority shareholders clearly have a fiduciary obligation toward minority shareholders. *Jones v. H.F. Ahmanson & Co.* (1969) 1 Cal.3rd 93 at 108.

ilar provision concerning his business in San Francisco except that he added ". . . that the business now conducted by me in this City, should after my death be continued by my two sons above named in the same place, with as little change and alteration as possible."

Caire built an enterprising island operation unique in California history. Those halcyon ranch days ended with his death in Oakland on December 10, 1897.[5] He was seventy years old. According to the obituaries, Justinian had suffered a partial stroke eighteen months before his death. Up until that time he was active in running his businesses. The *San Francisco Examiner* noted that Justinian "was a strong man who took great care of himself during his lifetime."[6] After he had his partial stroke, Justinian retired, and his two sons, Arthur and Fred, managed the businesses in which they had been actively involved since the early 1880s. During his eighteen-month retirement, the *Oakland Enquirer* reported that Justinian "lived very quietly and enjoyed comparatively good health until a few days ago when he was suddenly taken ill and gradually grew weaker until the end came."[7]

The *San Francisco Call* featured a large picture of Justinian Caire on the day of his death. The article described Justinian as ". . .one of the best known merchants of San Francisco, and he has always enjoyed first class commercial rating."[8] A similar accolade appeared in the *Santa Barbara Morning Press* on December 14, 1897. Curiously, all of the obituaries about Justinian Caire never mentioned his ownership of the Santa Cruz Island Company. It would be the company and its major asset, Santa Cruz Island, that would forever perpetuate his memory.

On January 13, 1898, Justinian Caire's will was filed for probate in Alameda County Superior Court.[9] The bulk of his assets, including the shares of stock of the Santa Cruz Island Company and the Justinian Caire Company, were not administered as assets

[5]Caire, "The History of the Holy Chapel," in *Chapel of the Holy Cross*, p. 21.
[6]*San Francisco Examiner*, Obituaries, December 11, 1897.
[7]*Oakland Enquirer*, Obituaries, December 11, 1897.
[8]*San Francisco Call*, Friday, December 10, 1897.
[9]The probate case was entitled, *In the Matter of the Estate of Justinian Caire.*

120 of his estate. According to the inventory and appraisement filed in Justinian Caire's probate estate, the only probate assets of Justinian's estate were fractional interests in parcels of mineral land located in Chili Gulch Mining District in the County of Calaveras, California. These estate assets were valued at $2,000.[10]

The lack of reported assets in Justinian Caire's estate raises questions as to the purpose of the transfers made before he died. Was it simply to avoid probate or was there another motive? Justinian's granddaughter, Helen Caire, observed that ". . .Some years before his death in 1897, Justinian Caire deeded his entire stock of the Santa Cruz Island Company to his beloved wife, Albina Maria Christina Molfina Caire. He intended that she and all her children should enjoy the island and continue ranching operations there. . ."[11] Caire's other assets including the family residence located on Madison Street in Oakland, and the shares of stock in the Justinian Caire Company were also transferred to his wife Albina prior to his death. The Articles of Incorporation, filed with the California Secretary of State on November 15, 1895, show that Justinian Caire then owned 340 shares of the Justinian Caire Company. Arthur Caire, using his father's power of attorney, signed the Articles of Incorporation. Sometime before his death in December 1897, the valuable capital stock of the Justinian Caire Company was transferred to his wife. It is unknown whether this transfer was done by Justinian himself or by his son Arthur. This also may have been the time when Justinian transferred his shares of the Santa Cruz Island Company to his wife. Shortly thereafter, he suffered a stroke.

POSTURING FOR CONTROL

Like the geological makeup of the island, events subsequent to the death of Justinian Caire fractured the Caire family into two distinct groups and plunged Justinian Caire's heirs into twenty years of litigation which lasted from 1912 to 1932 and involved

[10]Inventory and appraisement and decree of final distribution *In the Matter of the Estate of Justinian Caire.*

[11]Caire, *Santa Cruz Island,* p. 175.

eight appeals.[12] During this period there were four significant deaths among the Justinian Caire family: Goffredo Capuccio, Sr., a son-in-law, died in 1915; Amelie Caire Rossi, Caire's daughter, died in 1917; Albina Caire, Justinian's wife, died in 1924; and Helene Caire, the Caires' youngest daughter, died in 1928. The Caire conflict spanned a time in which the United States experienced World War I, the Roaring Twenties, Prohibition, the Great Stock Market Crash, and the ensuing Great Depression.

The litigation presented an unlikely scenario for the devoutly Catholic family in which Justinian Caire's own success allowed him the luxury of educating his children in European schools. Goffredo Capuccio, Sr., Justinian Caire's son-in-law, observed that the litigation was exactly what the gentle Justinian Caire would not have wanted. Problems appeared to surface in the 1880s and 1890s. Capuccio's unpublished memo, prepared sometime between 1913 and his death in July 1915, provided some insight:

> . . .In the flourishing and building up his fortune he [Justinian] was greatly helped by a faithful relative whom he had brought from France, Mr. [Adrian] Merle, now dead, who was in his employ and considered almost as Mr. Caire's partner, but who left when Arthur Caire and Fred Caire, who were being educated in Italy, came and entered their father's business about the year 1880 or perhaps later. Animosity, hostility, jealously, envy and hypocrisy it was said was seen shown by the young Caires against their relative who was compelled to quit.[13]

Events spun out of control after Justinian Caire's death. Some-

---

[12]Unpublished memo of Ambrose Gherini, 1937, p. 2. Gherini stated in his memo that he wrote a summary of litigation ". . . as I am the only surviving attorney, and the one who was connected with the litigation from its inception to its conclusion," p. 16. Gherini listed the eight appeals as follows: *Rossi v. Caire* (1916) 174 Cal. 74; *Rossi v. Caire* (1921) 186 Cal. 544; *Rossi v. Caire* (1922) 189 Cal. 507; *Capuccio v. Caire* (1922) 189 Cal. 514; *Rossi v. Caire* (1919) 39 Cal. App. 776; *Capuccio v. Caire* L.A. No 7709 (dismissed from the bench); *Capuccio v. Caire* (1929) 207 Cal. 200; and *Capuccio v. Caire* (1932) 215 Cal. 518.

[13]Unpublished memo of Capuccio Sr., p. 3.

122   time in 1905 and 1906, Albina and her oldest and youngest daughters, Delphine and Helene, visited Europe. While they were away, earthquakes and fires devastated San Francisco in April, 1906. The fire destroyed the Justinian Caire Company building, located on Market Street, with most of its contents, including Albina's will and many of the company records. Albina Caire's son-in-law, P.C. Rossi, whose business was not destroyed, allowed the Caires to continue business in a portion of his building.[14] After the San Francisco fire, Albina visited her daughter Aglae and her son-in-law Goffredo in Spezia, Italy. Years later, Goffredo Capuccio, Sr., recalled Albina complaining to him that her sons "were annoying her about making a new will as the old one was destroyed in the fire."[15] Helene related to Capuccio that her brother Arthur tried to get her to make a will but she refused.[16] Helene died intestate (without a will) in 1929.

    Frederic Caire contacted his close friend, Joseph R. Bluxome, the family attorney, to prepare a new will for his mother. The new will as drafted left Albina Caire's entire estate to her six children, except for Amelie Caire Rossi and Aglae Caire Capuccio, who were given their shares as a life estate with Frederic and Arthur as their trustees. This provision was indeed curious since the two married daughters' husbands were personally very close to Justinian Caire. The will was apparently sent by Arthur Caire to Italy with instructions for Albina to sign it. However, Goffredo Capuccio, Sr., Aglae's husband who was also in Italy, learned about the new will, obtained a copy of it, and sent a copy to P.C. Rossi.[17] Tremors began to rock the Caire family.

---

    [14]Unpublished memo of Ambrose Gherini, 1937, p. 13. It would be reasonable to assume that when Justinian signed his will in 1889, Albina also signed a similar will. This would have meant that all of their children would have shared equally in their parents' estate.

    [15]Unpublished memo of Capuccio Sr., p. 1. If Albina had no will, her estate would have gone equally to her children if Justinian did not survive her. Therefore, if members of the family didn't like the equal distribution, they would have had a reason to urge their mother to make a new will.

    [16]Ibid., pp. 1-2.

    [17]Ibid.

Upon receiving a copy of Albina Caire's new will, Amelie's husband, Rossi, wrote Capuccio on August 30, 1906:

> . . . I cannot do without remarking the insult that with such a document is hurled at Amelie as well as me, just as against Aglae and you and there is no doubt, that if such an indecency would come about, they would never live enough to regret the step taken. For the time being I would advise you not to even mention it to Aglae, because it would cause her too much sorrow, and it would be an unmerited humiliation, but when the opportune moment comes we will see what we will have to do.[18]

THE SEEDS OF DISCONTENT SOWN BY TRANSFER OF ASSETS AFTER JUSTINIAN CAIRE'S DEATH

After Justinian Caire's death, his widow, Albina, made several distributions of shares of stock of the Santa Cruz Island Company which issued a total of 100 shares. The distribution of the stock would prove to be historically significant. In the first round of distributions, Albina gave each of her six children seven shares of stock.[19] Albina retained 58 shares. This pattern of equal distribution to the Caire children was consistent with the way Justinian Caire had distributed the shares of stock of the Justinian Caire Company when it was incorporated in 1895.

Control of the Santa Cruz Island Company shifted in June 1911 as Justinian Caire's widow, Albina, made additional transfers of shares of the Santa Cruz Island Company. The transfers were in unequal amounts, and conflict ensued. After subsequent transfers, Albina retained 45 shares; Arthur and Fred Caire each held

---

[18]Letter from Rossi to Capuccio Sr., August 30, 1906. The letter was written in Italian on Italian Swiss Colony stationery. The letter was translated in 1982 by Fr. P. Carlo Rossi, S.J., who was the youngest of Amelie and P.C. Rossi's children. Father Rossi, a renowned scholar, spent fifty years as professor of Romance Languages at the University of San Francisco.

[19]Albina did not distribute shares at the same time. For example, stock certificate No. 6 in the Santa Cruz Island Company was issued on April 18, 1906, to Aglae Caire Capuccio for seven shares. Over four years later, she gave seven shares (certificate No. 8) in the company to Amelie Caire Rossi on December 21, 1910.

124

12 shares; Delphine Caire held 10 shares. Helene Caire, who had 7 shares of stock, felt that some shares "had been wrongly taken from her mother . . . had to be returned."[20] Helene nevertheless voted with her mother, brothers and sister Delphine. These shareholders, with 86 shares, were the majority and controlling shareholders of the corporation. Sisters Amelie Caire Rossi and Aglae Caire Capuccio with 7 shares of capital stock each were the minority shareholders.

Albina Caire died in Oakland on October 31, 1924, at the age of ninety-four. Although her will and codicil were offered to probate, there were no assets left to be administered since she transferred most of her assets to four of her six children during her lifetime.[21] Her will sheds some light on the transfer of the shares of stock. For instance, in her will dated April 17, 1912, Albina stated that she gave her two sons Arthur and Fred Caire an additional two shares each "in recognition of their generosity in turning over to me portions of their salary from time to time, and their devotion to my interests."[22] In addition, the will notes that Albina sold three shares each to Delphine, Arthur and Frederic. Albina's 1912 will also left the residue of the estate in equal shares, but the one-sixth interests to Amelie and Aglae were to be held in trust for them during their lifetime by Frederic and Arthur, who were also nominated as executors of her will.[23]

[20]Unpublished memo of Capuccio Sr., p. 2.

[21]A codicil is an amendment to a will which requires the same formalities as a will. Albina's will dated April 17, 1912, and codicil, dated June 18, 1913, were filed on November 7, 1924, *In the Matter of the Estate of Albina Caire*. Unpublished memo of Ambrose Gherini, 1937, p. 14. From his notes and records, it is apparent that Ambrose Gherini personally checked the estate file.

[22]Albina Caire's will. This is odd since Albina was the majority shareholder of the prosperous Justinian Caire Company. There is no evidence that Albina was in any financial trouble.

[23]Albina Caire's 1912 will also states that "to each of said six children I have heretofore given seven (7) shares each of the capital stock of the Santa Cruz Island Company, and have likewise given to each ten (10) shares each of the capital stock of the Justinian Caire Co." Albina's 1912 will further recited that she was disposing under her will of 45 shares of the Santa Cruz Island Company and 336 shares of the Justinian Caire Company. The statement by Albina in her 1912 will concerning her gifts of the Justinian Caire Company stock is puzzling since she made no gifts of this stock to her dauqhters Amelie and Aglae. The only shares they received of the Justinian Caire Company were the ten shares each

A year later on April 28, 1913, Albina, then eighty-three years old, transferred her remaining 45 shares of the Santa Cruz Island Company to Fred, Arthur, Delphine, and Helene.[24] This assignment gave Fred 23¼ shares, Arthur 23¼ shares, Delphine 21¼ shares and Helene 18¼ shares. About the time that Albina turned over her remaining shares of the Santa Cruz Island Company, she also conveyed all her 336 shares of the Justinian Caire Company to Fred, Arthur, Delphine, and Helene. In her codicil of June 13, 1913, Albina disinherited her only married daughters, Amelie and Aglae.

THE FORFEITURE OF THE COMPANY CHARTER:
AN OVERVIEW

In the words of P. C. Rossi, the "opportune moment" came when the Santa Cruz Island Company accidentally failed to pay a $5 license tax in November 1911. Ironically, those in control of the company precipitated the litigation by failing to pay the tax. At the time, Fred was president and Arthur was secretary of the company. Under section 6 of the Act of March 20, 1905, a corporation law, the non-payment of the license tax resulted in the forfeiture of the corporate charter. The law then stated that the directors were trustees for all the shareholders; therefore, they were obligated to liquidate the corporation and distribute the assets to the shareholders. As part of this liquidation, the trustees had to account for all the corporation's assets and make distribution to the shareholders.

When the company forfeited its charter in 1911, Justinian Caire's widow Albina and each of the Caire children owned shares of the Santa Cruz Island Company. At that time, the division of

---

received upon the incorporation of the Justinian Caire Company in 1895. They received no further shares of this stock from their parents. This left 4 shares unaccounted for since 400 shares were oriqinally issued. It is known that Arthur had an extra share. The inventory and appraisement filed in Amelie Caire Rossi's estate in 1917 showed only ten shares of the Justinian Caire Company. See Inventory and Appraisement filed *In the Matter of Amelie A. Rossi*. The ten shares were valued at par at $7,500.

[24]The 45 shares of the Santa Cruz Island Company were issued to Albina Caire on June 13, 1911, as evidenced by stock certificate No. 12. This certificate was subsequently canceled, and new certificates totaling 45 shares were issued to Arthur, Delphine, Fred and Helene on April 28, 1913.

126   the 100 shares of the Santa Cruz Island Company stock was as follows: Albina had 45 shares; Frederic and Arthur each had 12 shares; Delphine had 10 shares; and Helene, Amelie, and Aglae 7 shares each. Albina, and her children, Frederic, Arthur, Delphine, and Aglae were the company directors. The largest asset of the corporation was Santa Cruz Island, but the corporation also had substantial personal property. (See appendix for description of personal property.) Shortly after the forfeiture of the charter, the directors, with the exception of Aglae Caire Capuccio, attempted to rehabilitate the company under a law enacted in 1913 and continued to do business as the Santa Cruz Island Company.[25]

The marriage of the oldest of Amelie's fourteen children, Maria, would also prove to be historically significant. Maria, Justinian Caire's granddaughter, married Ambrose Gherini on October 30, 1906. Ambrose Gherini, born on October 19, 1878, in San Francisco, spent twenty years (1912-1932) representing Amelie Caire Rossi and Aglae Caire Capuccio's interest in the island litigation. Ambrose attended Stanford University for a year; went to Oregon to study at Mount Angel Abbey operated by the Benedictine Fathers and then transferred to Yale University where he obtained his bachelor and law degrees on the same day in 1902. He began a general practice of law in San Francisco in 1904 and later served as vice consul to the Russian government.[26]

Gherini later observed that the seven shares of stock of the Santa Cruz Island Company which Amelie and Aglae each received were the only assets that the two married Caire sisters received out of their father's vast island enterprise. The Santa Cruz Island Company paid no dividends and made no distributions to the shareholders. These shares, according to Ambrose Gherini, would have been worthless if the Santa Cruz Island Company had not forfeited its charter and if Amelie and Aglae had not

---

[25]Albina C.S. Caire et al. indenture to The Santa Cruz Island Company, January 30, 1917. By this indenture, Albina C.S. Caire, Arthur J. Caire, Fred F. Caire, and Delphine A. Caire as directors and trustees of the Santa Cruz Island Company quitclaimed any and all interest the defunct corporation had to the rehabilitated corporation.

[26]Unpublished interview of Marie Gherini Ringrose, June 24, 1983. Yale University still awards the Ambrose Gherini prize "for the student writing the best paper upon a subject of international law, either public or private."

Ambrose Gherini and Goffredo Capuccio Sr., (circa 1911-12). *Photo courtesy of Ilda Gherini McGinness.*

The Capuccio family figured prominently in the history of the island. From left to right: Goffredo Capuccio, Sr. (1866–1915), Aglae Caire Capuccio (1864–1943), and their children, Aglae E. "Cita" (1910–1994) and Goffredo, Jr. (1907–1986). *Photo courtesy of Ilda Gherini McGinness*

128 pursued their legal rights as shareholders of the company. Gherini concluded that Delphine, Arthur and Fred Caire had conspired to control the Santa Cruz Island Company and had prevailed upon their elderly mother, Albina, to make the unequal distribution of stock.[27]

This situation, coupled with the fact that Amelie and Aglae were virtually disinherited from the balance of Justinian Caire's fortune, served to heighten tensions within the Caire family. Out of 400 shares of stock of the Justinian Caire Company, Amelie and Aglae received only ten shares each. The shares later became worthless.

The litigation also compounded the personal losses of both Amelie Caire Rossi and Aglae Caire Capuccio. Amelie was widowed when P.C. Rossi died in 1911, leaving ten children. Aglae Caire Capuccio, whose husband died in 1915, had to raise two minor children. Aglae expressed her deep-seated feelings when she wrote that Edmund Rossi, one of Amelie's adult children, was to be "special guardian of my children; this is because I do not want those of my brothers and sisters who, in my most trying days caused me so much suffering, in any way to come in contact with or influence my children."[28]

The division of the Caire family was clearly defined. On one side, there were Albina, and her four children, Arthur, Frederic, Delphine, and Helene. They were the majority shareholders who held 86 shares of the company stock. Except for Helene, these shareholders were also the majority members of the board of directors and referred to during the litigation as "trustees."[29] It does not appear, however, that Helene actively joined the fray since she resisted suggestions to make a will and as a result of dying in 1929 without a will, her estate of $209,832 was divided equally among her siblings and their issue according to California

---

[27]Ambrose Gherini 1937 unpublished memo, p.14.

[28]Letter from Aglae Capuccio to Ambrose Gherini, June 1, 1916.

[29]Aglae was a minority director. Actually all the directors were legally considered trustees, but since the majority consistently voted aqainst Aglae, the majority directors for the purposes of this book will be referred to as the trustees. This is also consistent with the rule that majority directors have fiduciary responsibilities to the minority shareholders.

law.[30] On the other side of the family dispute there were sisters Aglae Caire Capuccio, who was the lone dissenting member of the board of directors, and Amelie Caire Rossi. On May 23, 1912, Amelie transferred her shares to her son, Edmund Rossi, to represent her.[31] Therefore, throughout the litigation the parties challenging the trustees were Edmund Rossi, Caire's grandson, and Aglae Caire Capuccio, Caire's daughter. The twenty years of litigation can be broken down into four areas: (1) the injunction lawsuit; (2) the accounting action; (3) the partition of the island; and (4) lawsuits concerning attorneys' fees.

(1) THE INJUNCTION LAWSUIT

In 1912, the Caire conflict entered the courtrooms. Then, the Eatons, who had lived on the island for many years, were still leasing the Pelican Bay Camp on the north side of Santa Cruz Island west of Prisoners' Harbor. It was the year that the scenes for the motion picture called "Heart of My Heart" were shot on the island. Bessie Holt was the leading lady and Edward Peil the leading man.[32] The use of the island for filming movies became routine and within a year the Eatons had obtained permission from the Caires to start a "resort" which would attract writers, film companies, and many people from across the country and which would last until 1937.[33]

Litigation quickly became routine for the Caires. On July 12, 1912, the first of many lawsuits was filed by Edmund A. Rossi, the son of Amelie, in San Francisco Superior Court.[34] The lawsuit

---

[30]The Inventory and Appraisement filed *In the Matter of Helene A. Caire* showed that in 1929 Helene owned a total of 94 shares of the Justinian Caire Company stock. This stock was appraised at $61,100. The estate file also reveals 10 shares were represented by certificate Nos. 5, and 84 were represented by certificate No. 14. Her estate also had 18¼ shares of Santa Cruz Island Company stock valued at $127,750 or $7,000 per share. This value was a $1,000 per share more than the $6,000 per share valuation in the partition case. The difference may be attributed to the dates of valuation. The partition date value was 1911. The date of valuation for the *Estate of Helene Caire* was her date of death, January, 1929.

[31]This transfer was an assignment of an equitable interest in the shares for the purposes of management. Legal ownership remained with Amelie Caire Rossi, and the shares were inventoried and taxed in her estate.

[32]Eaton, *Diary of a Sea Captain's Wife*, p. 185.   [33]Ibid., pp. 193-250.

[34]*Edmund A. Rossi v. Arthur Caire, et al.*, San Francisco Superior Court, No. 43295.

130 sought to enjoin the directors of the Santa Cruz Island Company from carrying on the business of the corporation and to compel them to wind up the affairs of the corporation by paying all of its debts and by distributing the corporate assets to the shareholders in proportion to their interest.[35] The position of Rossi was that the corporation had to be liquidated since its charter was forfeited.

Arthur, Fred, and Delphine Caire and their mother Albina, as the majority directors of the corporation, vigorously resisted this lawsuit from the outset. They would have preferred to reinstate the Santa Cruz Island Company's corporate charter so that they could continue to control the company. The injunction litigation

[35]*Rossi v. Caire* (1916) 174 Cal. 74 at 76.

Pelican Bay Resort made famous by the Eatons who leased the area from the Santa Cruz Island Company (1912-1937). Note the snake and alligator head.
Photo taken by F.F. Flournoy survey team; Pier Gherini family collection.

lasted from 1912 to 1930 when the parties finally dismissed it. Aglae Caire Capuccio, after having hired attorney David Freidenrich to act as co-counsel with Ambrose Gherini, filed a similar lawsuit on March 20, 1913, but the court stayed it pending the outcome of the Rossi suit.[36]

A trial was held in San Francisco before Superior Court Judge George A. Sturtevant. Judge Sturtevant ruled on June 9, 1913, for Edmund A. Rossi. The court initially determined that the controlling corporate directors (Albina, Arthur, Fred, Delphine) were trustees and were charged with the duty of settling the affairs of the corporation since the company forfeited its charter. The court stated that all the shareholders were entitled to an accounting, and after all of the debts of the corporation were paid, the shareholders would be entitled to a distribution according to their respective shares at the time of forfeiture of the company charter in 1911.[37] On June 13, 1913, four days after Judge Sturtevant's ruling, Albina Caire signed a codicil to her will disinheriting her two married daughters, Amelie and Aglae.

After his initial order, Judge Sturtevant on April 3, 1914, further ordered the trustees to distribute $35,000 derived from the property of the corporation. He also ordered the trustees to sell the real and personal property of the company at a public sale. The trustees objected to the ruling and moved for a new trial; this motion was denied.[38] Arthur Caire and the other corporate directors, except Aglae, appealed the orders made by Judge Sturtevant. The California Supreme Court eventually decided to hear the case.

Edmund Rossi, at the urging of his brother-in-law, Ambrose Gherini, hired prominent San Francisco attorney, Orrin Kip McMurray, to act as co-counsel along with Gherini on appeal. McMurray, known for his encyclopedic knowledge of California law, was born in 1869, the same year ten investors formed the Santa Cruz Island Company. He practiced law for ten years in San

---

[36]*Capuccio v. Caire*, San Francisco Superior Court Action No. 48031.
[37]*Rossi v. Caire* (1916) 174 Cal.74 at 77.
[38]Ibid.

Francisco where he met Ambrose Gherini in the early 1900s. McMurray joined the faculty at the School of Jurisprudence at the University of California and later became its dean, serving from 1923 to 1936.[39] McMurray, along with Ambrose Gherini, were attorneys of record throughout all the appeals.

In 1916, the California Supreme Court reversed Judge Sturtevant's ruling that the trustees had to distribute the cash and sell the other corporate property. The Supreme Court felt that it was unnecessary for the lower court to intervene in and supervise the liquidation of the corporation. If there were sufficient monies to pay the corporate debts, the Supreme Court observed that there would be nothing improper in distributing the assets, including the land in kind, to the shareholders rather than force a sale of the assets.[40] Ironically, because of the steadfast resolve of the trustees to prevent the break-up of the company, the courts would later have to supervise the ultimate dissolution of the island enterprise.

The Supreme Court, however, did not intend to foster any notion that the trustees could be dilatory in winding up the affairs of the company. To the contrary, the Court tried to define the duties of the trustees and the rights of the shareholders. It stated in unequivocal terms that upon forfeiture, the corporation died and could not hold title to property which belonged to the shareholders. The Court also noted that directors became trustees "for the corporation and its stockholders to settle its affairs."[41] The Court gave a clear message. The corporation had to be liquidated. The Supreme Court also significantly pointed out that ". . .neither the trustees nor the majority stockholders can compel the minority to join in the formation of a new corporation and transfer their shares to it. . ."[42]

Arguably, the case should have ended and settled after the first Supreme Court decision in 1916. Ambrose Gherini pointed out

---

[39]McMurray taught Ambrose Gherini's son, Pier, when he attended law school in the 1930s a standard law course called "Conflicts" which dealt with conflicting laws of different jurisdictions.
[40]*Rossi v. Caire* (1916) 174 Cal. 74 at 82.
[41]Ibid., p. 81.
[42]Ibid., p. 83.

that the first case "settled all of the law involved in this unnecessarily prolonged litigation." Gherini observed that in form the case was won by the trustees, but in substance, Rossi and Capuccio were the victors.

Why did the litigation continue for the next 16 years? Frank P. Deering, the attorney for the trustees, told Gherini that "his clients would rather pay their attorneys than us."[43] The court's decisions, which clearly defined the rights and liabilities of the parties, together with the underlying documents and the records of the Santa Cruz Island Company, suggest that the trustees, led by Fred, Arthur and Delphine Caire, tried to retain their right to control the Santa Cruz Island Company and its major asset, the island of Santa Cruz. For this reason, the trustees refused to liquidate the company and distribute its assets to its shareholders, and this unnecessarily prolonged the litigation.

Rossi raised this very issue before Judge Sturtevant. Even though he ruled in favor of Rossi, Judge Sturtevant determined that the trustees had not been negligent in liquidating the corporation, and were not trying to carry on the business since the forfeiture of the charter in 1911. The Supreme Court declined to overrule this factual determination.[44] The court's ruling played into the hands of the trustees who wanted to continue running the company and blazed the path for future litigation.

While the first lawsuit for injunctive relief was pending, the California Legislature in 1913 amended Section 6 of the Act of March 20, 1905. The amendment allowed for the revival of the forfeited charter of any corporation that had failed to pay the license tax under the Act of March 20, 1905, by payment of the tax and any penalties prescribed by the act.[45] The trustees of Santa

---

[43]Unpublished memo of Ambrose Gherini, 1937, p. 3-4.

[44]*Rossi v. Caire* (1916) 174 Cal. 74 at 80. Gherini later reflected that Judge Sturtevant's failure to find that the trustees were negligent in refusing to liquidate the corporation actually promoted the litigation. In short, Gherini felt that, had the court forcefully intervened at the outset to dissolve the corporation, years of litigation would have been avoided. Unpublished memo of Ambrose Gherini, 1937, p. 3.

[45]Reporter's Transcript in *Capuccio v. Caire*, Santa Barbara Superior Court Case No. 10812, pp. 53-55.

134   Cruz Island Company thereupon paid the tax and penalties from the corporate funds in an attempt to revive the corporation. On January 26, 1914, these shareholders, representing 86 percent of the company stock, voted to make Fred, Arthur, and Delphine the directors of the revived corporation. The directors elected Fred as president and Arthur as secretary. Since their election, they along with their sister Delphine, managed the island and made the decisions relating to the on-going litigation.[46] The trustees then held a meeting on January 27, 1916, to authorize the transfer of the assets of the defunct corporation to the "revived" corporation. Aglae, although still a director, refused to attend. The trustees made the transfer on January 30, 1917.[47] In addition, the trustees voted themselves fees in the amount of $200 per month for their work as trustees from January 1912 to January 1914. Amelie and Aglae did not consent to any of these actions.

Even though the company stopped advertising in the San Francisco business directory in 1912, the island operation continued as though nothing had happened to the corporate charter. The company's records indicate that there was no termination of business operations. Boat logs showed frequent boat trips being made to supply the island. The schooner *Santa Cruz* held to its regular weekly schedule of leaving from Santa Barbara for the island on every Thursday. The island vineyards were in full production. In 1916, the superintendent reported 62,539 gallons of wine produced.[48] Despite the coming of Prohibition, wine production, even at the time of the last vintage in 1918, was a substantial 63,000 gallons of wine.[49] On January 1, 1919, the company inventory showed 79,043 gallons on hand and had a yield of 137 tons of grape. Prohibition was in a sense a boon to the vineyards from 1920 to 1926 because raw grapes could be sold for home con-

---

[46]See Judge S.E. Crow's decision filed on September 21, 1920 in *Capuccio v. Caire*, Santa Barbara Superior Court No. 10812.

[47]Ibid., pp. 62-64. Aglae, a dissenting trustee director, was not an officer of the company and received no fees.

[48]Superintendent's report, October 26, 1916.

[49]Pinney, *The Wine of Santa Cruz Island*, p. 87.

sumption. This was perhaps a more difficult operation for the company because of the transportation involved.[50]

The company records also showed that there was no "winding down" of the livestock operation. In 1917, there were 15,000 sheep reported on the island.[51] According to the superintendent's June 1919 report, the shearers clipped 13,206 sheep producing over 100,000 pounds of wool packed in 256 sacks with weights ranging from 318 to 476 pounds. The company inventory recorded 1,147 cattle as of December 31, 1918.[52] These figures demonstrate that there were substantial company assets that the trustees had to account for and eventually divide among the shareholders.

Meanwhile, Hollywood's greatest and most glamorous stars continued to visit the island. The Eatons' Pelican Bay camp was the headquarters for the movie operations which were charged $100 per week by the Santa Cruz Island Company. The use of the island seemed to go from the sublime to the ridiculous. The movie "Undine," directed by Henry Otto, involved fifty diving girls who spent days posing and diving off rocks and swimming around the beaches. In another instance, a movie company wanted to shoot a scene of a horse jumping from a 110-foot cliff.[53] The superintendent selected an island horse called Saturno because the ranch hands considered it an "outlaw" or wild horse. The superintendent figured it was a good way to get rid of the horse and earn some money for the company. Saturno had other ideas. The horse refused to jump, bucked the stunt man, and galloped back to the pasture.[54] The real drama, however, was not on the silver screen but in the courtrooms. The litigation continued.

(2) The Accounting Action

Edmund Rossi filed an accounting action in San Francisco on

[50]Pinney interview, August 20, 1993.

[51]Letter to Chicago Flexible Shaft Co. from Superintendent Swain, December 14, 1917. Mr. Swain was inquiring about a shearing machine and explained the island shearing situation.

[52]Superintendent's Report, June 8 and 11, 1919.

[53]Eaton, *Diary of a Sea Captain 's Wife,* pp. 205-207 .

[54]McElrath, *On Santa Cruz Island,* pp. 78 79.

136   August 28, 1917, that lasted until April 22, 1930.[55] Here again, the extensive nature of the litigation can be seen by the registry of filings in that action. The majority of the directors as trustees, led by Arthur and Fred Caire, resisted any accounting of the Santa Cruz Island Company.

Initially, after the first Supreme Court decision became final and the case was sent back to the trial court in San Francisco, the trustees requested the trial court to dismiss the lawsuit filed by Rossi for accounting. The trustees thought they had won the first case based on the language of the Supreme Court in its first decision. On February 23, 1917, Judge George A. Sturtevant agreed with them and dismissed the accounting action.[56]

Edmund Rossi, joined by Aglae Caire Capuccio, appealed. On February 17, 1919, the California Appellate Court reversed Judge Sturtevant by stating that the effect of the Supreme Court's previous ruling in the injunction case was to leave the parties where they stood before the ruling and that Rossi and Capuccio were entitled to a trial on the accounting issues.[57]

After the Court of Appeal decision, Edmund Rossi filed an amended complaint for accounting. Rossi contended in his lawsuit that he continuously objected to the trustees carrying on or conducting the business of said corporation; he demanded they wind up the affairs of the company and distribute the property and assets to its stockholders. The trustees refused to do so.[58]

Arthur Caire and the other majority trustees answered. They relied on the 1913 amendment to section 6 of the Act of March 20, 1905. This amendment allowed a corporation to pay the tax and penalty to revive the corporate charter. As if giving symbolic meaning to the island's translated name as the "Island of the Holy Cross," the trustees took the position that the corporation was resurrected or revived under the 1913 amendment. They contended that all of the directors of the corporation except Aglae voted to revive the corporate charter on August 25, 1913. They

---

[55]*Rossi v. Caire*, San Francisco Superior Court No. 84070.

[56]See Transcript on Appeal in *Rossi v. Caire*, S.F. No.8326 (39 Cal.App. 776), pp. 70-71.

[57]*Rossi v. Caire* (1919) 39 Cal.App. 667 at 778.

[58]Second Amended Complaint filed by Rossi in *Rossi v. Caire*, San Francisco Superior Court No. 84070, paragraph IX.

also asserted that the assets of the defunct corporation were transferred to the new revived corporation that was approved by 86 percent of the shareholders.

Arthur Caire testified at the accounting trial about the intentions of the trustees. Arthur was asked: "You have no intention, Mr. Caire, and so far as you know, the trustees of the defunct corporation have no intention of winding up the business of the defunct corporation, or returning the property to the stockholders?" He answered: ". . . feeling that our corporation is revived, we see no reason why we should wind up the affairs . . . The corporation is conducting the business with the intention of continuing . . ."[59]

Additional facts at trial established that on January 2, 1919, the majority directors of the Santa Cruz Island Corporation adopted a resolution to continue to extend the life of the corporation for an additional fifty years. The original documents of incorporation of the Santa Cruz Island Company which were filed in 1869 provided for a corporate life of fifty years. The shareholders holding 86 shares of the stock approved this action which assumed the validity of the revival of the corporation. At this time the breakdown of the shareholders holding the 86 shares was as follows: Fred as president had 23.25; Arthur as secretary had 22.25, William J. Martin had 1; Delphine had 21.25; and Helene had 18.25.[60] The majority directors further contended that there was no action to set aside the revived corporation.[61]

The line was again clearly drawn. The majority trustees of the island company led by Arthur and Fred Caire were not going to relinquish ownership and control of the company despite the clear direction of the first Supreme Court decision. Instead, by resurrecting the corporation through the revival statute, they embarked on a strategy to circumvent the first Supreme Court decision and to continue to do business.

[59]Transcript on Appeal, *Rossi v. Caire*, S.F. No.9402 (186 Cal. 544), pp. 67-68. Arthur Caire's statement contrasts with his testimony in the injunction lawsuit. There he testified that "we will obey the law and wind up the affairs of the corporation." Transcript on Appeal in *Rossi v. Caire*, S.F. 7101 (174 Cal. 74), p. 58.

[60]Ibid., pp. 69-71. It is not known who William J. Martin was or why he received one share of stock.

[61]Answer to Second Amended Complaint filed by Arthur Caire et al., in *Rossi v. Caire*, San Francisco Superior Court No. 84070, paragraphs 1, 3 and 6.

138   Judge James M. Troutt took the matter under submission and then on October 20, 1919, ruled in favor of the trustees. He concluded that the trustees had not neglected their duties and that Rossi did not take any action to set aside in a timely fashion the revivor of the corporation.[62] Again the accounting issues were left undecided. Rossi and Capuccio again appealed.

Island operations kept on going. Despite the effects of Prohibition, the company maintained the vineyards by pruning, plowing, harrowing and removing the rocks. "Lopez is putting the crusher in shape and tightening the hoops on the fermenting tanks," the superintendent wrote in his report for August 16, 1920. "Leon will start the cleaning of the tanks as I want to keep Dianaz on the hay press the remainder this week after which he will take over the cellar work."[63] The company also contracted to sell the entire production of grapes for 1920 to Joe Ardeno who reportedly paid a very good price of $45 per ton for the raw grapes.[64] The sheep operation also continued. The ranch hands sowed 523.49 acres in barley, oats and wheat. At Scorpion, workers routinely plowed and planted the hay fields, built and repaired fences and mowed the alfalfa fields. The Superintendent reported that "the hay in Campo la Cruz is being baled and promises to yield about 1,000 bales of very good hay.[65] The company shipped a large supply of lumber to Scorpion in order to build a roof for the reservoir.[66] Every indication showed that the corporation and its business were alive and well.

The oral argument before the Supreme Court took place on January 10, 1921, in San Francisco. The courtroom of the Supreme Court with its high ceilings and ornate fixtures punctuated the solemn and serious nature of the arguments which at times seemed like a religious debate. In a sense they were. They were discussing the "Island of the Holy Cross." The debate was spirited. Professor Orrin Kip McMurray argued on behalf of

---

[62]Decision filed in *Rossi v. Caire,* San Francisco Superior Court No. 84070.

[63]Superindendent Report, August 16, 1920.

[64]Pinney, *The Wine of Santa Cruz Island,* p. 87-89.

[65]Superintendent's Report, September 13, 1920.

[66]Superintendent's Report, May 10, 1920.

Edmund Rossi and Aglae Capuccio. Frank P. Deering pleaded the case on behalf of Arthur Caire and the other trustees. The issue before the Supreme Court centered on the effect of the legislation allowing revival of a corporation whose charter was forfeited. In short, the life and death of the corporation would be the focal point of the arguments.

Professor McMurray, after giving a brief description of the events leading up to the appeal, boldly stated that because of the non-payment of the license tax, the corporation had died.[67] Chief Justice Frank Angellotti then asked Professor McMurray whether the legislature passed a statute covering the period when "this corporation ceased to live?" Professor McMurray responded that there was no such revival statute in 1911 when the forfeiture occurred. He then argued:

> . . . Assume, however, that the forfeiture could be and was relieved from, how about the property of the corporation? Our position is that upon the death of the corporation, its soul and body were divided, its property vested in its stockholders, subject to the power of the trustees to settle its affairs . . . In other words, we were tenants in common, very analogous to the case of the individual who dies . . .[68]

Justice Lucien Shaw then asked, "Your position is the reviving effect of the statute would restore to the corporation its corporate franchise but did not affect its corporate property?" Professor McMurray responded, "Yes."[69]

Frank P. Deering responded by arguing that the corporate charter, forfeited in 1911 by failure to pay the license tax, was revived when the majority of trustees complied with the Rehabilitation Act of 1913. The trustees, he asserted, properly transferred the corporate assets to the rehabilitated corporation.[70] Deering explained that the legislature must have intended by passing the Rehabilitation Act to give the trustees not only the authority to

---

[67]Transcript of oral argument of Orrin K. McMurray in *Rossi v. Caire*, S.F. No. 9402 (186 Cal. 544), p. 2.

[68]Ibid., pp. 3-5.

[69]Ibid., p. 5.

[70]Transcript of oral argument of Frank P. Deering in *Rossi v. Caire*, S.F. No. 9402, pp. 1-2.

140 revive its franchise but also the power to re-transfer the property to the revived corporation.[71]

Deering then challenged the argument of Professor McMurray by pointing out that there is a distinction between a person who dies and the forfeiture of a corporate charter. In the former case, the law says that the property passes to the devisees. In the latter case, the License Tax Act did not say that the property passes to the stockholders.[72]

Professor McMurray replied by stating that the distinction was one without a difference. "When its corporate franchise was removed, where did this property go, if it did not go to the stockholders?" asked McMurray.[73] The Supreme Court submitted the matter for decision.

On July 28, 1921, the Supreme Court ruled against the trustees. In its decision, which reversed the decision of Judge Troutt, the Supreme Court stated that the effect of the nonpayment of the license tax resulted in the forfeiture of the corporate charter and "it was not a case simply of suspended animation . . . but one of absolute death . . ."[74] In short, there could be no resurrection of the original corporation. This meant that the shareholders were immediately entitled to have the corporation liquidated and its assets distributed.[75]

The attempted revival of the original corporation also failed. The Supreme Court explained that the attempt to revive the corporation under California law ". . . against a non-consenting former stockholder who diligently asserted his rights, would be an impairment of a vested right in property prohibited by both state and federal constitutions."[76] The Court noted that there was no lack of diligence on the part of Rossi or Capuccio in complaining about the actions to revive the corporation against their wishes.[77]

---

[71]Ibid., p. 5.

[72]Ibid., p. 14.

[73]Transcript of oral argument of Orrin K. McMurray in *Rossi v. Caire*, S.F.No. 9402, p .8.

[74]*Rossi v. Caire* (1921) 186 Cal. 544 at 549.

[75]Ibid., p. 550.

[76]Ibid., p. 552.

[77]Ibid.

The case was again sent back to the trial court to hear the accounting issues. On December 7, 1921, Judge James M. Troutt ruled against the trustees and in his ruling stated that for more than nine years:

> ... defendants Arthur J. Caire, Fred F. Caire, Albina C.S. Caire, Delphine A. Caire, have neglected their duties as trustees and have violated their trust obligations by failing to liquidate and settle the affairs of the dissolved corporation...[78]

Judge Troutt, thereupon, ordered the trustees to file an inventory and to render an accounting of the island company. The finding that Ambrose Gherini sought in the injunction action in 1913 was finally given by the court in 1921 in the accounting action.

The trial court, on February 3, 1922, appointed Leslie W. Symmes, an agricultural engineer, to verify the accuracy of the inventory filed by the trustees and make an assessment of the ranch operation. In his report Symmes observed that "the island is a good livestock property, and with certain needed improvements, and development, will produce a satisfactory return." He felt in order to produce a satisfactory return there would have to be a complete change in the company's system of operation. With this change, the island could be brought into full production in three years. Some of the fields would not be used so that they would reseed themselves. The company should extend the vineyards and trap the wild sheep.[79] In his report Symmes estimated a profit of $62,000 for the year 1923; somewhat less profit in 1924 because of the small number of young cattle and the reduced number of wild sheep rounded up before the flock is built up with tame sheep; by the third year, the operating net profit should be $80,000. He predicted full production by 1926 with an operating profit of $136,200 and after payment of taxes a net annual profit of $124,200.[80] Lastly, Symmes opined that Santa Cruz Island "has very great possibilities in resort development from which it is

---

[78]Interlocutory Judgment filed in *Rossi v. Caire*, San Francisco Superior Court No. 84070.

[79]The unpublished report prepared by Leslie Symmes in 1922 was entitled: "Santa Cruz Island, estimated operating cost and returns." pp. 1-2.   [80]Ibid., p. 4

142 believed substantial revenues could be derived on leases, and the sale of shore frontages."[81]

Undaunted, the trustees, led by Arthur and Fred Caire, appealed the December 7, 1921, decision of Judge Troutt. The case again found its way before the California Supreme Court. The Court, however, did not decide the merits of the case because a motion was made to dismiss the case as an appeal from an interlocutory judgment which is normally not appealable unless specified by law. The Supreme Court granted the motion to dismiss the appeal on September 13, 1922.[82]

From 1923 until 1928 there appears to be a hiatus in the legal maneuvering in the accounting lawsuit. The reason for this is that the parties switched legal battlefields to Santa Barbara where they litigated the partition action. Then on November 16, 1928, 11 years after the filing of the accounting lawsuit, Judge Troutt entered his decree settling the accounting aspect of the case. He approved the trustees' accounting with certain significant exceptions. He disallowed over $22,000 in attorneys' fees and costs which the trustees attempted to portray as corporate expense. He also disallowed $26,800 in salaries paid to the officers of the corporation and the trustees. The state and federal taxes paid by the corporation in the amount of $12,383 were also disallowed as were the cash payments paid in 1922 to unspecified employees in the amount of $10,706. After the deductions were made, the court ordered the trustees to pay the sum of $9,807.68 plus interest each to Edmund Rossi and Aglae Capuccio.[83]

The court's involvement in the island operation became far more pronounced than the Supreme Court in its original decision anticipated. Even the schooner *Santa Cruz* did not escape entanglement in the legal proceedings. On August 7, 1929, the court ordered the schooner sold for $4,000 to Arthur Caire. The court even controlled the expenditure of funds as shown by the order authorizing the trustees to spend $200 for cattle feed.[84]

[81]Ibid., p. 5.

[82]*Rossi v. Caire, et al.,* California Supreme Court No. S. F. 10233.

[83]Decree entered on November 16, 1928, in *Rossi v. Caire,* San Francisco Superior Court No. 84070.

[84]See Record of filings in *Rossi v. Caire,* San Francisco Superior Court No. 84070.

(3) The Partition of the Island

The marathon legal wrangling over the island continued in Santa Barbara. While the accounting action was being litigated in San Francisco, Edmund Rossi and Aglae Caire Capuccio filed a partition action in the County of Santa Barbara on May 16, 1918, and recorded a *lis pendens*.[85] They took this action because the trustees had attempted to revive the corporation and had been occupying the island since the year 1913. Rossi and Capuccio feared that the trustees might claim title to the property by adverse possession.[86] Their attorneys at the time were David Freidenrich, Orrin Kip McMurray, Ambrose Gherini, and James E. Lyons.

The trustees, again led by Arthur and Fred Caire, resisted the partition action. In their answer filed in July 1919, the trustees raised the same issues which they raised in the accounting action being litigated in San Francisco. The trustees steadfastly maintained that since August 28, 1913, they revived the corporation; hence they were entitled to conduct business and had no obligation to liquidate the company. The trustees asserted that the corporation and not the individual shareholders owned the island and the personal property of the company. Arthur Caire testified that based on his forty years of personal experience with the island "that said Island is so situated that partition cannot be made without great prejudice to the owners thereof..."[87]

Veteran Judge Samuel Eugene Crow (1860-1940) presided over the partition lawsuit. Judge Crow, born in Ashland, Illinois, came West as a teenager eventually settling in Santa Maria, California. He attended Hastings College of Law, served as justice of the peace and later as district attorney. He was appointed to the Supe-

---

[85]Partition action is a legal proceeding to divide or sell the property under court supervision when joint owners cannot agree on the management or use of the property. The lawsuit for partition is required to be filed in the county where the property is located. *A lis pendens* is a recorded notice that there is pending litigation involving the property.

[86]Under California law, one who occupies the property of another adversely for five years can claim title to the property. The occupation must be hostile, open, notorious and for the prescribed period of time.

[87]Affidavit of Arthur J. Caire, filed in the partition case, *Capuccio v. Caire*, Santa Barbara Superior Court No. 10812.

144 rior Court bench in 1906 and served for twenty-six years.[88] He was well qualified to hear the historic case.

Judge Crow had to initially decide various procedural issues raised by the trustees. On September 21, 1920, he ruled that the partition action was proper, that the individual shareholders owned the island in their individual capacities and that the Santa Cruz Island Company had no title or interest in it. He decided that the partition action was not barred by any statute of limitations as claimed by the trustees. He also determined that the island should be partitioned in kind, that this could be done without great prejudice to the owners thereof and that the partition should be made according to the parties' respective interests. A few weeks later on October 6, 1920, Judge Crow appointed surveyor Frank F. Flournoy, George W. McComber, and Frank M. Whitney as the referees to make the partition. The trustees, however, appealed Judge Crow's decision.[89] Again, the case wound its way up to the California Supreme Court.

The Supreme Court rendered another decision in the case on September 14, 1922, and affirmed Judge Crow's decision in all particulars. The trustees raised numerous objections on appeal. The first objection was that the plaintiffs, Edmund Rossi and Aglae Caire Capuccio, were not in possession of the property, and therefore, a partition action could not be maintained by them. The Supreme Court rejected this argument by stating that the Court had previously determined that Rossi and Capuccio had vested rights in the property of the defunct corporation. Because of the forfeiture, the court explained that the corporation could not hold title to the property. The court also pointed out that at the time of the filing of the partition action all the claims against the defunct corporation had been satisfied and, therefore, the shareholders were entitled to possession. That being the situation, they had a right to file the partition action.[90]

The trustees also asserted that the partition case was barred by

---

[88]Tompkins, *Santa Barbara History Makers,* pp. 313-315.

[89]Reporter's Transcript in *Capuccio v. Caire,* Santa Barbara Superior Court No. 10812, p. 48-65.

[90]*Capuccio v. Caire* (1922) 189 Cal. 514 at 524-525.

the statute of limitations. The Supreme Court rejected this argument by stating that Edmund Rossi and Aglae Caire Capuccio were in the same position as any other owner of real property seeking to have the property divided between the co-owners.[91]

The last contention urged upon the Court by the trustees was that the partition actions could not be maintained because of the existence of the two lawsuits filed in the Superior Court of San Francisco. The Supreme Court rejected this contention and characterized it as a "belated defense" that was apparently made before the trial court a year and a half after the filing of the partition action and was properly rejected by Judge Crow. The Supreme Court explained that the two lawsuits filed in San Francisco were not partition actions but equitable actions for accounting and injunctive relief and could not have been partition lawsuits since a partition action can only be filed in the county where the property is located.[92]

While these appeals were pending, the trustees filed a motion in the Santa Barbara Superior Court to dismiss the entire partition proceedings on the ground that the court lacked jurisdiction. The legal basis of the motion was that the original patent of the United States to Castillero contained a reservation of 100 acres to the United States for the purposes of a lighthouse. They argued, therefore, that the United States government should have been made a party to the partition action because of the government's potential ownership interest in the island. If this were the case, the Federal Court in Los Angeles would have jurisdiction over the case.[93] Judge Crow denied the trustees' motion, and the trustees thereupon filed a partition action in the Los Angeles Federal Court.[94] The United States Federal Court eventually dismissed this lawsuit on July 14, 1924, since the trustees did not pursue it.[95]

The parties unsuccessfully attempted to settle the case.

---

[91]Ibid., pp. 526-527.   [92]Ibid., pp. 527-528.

[93]Reporter's Transcript in *Capuccio v. Caire,* Santa Barbara Superior Court No. 10812, pp. 68-71.

[94]The trustees recorded a *lis pendens* concerning the federal suit on June 9, 1923 in Book F (Notice of Actions), p. 56 in the Official Records of Santa Barbara County.

[95]Unpublished memo of Ambrose Gherini, 1925, p. 6. See also Reporters Transcript in *Capuccio v. Caire,* Santa Barbara Superior Court No. 10812, p. 71.

146 Ambrose Gherini, representing Edmund Rossi and Aglae Caire Capuccio, and Frank Deering, representing the trustees (except Capuccio), met sometime in 1922 to try to explore ways to settle the case before a partition or sale of the island. Arthur Caire placed a value on the island of $2,720,000. Gherini's clients offered to sell their interest for $500,000, which included damages for loss of use of their investment for eleven years. In the discussions, the attorneys talked candidly about the possibility that the prevailing party might be entitled to attorneys' fees. Ambrose Gherini and Frank Deering talked about what the physical partition of the island would involve. "You are aware, of course, that the partition in kind will involve: a) a topographical survey to show acreage; b) land classification; and c) careful survey of the water supply to ascertain the possible use for irrigation as well as for watering the stock ranges," Gherini explained to Deering.[96] "He [Deering] again wanted to know if the matter could not be ended because he wanted to end it," Ambrose Gherini recalled. "I informed him that was our point also, and that we were very much surprised that he had not come back to us with a counter proposition."[97] Settlement negotiations failed and the litigation continued.

Meanwhile, Whitney resigned as a referee, and on February 5, 1923, Judge Crow selected H. J. Doulton in Whitney's place.[98] The way was now paved for the historic survey of the island. The three referees appointed by the court, F.F. Flournoy, George W. McComber, and H.J. Doulton, had extensive experience. Flournoy, a former Santa Barbara County Surveyor from 1895-1915, was a civil engineer and surveyor. McComber, a longtime advocate of a deep port in Santa Barbara, was a real estate and insurance broker with a large business. H. J. Doulton was the proprietor of the Miramar Hotel near the city of Santa Barbara.[99]

Monumental tasks, some extremely difficult and dangerous,

---

[96]1922 Deering memo, p. 3.

[97]Ibid., p. 5.

[98]Transcript on Appeal, in *Capuccio v. Caire*, (207 Cal. 200), p. 116.

[99]Ibid., p. 127; See also Bookspan, *Santa Barbara by the Sea*, pp. 54, 74; Referee's Report filed in *Capuccio v. Caire*, No. 10812.

Frank F. Flournoy, civil engineer and surveyor, headed the
Santa Cruz Island surveying team in 1923-1924.
Photo taken by F.F. Flournoy survey team; Pier Gherini family collection.

confronted the survey team. The surveyors battled treacherous
ocean swells and scaled steep mountains and ridges. Before plot-
ting the interior of the island, the surveyors had to measure 70.47
miles of coastline marked by precipitous cliffs rising almost 200
feet vertically from the water's edge. The survey team used expert
surf men and ". . . in some places even this was impossible and life-
lines were let down from above or detours were made inland
sometimes to the distance of one mile in order to reach an outlet
to the shore."[100] The team made a ground check of the exterior
boundary lines by triangulation with old government monuments
erected by United States government surveyors in the years 1853
and 1874.[101]

[100]Referee's Report in Partition of Santa Cruz Island, December 30, 1924. p. 5.
[101]Ibid .

Surveying party battled the rugged island coastline. Note the natural face on the cliff. *Photo taken by F.F. Flournoy survey team; Pier Gherini family collection.*

Members of the surveying party.
Photo taken by F.F. Flournoy survey team; Pier Gherini family collection.

The referees unanimously recommended the division of the island into seven parcels or tracts so that there would be one parcel for each shareholder who owned shares of the Santa Cruz Island Company on the date of its forfeiture on November 30, 1911. Each parcel equated to what the referees thought would be the percentage interest that a shareholder owned on the date of forfeiture of the company. The 1925 breakdown of the parcels was as follows:

Parcel 1 was allocated to Helene, the youngest Caire daughter. This parcel of 3,867.39 acres had a value of $42,000. Parcel 1 which was located on the west end of the island contained 100 acres of valley land around Forney's Cove where there was a harbor and beach but no wharf and 350 acres of mesa land on the north side of the island above the cliffs. It also contained 3,117.30 acres of grazing land and 300 acres of waste land.

The referees set aside 3,667.12 acres as parcel 2 for younger son, Fred Caire. They valued his 12/100ths at $72,000. Parcel 2 consisted of 200 acres of valley land, including a portion of the Christy Ranch with the barns and shearing sheds and Dr. Shaw's house, 300 acres of mesa land, 3,017.12 acres of grazing and brush land, and 150 acres of wasteland. Some of the area was tillable land and alfalfa was grown. Parcel 2 had a beach and Christy was its harbor. Because of the wind, it was not available most of the year. Historically, the wool shorn at the Christy Ranch was taken by road to Prisoners' Harbor.

Parcel 3, earmarked for Delphine, the oldest Caire daughter, comprised 6,024.70 acres that was valued at $60,000 for her 10/100ths interest. This parcel has a harbor known as Cueva Valdez, but it was not accessible because of the high ridge in back of the harbor. Delphine's acreage was broken down as follows: 200 acres of valley land; 300 acres of mesa; 5,324.70 acres of grazing and brush land; and 200 acres of wasteland.

The referees designated parcel 4 for Arthur, the oldest Caire son. His portion was 6,639.77 acres located primarily on the south side of the island between Punta Arena and the Christy

Ranch. His 12/100th interest was valued at $72,000. It consisted of 300 acres of valley land, including the main Christy Ranch House, 400 acres of mesa land, 5,539.77 acres of grazing and brush land and 400 acres of wasteland including Mt. Blanco. There were no harbors on this tract of land. The referees also recommended a right of way for parcels 1, 2, 3, and 4 to Prisoners' Harbor.

The referees proposed that 34,289.27 acres go to Justinian Caire's widow, Albina, for her 45/100th interest in the stock of the defunct Santa Cruz Island Company. This acreage, called parcel 5,

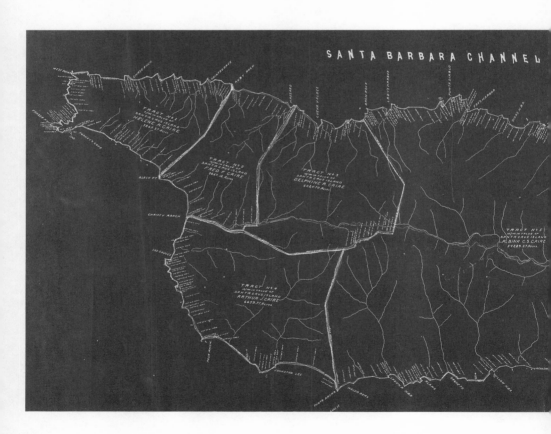

included the 500 acres of the Central Valley as well as the vineyards and was valued at $270,000. Of this acreage, 23,089.27 were usable for grazing; 700 were poor mesa land and 10,000 were wasteland including Santa Cruz Island's highest peak, Mt. Diablo. This tract contained Prisoners' Harbor, the main harbor of the island. It also encompassed other anchorages and harbors such as Willows, Ladies, Punta Diablo, Fry's, Dicks, Twin Harbor, Pelican Bay where the Eatons had their "resort" camp, Tinkers, and Chinese Harbor. As previously noted, Albina had transferred in April of 1913 her 45 shares of the Santa Cruz Island Company to Arthur,

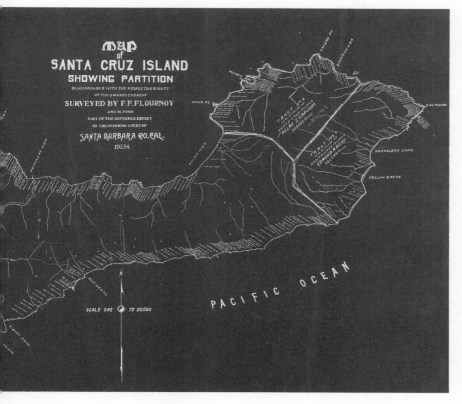

Partition Map prepared by F. F. Flournoy. *Pier Gherini family collection.*

152   Fred, Delphine, and Helene. She reconfirmed these gifts to them
and, in essence, disinherited daughters, Amelie and Aglae, in her
codicil dated June 13, 1913. Her codicil and the will were admitted to probate, but there were no assets of the estate to be administered. The trustees (Fred, Arthur, and Delphine) and Helene,
who had cooperated with them over the years in the litigation,
ended up with nearly 90 percent of the island.

The referees awarded to Edmund Rossi and Aglae Caire Capuccio parcels 6 and 7 located on the east end of the island. Since
each had seven shares of stock at the time of the forfeiture of the
charter, they each owned a 7 percent interest in the island. Had
Justinian Caire's intent that his children share equally been realized, his married daughters' share would have been 16.6 percent
each.

According to the referees' recommendations, Aglae Caire
Capuccio would receive parcel 6 which encompassed 3,035.60
acres, including 150 acres of Scorpion Valley and ranch facilities,
and was valued at $42,000. It also included 300 acres of mesa,
2,200.60 acres of grazing and brush land and 385 acres of wasteland. The main features of this tract were Scorpion Harbor and
the mesa where good crops were raised. Flournoy testified that
Scorpion Harbor was practically the same size as Prisoners' Harbor and it is about as accessible. The best soil on the island was on
parcel 2, but because of the wind conditions it was not good for
crops.

The referees selected parcel 7, consisting of 3,217.89 acres, for
Edmund Rossi who represented the Amelie Caire Rossi interest.
The centerpiece of this area was Smugglers' Cove and the buildings located there. Parcel 7 was valued at $42,000 and included
150 acres of valley, with a well and an old dwelling; 350 acres of
mesa, including San Pedro point; 2,414.89 acres of grazing and
brush land; and 303 acres of wasteland. The referees did not provide any access to parcels 6 and 7 across the other parcels, but the
owners would have a right of way to use Scorpion and Smugglers
harbors respectively.

The entire island totalled 60,741.74 acres and the referees valued it for agricultural purposes at $600,000 for the year 1911.[102] The referees' work took 238 work days in 1923-1924, and the parties stipulated that their fee of $37,500 was reasonable.[103] All three of the court appointed referees testified at the partition trial to explain their recommendations. Excerpts of their testimony give some insight as to the complexity of their task.

Flournoy, the first witness, testified that the referees took into account many factors in partitioning the island including the value of each parcel as a residential resort. "We tried to give as fair and as equitable a division as possible," Flournoy explained. "We had no thought of intentionally giving any one party more than just what was coming him."[104] On being asked to define the term "value" he stated that the appraisal team divided the island into different classes of land: valley land, mesa, irrigable, brushy, grazing, recreational and scenic, and wasteland including cliffs, volcanics and cacti. He pointed out that they took into account possible sites for pleasure resorts, hotels and harbors. He felt that parcels 6 and 7 "are suited to about the same purposes as the rest of the island." He could not differentiate which part of the island was best suited for residential purposes. He explained that all the island "is objectionable on account of high winds," and that there was not enough water along those resort sites for irrigation of lawns."[105]

Access was also a key issue. Flournoy testified that there is a historic trail from parcels 6 and 7 (the east end of the island) to Prisoners' Harbor. Flournoy also admitted that to build a road over the historic trail from parcel 6 to Prisoners' Harbor would cost about $120,000.[106] He opined that the cost to build a 300-foot long and 15-foot wide wharf at Scorpion Harbor which had none would be about $25,000.[107]

---

[102]Transcript on Appeal, in *Capuccio v. Caire*, (207 Cal. 200), pp. 150-152.
[103]*Cappucio v. Caire* (1932) 215 Cal. 518 at 529.
[104]Transcript on Appeal, in *Cappucio v. Caire*, (207 Cal. 200), p. 156.
[105]Ibid., pp. 138-155.
[106]Ibid., p. 146.
[107]Ibid., p. 148.

154   There was a bit of spice added to the trial. Clifford McElrath, the superintendent of the island for several years for Arthur and Fred Caire, testified on behalf of Edmund Rossi and Aglae Caire Capuccio. In fact, he testified that during the partition trial he had been sitting next to Ambrose Gherini and "prompting him during the entire hearing." "I want it understood that I have nothing but kindly feelings toward the Caires, but I feel more friendly toward Mr. Gherini and the side he represents," he explained. "I had to get up here to tell the truth and I will answer it honestly."[108] He testified that there was no wharf at Scorpion which as a result was of less value. The cattle, he stated, could not be exported from Scorpion Harbor but had to be herded over the historic trail to Prisoners' Harbor.

McElrath discounted the resort potential of the east end (parcels 6 and 7) because of lack of water. He was of the opinion that the property from Prisoners' Harbor on the east and Punta Diablo on the west would be valuable for resort purposes because of water. He conceded that it would not be a resort like Catalina "but it was sufficient to make a rich man's resort, and as a hunting reserve it would be unsurpassed."[109]

H.J. Doulton took the stand. Judge Crow observed that Doulton "has lived [in Santa Barbara] practically all his life and is very familiar with real estate values and building of public roads."[110] Doulton pointed out that since the majority of the heirs wanted to remain united, "everything was taken into consideration that could be thought of: wharves, water, conditions of the land and . . . the building of that road from tracts 6 and 7 to the wharf at Prisoners' Harbor and the expense was so great that we abandoned it."[111]

Doulton, as noted by Judge Crow, had experience in supervising the cost of building wharves. In his opinion, the eucalyptus grove in Scorpion Valley would provide the necessary tree trunks for pilings to construct a wharf. In his view, they were fine, "none better." He opined that a wharf at Scorpion Harbor could be com-

---

[108]Ibid., pp. 157-161.   [109]Ibid., pp. 158-159.
[110]Ibid., p. 161.   [111]Ibid., p. 162.

pleted with 50 piles. He estimated that with a steam pile driver it would cost $10,000 to build a 300-foot wharf. At Smugglers' Cove, he explained that a 1,000-foot wharf could cost between $12,000 to $15,000. A longer wharf would be needed at Smugglers' because of the breakers close to shore.[112]

Doulton offered an interesting perspective on the valuation of the east end. His testimony contrasted with the arguments that Ambrose Gherini was making on behalf of his clients. Gherini contended that a greater amount of land should be allocated to Edmund Rossi and Aglae Caire Capuccio because it did not have the development potential of the rest of the island and was isolated because parcel 6 and 7 did not have a wharf or access to Prisoners' Harbor. Doulton observed that the east end of the island that was going to be allocated to Gherini's clients has better climate, soil, topography and harbors than the rest of the island.[113] Concerning the resort capabilities, Doulton noted that "it would astonish people to know the amount of money it would take to develop this island for residential or resort purposes."[114]

The repeated questioning began to pique Doulton. Raising the pitch of his testimony, he stated, "If I may say it, they [referring to Mrs. Capuccio and Mr. Rossi] are getting the cream of the whole thing and we thought so at the time and we figured it out just that way and we thought these other people would be the ones, if anybody, who would say they were not getting a square deal . . . Why you people [referring to Rossi and Capuccio] have a principality on that island and you don't know it."[115]

The third referee, McComber, then testified. "Mr. McComber is one of our leading real estate men here," Judge Crow commented. "He knows values as good as any man here, I should think. He has a large and well-established real estate business here."[116] McComber believed that the land extending from Prisoners' Harbor to Punta Diablo was especially adapted for residential purposes, country estates, pleasure resorts, and similar

[112]Ibid., p. 163.   [113]Ibid., pp. 163-164.
[114]Ibid., p. 167.   [115]Ibid., p. 168.
[116]Ibid., p. 161.

156 purposes. He felt this area of the island possessed unsurpassed scenic beauty.[117]

Judge Crow, after hearing the testimony, accepted the survey and valuation by Flournoy, McComber and Doulton *in toto* and entered his final decree which was recorded on December 4, 1925, the year that a devastating earthquake wrecked Santa Barbara. The island was now divided into seven legal parcels, and each of Justinian's children had an individual ownership interest. Rossi and Capuccio moved the trial court to modify and change the referees' findings. Judge Crow refused, and Rossi and Capuccio appealed unsuccessfully.[118]

With the conclusion of the partition litigation and the physical division of the island rancho, the struggle of Arthur, Fred, and Delphine Caire to maintain control of the island through the Santa Cruz Island Company was over. The litigation, however, was not!

(4) LAWSUITS CONCERNING ATTORNEYS' FEES

Since the inception of the island litigation in 1912, the Rossi and Capuccio families were unable to pay attorneys' fees. As a result, Ambrose Gherini and David Freidenrich, Sr., entered into agreements in January 1921 with the heirs of Amelie Caire Rossi and Aglae Caire Capuccio concerning the payment of fees. The agreements were negotiated by Edmund Rossi and drafted by David Freidenrich, Sr.[119] Under the agreements, Rossi and Capuccio gave a total 4.5 shares of their 14 shares in the Santa Cruz Island Company to Gherini and Freidenrich since they ". . . have received no compensation for the services rendered by them in

---

[117]Ibid., p. 170.

[118]See *Capuccio v. Caire* (1929) 207 Cal. 200 at 211. Rossi and Capuccio contended that the referees might have made a more equitable division of the property. They argued that the referees should have provided more ingress and egress to the parcels awarded to them. The Supreme Court decided that these were factual issues to be decided by the trial court and that there was no showing of abuse of discretion on the part of the trial court in deciding the issues.

[119]Letter from Ambrose Gherini to Henry E. Monroe, dated December 7, 1929. Aglae Capuccio and Edmund Rossi were independently represented by Henry E. Monroe in the settlement of the Freidenrich litigation.

said litigation." The fee was contingent and provided that if Edmund Rossi and Aglae Caire Capuccio did not obtain such an interest in the assets of the Santa Cruz Island Company, the contract provision providing for a fractional interest was voided. The agreements further provided that Edmund Rossi and Aglae Caire Capuccio were entitled to the right of "first privilege to purchase" back the fractional interest which they were giving to Ambrose Gherini and David Freidenrich, Sr., of the assets of the defunct Santa Cruz Island Company. If Rossi and Capuccio were not successful, each of them was obligated to pay Gherini and Freidenrich only $2,500.[120]

The final decision in 1925 in the partition case did not end the litigation. There were not only continued disputes among the Caire family concerning who would pay the attorneys' fees for the partition case (1918-1925) but also new suits filed by David Freidenrich, Jr., against Ambrose Gherini and his clients for work his father did in the other island cases, the first of which started in 1912. Freidenrich, Sr., who was co-counsel with Gherini in the ongoing litigation, died in January 1924, before the conclusion of the partition suit.

Edmund Rossi and Aglae Caire Capuccio filed a motion in September of 1925 in the trial court seeking attorneys' fees for work involving the partition action which they were compelled to file in 1918 to protect the rights of the minority shareholders of the Santa Cruz Island Company. This application for fees was only for the partition case and was not for legal work for the other years of work in the Caire litigation. The trustees objected to Rossi and Capuccio's claim for fees. Judge Crow, denying Rossi and Capuccio's request for fees, ruled that fees could not be awarded in a contested partition action because the fees were not rendered for common benefit. Rossi and Capuccio appealed.

Meanwhile outside the courtroom, island history was also

---

[120]Memorandum of Agreements, January 28, 1921. The agreements provided that Gherini and Freidenrich, Sr., would receive a total of 5/14 interest from Rossi (i.e., 2.5 shares of the 7 shares owned by Rossi), and a total of 2/7 interest from Capuccio (i.e., 2 shares of the 7 shares owned by Capuccio).

158   being made. In 1927, Santa Cruz Island Company contracted with Merritt-Chapman & Scott Corporation to supply from Fry's Harbor the quarry rock required to build 600 feet of the Santa Barbara breakwater.[121] Over the years many had discussed and debated the idea of a breakwater. The project did not become a reality until Major Max C. Fleischmann, an ardent yachtsman and community benefactor, donated at least $550,000 for its construction. The project was completed in the early 1930s.[122]

The other historic island event occurred on April 17, 1928, when America's pioneer air mail pilot, Earle L. Ovington (1879-1936), made the inaugural flight to Santa Cruz Island. On this occasion, Ovington, who carried the first air mail in the United States in 1911, delivered the first and perhaps only official air mail letter addressed to Santa Cruz Island.[123] On this historic flight, Ovington flew from a private field called Casa Loma and landed on the Campo Grande field near Scorpion Ranch on the east end of the island.[124]

Back in the courtroom and five years after the death of his father, David Freidenrich, Jr., filed in Santa Barbara Superior Court two separate lawsuits in 1929 against Aglae Capuccio and Edmund Rossi and their attorney, Ambrose Gherini.[125] He sought compensation for his father's work in the island cases and alleged that the reasonable value of the services rendered by his father was $150,000. The lawsuits were quiet title actions since Freidenrich, Sr., along with Gherini, under the 1921 fee agreements received a fractional interest in the property for services rendered in the Caire litigation.

---

[121]Bookspan, *Santa Barbara by The Sea,* p. 75.

[122]Letter from Julius Bergen of the Max C. Fleischmann Foundation of Nevada to Edward S. Spaulding, June 1, 1961. Fleischmann, who made substantial contributions to Santa Barbara, wanted a harbor for his five luxury cruisers, all named *Haida.* He felt a good harbor would be an important asse' for the resort city. Bookspan, *Santa Barbara by the Sea,* p. 75. See also Tompkins, *Santa Barbara History Makers,* pp. 339-340.

[123]Letter from Earle Ovington to Ambrose Gherini, April 17, 1928. Ovington is also credited with pioneering the idea of establishing a municipal airport. Today, Santa Barbara Municipal Airport is named for him. Tompkins, *Santa Barbara History Makers,* pp. 369-371.

[124]*Santa Barbara Morning Press,* April 18, 1928.

[125]*David Freidenrich v. Ambrose Gherini and Aglae S. Capuccio,* and *David Freidenrich v. Ambrose Gherini and Edmund Rossi, et al.*

A demurrer was filed by Edmund Rossi, Aglae Capuccio and Ambrose Gherini.[126] David Freidenrich, Jr., opposed the demurrer and his attorneys argued:

> . . .Possessed of these muniments of title, and with nine years united work behind them, shoulder to shoulder, the two able attorneys plodded on, "cheek by jowl", for three more years of strenuous litigation till the 20th day of January, 1924, at which time Providence called D. Freidenrich away from strife of any kind, and ended his twelve years efforts for the defendants. At the time of his demise, the results of his twelve years effort were not fully declared by the appellate court . . . In other words, when D. Freidenrich died, the trees that he had planted were all in fruit, but it was not all quite ripe enough to fall and it remained for Ambrose Gherini to do the picking.[127]

On August 26, 1929, the trial court sustained the demurrer but allowed David Freidenrich, Jr., to amend his complaint. The matter was later settled when Ambrose Gherini paid the sum of $25,000 to David Freidenrich, Jr. In exchange, Freidenrich, Jr., relinquished to Gherini any right, title and interest in Santa Cruz Island and the Santa Cruz Island Company, and the lawsuits were dismissed on December 13, 1929.[128] Ambrose Gherini had agreed with Edmund Rossi and Aglae Capuccio that he would be fully responsible for any payment due to David Freidenrich, Jr.[129] In the end, Ambrose Gherini owned 4.5 shares of the defunct Santa Cruz Island Company.

In the same year, the Supreme Court decided the fee issue in the partition case by reversing Judge Crow's ruling denying the fees. The Court determined that Rossi and Capuccio, as minority

---

[126]A demurrer is a legal motion which challenges the sufficiency of the complaint; that is, whether enough facts, assumed to be true for the purposes of the motion, have been set forth to give rise to a lawsuit.

[127]Brief opposing demurrer filed by David Freidenrich, Jr., August 26, 1929 in both lawsuits. David Freidenrich, Jr., was represented by Aaron Cohen and Vincent Surr.

[128]Indenture from Freidenrich, Jr. to Ambrose Gherini relinquishing any and all interest in the island to Ambrose Gherini was dated December 11, 1929.

[129]Letter from Ambrose Gherini to Henry E. Monroe, December 7, 1929.

160   shareholders, had the right to make an application for fees for work in the partition case even though there were contested issues. The Supreme Court took into account the history of the prolonged Caire litigation and held that Rossi and Capuccio were entitled to fees which they could prove were for the common benefit.[130] The matter was then sent back to the trial court and heard by another judge, Frank C. Collier. After hearing the evidence, Judge Collier awarded Ambrose Gherini $75,000. The trustees appealed again, and in 1932 the Supreme Court upheld the award.[131] The Supreme Court observed that the trustees "offered no evidence to controvert plaintiff's showing as to the reasonable value of the services rendered by plaintiff's counsel for the common benefit."[132] Twenty years of litigation from 1912 to 1932 ended, but two new family eras would soon emerge in the island's history.

The Caire era (1880–1937), the period when the Caire family controlled the entire island, will be remembered not only for its legacy of litigation but also for the diverse development of a unique California ranch which included the building of many historically important structures.

---

[130]*Capuccio v. Caire* (1929) 207 Cal. 200 at 208-209; 73 A.L.R. 8. Here the Court held that fees would be proper if they were determined to be for the common benefit regardless of whether or not there had been litigated controversies concerning the partition action. The case was the subject of an American Law Reports, annotated (A.L.R.) article entitled "Allowance and apportionment of counsel fees in suit for partition." (73 A.L.R. 16).

[131]*Capuccio v. Caire* (1932) 215 Cal. 518 at 527-531. The Court also noted that the fee of $37,500 to the referees for work over a comparatively short period ". . . is also somewhat indicative of the reasonableness of the fee allowed by the court below for legal services performed 'for the common benefit' over an extended period of time." (529). The Court also noted that there was other expert testimony presented that reasonable value of the fees was $87,500 (527).

[132]Ibid., p. 527.

Chapter 7

The Stanton Family Era: 1937-1987

THE STANTON FAMILY AND ITS PURCHASE OF 90 PERCENT OF THE ISLAND

The Caire litigation took its financial toll on the defunct Santa Cruz Island Company which was operated by its trustee directors (Fred, Arthur and Delphine Caire). Debts kept mounting, and the company kept borrowing. The public records show that from 1930 to 1935 the Santa Cruz Island Company borrowed $230,000. From this amount, the company paid $25,000 in April 1930 to satisfy the judgments entered in the accounting action against the trustees; accordingly, both the injunction and accounting lawsuits were dismissed.[1] In addition, the trustees paid their proportionate share of attorneys' fees as ordered in 1932 by the California Supreme Court in the last of the Caire cases. The trustees also borrowed to finance the operation of the company.

On April 10, 1937, five years after the end of the litigation, the Santa Cruz Island Company sold parcels 1-5 consisting of 54,500 acres or 90 percent of the island to Edwin L. Stanton of Los Angeles

---

[1] Letter of Ambrose Gherini to Oakland Title Insurance & Guaranty Co., dated April 21, 1930. This money was actually paid to Maria Gherini since she bought all right, title, and interest from Aglae and the heirs of Amelie Rossi. The amount also probably included an agreed upon amount of interest.

162   for $750,000.[2] The schooner *Santa Cruz* was included in the sale. In
the same year, Stanton inquired of the National Park Service if it
was interested in Santa Cruz Island as a park. He did not receive a
reply.[3] Why Stanton initiated the inquiry is unknown. Possibly he
was looking for a quick sale or simply inquiring of their future plans.
The Caires maintained the Santa Cruz Island Company name until
December 1946 when they dissolved the corporation.[4]

One of the first actions taken by Ed Stanton was to give the
Eatons notice in May 1937 to vacate the famous Pelican Bay resort
run by them for nearly 25 years. By this time, the Eatons had
already abandoned the resort leaving behind dilapidated buildings and many vivid memories. Margaret Eaton signed a quitclaim deed which formally terminated their lease.[5] Ira Eaton died
August 13, 1938. Margaret observed:

> And that was the end of a time that would never be again.
> "No Trespassing" signs are up at Santa Cruz Island, but I am
> sure that the blue heron or his descendant—undisturbed by
> wars or other human sorrows—still sits on his perch guarding
> what we had once called our beautiful Pelican Bay.[6]

Ed Stanton also initiated a program to eliminate the pigs by
introducing "hog cholera" and to eradicate the ravens by poison-
ing them.[7] He observed that the island was improperly grazed
and over-stocked. He felt the cattle were an inferior breed. Therefore, he decided to sell off all the livestock he purchased from the
Caires.[8] So began the Stanton era, but not without human sorrow.

Edwin Stanton was born in San Diego on July 12, 1893, the year

---

[2]Santa Cruz Island Company corporation grant deed to Edwin Stanton was recorded on
April 22, 1937. A sale of $1 million was erroneously reported in the *Los Angeles Times* and
Santa Barbara News-Press on April 23, 1937.

[3]Ehorn, "The Establishment of Channel Islands National Park," unpublished article,
April 1994.

[4]The Certificate of Winding Up and Dissolution of The Santa Cruz Island Company, A
California Corporation, filed on December 30, 1946.

[5]Eaton Quitclaim Deed was recorded on May 28, 1937.

[6]Eaton, *Diary Of A Sea Captain's Wife*, p. 252. Margaret Holden Eaton died in 1947.

[7]Letter from Edwin L. Stanton to Ambrose Gherini, December 5, 1938.

[8]Ibid.

of the maiden voyage of the *Santa Cruz* to the island. He attended the University of California where he was a track star and Olympic contender. During World War I, he served in France as a First Lieutenant in the Field Artillery Division.[9] Stanton was a successful Los Angeles businessman who had formed the Stanton Oil Company which owned certain Signal Hill oil producing properties and the Edwin L. Stanton Company. He also owned the Stanton Axle Works which produced axles for Chevrolets in the Long Beach area.[10] Ed, as he was known, was a rugged outdoorsman and a good story teller. He had a forceful, yet delightful, personality and a good sense of humor.[11] Ed married twenty year old Evelyn Carey, who was born July 26, 1895 in Detroit, Michigan. Although they lived in exclusive Hancock Park in Los Angeles, the couple made many trips to the island aboard the famous schooner *Santa Cruz*.[12]

Ed and Evelyn had two children, Edwin, Jr., and Carey. The elder son, Edwin, Jr., born on April 16, 1918, was designated by his parents to take over and run the island.[13] Tragically on July 11, 1944, First Lieutenant Edwin Stanton, Jr., was killed in World War II combat at Normandy, France. Edwin, Jr., left a small child, Edwin Stanton III, born June 23, 1944, whom Edwin, Jr., did not live to see.

The Stanton's younger son, Carey, was born on February 20, 1923, in Los Angeles. Like many of the Caires, Carey as a youngster spent much of his school vacation and other free time on the island. Carey eventually was graduated from Stanford University School of Medicine. He interned at Los Angeles County Hospital where he contracted polio while caring for polio patients. He

---

[9]Daily, "Cemetery of the Holy Cross," pp. 30-31.

[10]McComb interview, September 7, 1993, pp. 2-4. McComb recalls that Ed sold the axle business to General Motors and used the proceeds to buy Santa Cruz Island. See also *Los Angeles Times*, April 23, 1937. McComb was a personal friend of the Stantons and a relative by marriage.

[11]Bergen interview, March 11, 1992, pp. 1-2. Mr. Bergen died on May 3, 1992. He was a partner with the Los Angeles law firm of O'Melveny & Myers and the Stanton family attorney.

[12]Daily, "Cemetery of the Holy Cross," p. 33.

[13]Bergen interview, p. 1.

164 worked in internal medicine and pathology for about ten years.[14] As Carey would later describe it, "overtaken by good sense . . . [he] returned to Santa Cruz Island" on April 10, 1957, to operate the ranch.[15] As fate would have it, the younger Stanton son, like Dr. Shaw a century before him, gave up his medical practice to operate an island ranch. Carey, who never married, was small in stature and exhibited a feisty personality. He quickly developed the reputation of being a zealous guardian of the island. One could easily incur his wrath for trespassing on the island or providing misleading information about it. Behind this veneer, Carey was a sensitive individual who had a genuine love of people and the island. Over the years, he developed a passion for collecting island memorabilia and had an avid interest in the island's history.[16] He wrote in 1984 a short but interesting essay called *An Island Memoir*.[17]

Ed Stanton died of a heart attack on June 5, 1963. At the time of his death, the Stanton portion of the island was not incorporated. Under his will, Ed Stanton directed that the Santa Cruz Island Company be recreated.[18] The company was again incorporated on July 13, 1964, by the filing of new Articles of Incorporation with the California Secretary of State.[19] Shortly thereafter, the directors of the company (Carey Stanton, Evelyn Stanton and family attorney, Richard Bergen) amended the articles to increase the capital structure of the corporation from $25,000 to $3,000,000 and created two classes of stock, common and preferred.[20]

---

[14]McComb interview, p. 6. McComb states that Carey worked for Aetna Life Insurance Company as pathologist.

[15]Stanton, *An Island Memoir*, p. 11.

[16]Daily, "Cemetery of the Holy Cross," p. 49.

[17]Stanton, *An Island Memoir*.

[18]Declaration of Carey Stanton attached to Points and Authorities in the case entitled *Edwin L. Stanton III v. Carey Stanton, et al.*, Los Angeles Superior Court No.C 152947.

[19]Articles of Incorporation filed in the office of the Secretary of State, July 13, 1964.

[20]A Certificate of Amendment of Articles of Incorporation of Santa Cruz Island Company was filed in the office of the Secretary of State on December 8, 1964. The amendment authorized the issuance of 2,000 shares of stock, half to be common and the other half to be preferred. In addition to priority dividend rights, the preferred stockholders were given a 3 to 1 voting advantage over the common stockholders.

Russ Vail, John Gherini, Pier Gherini, Carey Stanton and Al Vail at Santa Rosa Island, 1987. This photo is the only known photo of the island owners together at the same time on one of the Channel Islands. Stanton died later that year and Pier Gherini passed away in 1989. *Photo taken by William Ehorn.*

The company was again resurrected. The Santa Cruz Island Company had originally been incorporated in 1869 and died in 1911 as a result of failure to pay a $5 license tax. Some of the Caires revived the corporation and elected in 1919 to extend its life for another 50 years. This revival was held to be ineffective against the dissenting shareholders, and the majority shareholders dissolved the Santa Cruz Island Company in 1946. The corporation in the Stanton era was given new life but would eventually succumb to more dissension over who would control it.

In their wills, Ed and Evelyn laid the groundwork to control the

166 company but at the same time planted the seed from which more island conflict would grow. According to the testamentary plan of Ed Stanton, an undivided interest in the island was transferred to the new company and common stock in the company was issued.[21] Carey was distributed two-thirds of the common stock, and he held the other one-third of the common stock in trust for his nephew, Edwin Stanton III. From the estate, Ed's wife Evelyn received fractional interests in Ed's assets, including the island.[22] Her share of the island was later transferred to the corporation in exchange for all of the company's preferred stock. Evelyn died on November 20, 1973. Under her estate plan, Carey received two-thirds of the preferred stock and held all but one of the remaining shares for the benefit of Edwin Stanton III. In short, Carey owned two-thirds of the Santa Cruz Island Company and Edwin III owned or had a beneficial interest in one-third of the company.[23]

The Stanton era lasted fifty years (1937-1987). During this time the Stantons, like the Caires, made many diversified uses of the island but not without experiencing its burdens. Ed Stanton abandoned the sheep operation and the flock became known as "feral" or wild sheep (*Ovis aries*). He continued a cattle business with new livestock, most of which had to be evacuated from the island during the 1948 drought. As a hedge against future droughts, he planned to build a large lake or reservoir in the central mountains of the island. The scheme, which would have been Santa Barbara County's largest water conservation project, was never carried out.[24] Stanton replenished his herd and ran a cow/calf operation of registered polled Herefords. In order to generate income, Ed leased portions of the island. He rented a hilltop loca-

---

[21]*Estate of Edwin L. Stanton, deceased,* Los Angeles Superior Court No. 470036. The order authorizing Carey Q. Stanton as executor of his father's estate to exchange assets was entered on December 14, 1964, and recorded. The order authorized the executor to convey fractional interests in the island, the Stanton Oil Company and the Edwin L. Stanton Company to the Santa Cruz Island Company in exchange for 1,000 shares of company stock.

[22]Order Authorizing Preliminary Distribution in the Estate of Edwin L. Stanton. The order was filed on December 14, 1964, and recorded.

[23]Declaration of Carey Stanton filed in *Edwin L. Stanton III v. Carey Stanton, et al.,* Los Angeles Superior Court No. C. 152947.

[24]*Los Angeles Times,* June 25, 1950, p. 34.

tion west of the Montañon in February 1949 to the United States government for the purposes of establishing a missile tracking station. About thirty Navy and civilian technicians maintained and operated the radar facility.[25] Not only did the lease provide needed income ($60,000 annually in later years), but also the government helped maintain some of the roads and the pier at Prisoners' Harbor and hauled heavy equipment and supplies to the island at the government's expense.[26] Subsequently, in 1950, a fire gutted the historic winery and the wooden main ranch house. The Chapel had fallen into disrepair from normal deterioration caused by weathering and earthquake activity.[27] In the same year, Stanton, perhaps burdened by island ownership, listed his 54,500 acres for sale at $2,725,000 ($50 per acre) claiming it to be an outstanding cattle ranch lending itself "ideally for a large colony or subdivision."[28] The island did not sell and operations continued but so did the problems. Regretably in 1960, the schooner *Santa Cruz* sank, and the historic adobe at Prisoners' Harbor was dismantled after being damaged by flooding.

During the second half of the Stanton era, the Santa Cruz Island Company in 1965 let a small area (approximately 1 acre) to General Motors Corporation for research; by 1983 when Maripro Inc. took over the lease, it generated $91,800 annually.[29] In 1965, the Santa Cruz Island Company also contracted with the Santa Cruz Island Hunt Club, owned and operated by William E. Huffman and Richard A. Lagomarsino. Under this agreement the club was given the non-exclusive right to hunt and kill feral sheep and pigs and paid the Santa Cruz Island Company twenty-five percent of the gross receipts.[30] In some years, the company received

[25]Hillinger, *The California Islands,* p. 93.

[26]Board of Directors minutes of Santa Cruz Island Company, November 4, 1987.

[27]Daily and Dewey, "Pictorial Restoration," p. 105.

[28]Coldwell, Banker & Company listing memo, March 6, 1950. Listing price was $50 per acre. Letter from Edwin Stanton to Ambrose Gherini, June 22, 1950.

[29]Minutes of Santa Cruz Island Company Board of Directors meeting, March 16, 1983.

[30]Copy of leases are contained in Santa Cruz Island Company, *Sale of Stock and Assets to The Nature Conservancy* (1977), vol. 1, No. 23. See also, unaudited financial statement of the company for the year 1976 contained in Santa Cruz Island Company, *Sale of Stock and Assets to The Nature Conservancy* (1977), vol. 1, No. 22.

168   nearly $150,000 annually.[31] The University of California, under a 1966 license agreement with the Santa Cruz Island Company, established a research station on the island for "educational and scientific activities." The company also leased in 1973 two communication sites to the Santa Cruz Island Communications Company which was owned by Carey Stanton, Ted Green, Rick Lagomarsino and Henry Duffield. The company in turn sublet space to others desiring a communication system on the island's high mountains.[32] Stanton, in 1980, guided a major restoration of the historic Casa Vieja at the Christy Ranch.

CONFLICT AMONG THE STANTON FAMILY

Conflict in the Stanton era took on an eerie resemblance to the conflict in the Caire years. In both cases, disputes arose over who would control the island and who would be excluded. The name of the Santa Cruz Island Company was resurrected only to be engaged in more costly family strife.

Since the formation of the resurrected corporation in 1964 after the death of his father, Carey was in control and was not about to relinquish it.[33] He was president, a director, and a majority shareholder. The shareholders of the company received no dividends although Carey received a salary to manage the ranch. The reason advanced by Stanton was that his parents' deaths triggered a tremendous estate tax liability which in 1976 still showed a balance of approximately $700,000. To extricate his mother's estate from the tax dilemma, the company purchased back some of the estate's preferred stock in order to provide cash to pay the taxes.[34]

Despite the estate tax burdens which plagued the owners of the island over the years, the fact remained that Carey was in control which, as the island's historical record showed, proved costly. Irre-

---

[31]Rick Lagomarsino and Bill Huffman interview. The Santa Cruz Island Company earned $149,230 in 1984 and $148,996 in 1985 from the hunt club. Over the years the hunt club provided substantial income to the Company.

[32]Green interview, January 9, 1995.

[33]Bergen interview, p. 6.

[34]Stanton declaration in *Edwin L. Stanton III v. Santa Cruz Island Company, et al.,* Los Angeles Superior Court No. C. 152947.

spective of his own modest living habits, Carey was living on the island in what was perceived by his nephew as a lifestyle of the "rich and famous"; the company was making some money, and Edwin III felt excluded. There were all the ingredients for another island family fight. Three years after the death of his grandmother Evelyn, Edwin III filed his lawsuit on November 12, 1976, to dissolve the corporation and to require an accounting.[35]

At the time of the filing of the lawsuit, Edwin III was a director and minority shareholder of the Santa Cruz Island Company. The lawsuit filed by Edwin III alleged that his grandmother Evelyn and his uncle Carey had conspired to control the corporation and the assets of the Stanton family. Of particular concern was the fact that the non-island assets, such as the Stanton Oil Company which was a partnership of valuable oil producing properties, were transferred to the Santa Cruz Island Company in exchange for the island company stock. This meant that the oil producing assets would be under the control of the corporation rather than Edwin III owning his one-third interest outright.[36]

Edwin III also alleged that he was excluded from the corporation despite his one-third interest in it. He further claimed that his grandmother Evelyn and his uncle Carey had been "using the corporation for their own selfish purpose of keeping the island for their personal power, vanity, pleasure and aggrandizement without regard to profit motive or benefit to the minority shareholder."[37] The lawsuit alleged that the island cattle operation had

[35]The lawsuit was entitled *Edwin L. Stanton III v. Santa Cruz Island Company, et al.,* Los Angeles Superior Court No. C180228, filed January 2, 1976.

[36]Edwin III alleged that the corporation was mismanaged and that the cattle operation had lost approximately $930,000 since 1965. During the same period of time, the oil properties generated approximately $454,000, and it was claimed that the oil interests were in fact subsidizing the island operation. First cause of action of complaint, paragraph 5, p. 15 and paragraph 9(3), p. 19. By the time Edwin III filed his lawsuit in 1976, the Santa Cruz Island Company reported substantial gross income of $387,337 and a total net income of $80,101. The agricultural operations, both operating and non-operating, totaled $323,624 and oil and gas revenues totaled $63,713. Unaudited financial statement of the company for the year 1976 contained in Santa Cruz Island Company, *Sale of Stock and Assets to The Nature Conservancy* (1977), vol. 1, No. 22.

[37]First cause of action of complaint, paragraph 24, p. 9.

170 incurred substantial losses since 1965. Despite the losses, Edwin III contended that Carey and Evelyn had continued to hold the island because of the ". . . power and prestige derived from controlling one of the largest islands off the coast of California and the personal benefits flowing from such control."[38]

Carey Stanton filed a verified answer to the complaint denying many of the allegations. Some feel the allegations that Carey led a lavish lifestyle or that he would intentionally mismanage island finances were exaggerated and that Carey was too conservative in his manner and demeanor and simply too parsimonious.[39] Nevertheless, Carey had an interesting lifestyle. He often traveled between his house in Sierra Madre and his island ranch residence, each of which contained his own fine paintings, antique silver and other valuable furnishings.[40]

Stanton's lifestyle, however, was not the real problem, and it is doubtful that there is any basis to the claim of his mismanaging the company. The allegations filed by Edwin III, raised broader historical issues. Edwin III knew that he was a beneficial owner of a very valuable asset, but had no power or ability to realize anything from it. Carey on the other hand loved the island and was not about to relinquish control which his parents had given to him.[41] The lawsuit raised shadows of the past. Edwin III's position was similar to that of Amelie Caire Rossi and Aglae Caire Capuccio. History was indeed repeating itself!

SALE OF THE STANTON INTEREST TO THE NATURE CONSERVANCY

Carey Stanton realized his dilemma. He was faced with the prospect of expensive litigation which in the words of Helen Caire would have been "self defeating." He knew that he did not have the liquid assets to buy out Edwin III. Carey not only wanted the island to be preserved, but he also wanted to control it.[42] These

---

[38]Ibid., first cause of action of complaint, paragraph 27, p. 11.

[39]Daily interview, September 2, 1993. See also Bergen interview, p. 8.

[40]Daily observes that Carey Stanton always was careful in making a distinction between his personal assets and those of the Santa Cruz Island Company.

[41]Bergen's interview, p. 12.   [42]Ibid.

goals would be the catalyst which eventually led to a settlement of the litigation and the sale of 90 percent of the island to The Nature Conservancy.

The Nature Conservancy, a nationally known private non-profit conservation organization,[43] and the National Park Service were both interested in the long term preservation of the island. As early as 1973, The Nature Conservancy had targeted Santa Cruz Island for acquisition, but it was not until 1975 that Stanton became interested in the Conservancy. The following year, before the lawsuit was filed in November of 1976, Stanton invited to Santa Cruz Island representatives of the National Park Service, including William Ehorn, then superintendent of the Channel Islands National Monument, Howard Chapman, the National Park Service western regional director and Gary Everhardt, the director. At this island meeting, Everhardt asked Stanton if he was interested in donating his interest in the island to the National Park Service. Stanton emphatically declined and expressed his opinion that he thought he had done a better job managing the island than the Park Service had done in managing Anacapa and Santa Barbara Islands which were then part of the Channel Islands National Monument.[44]

After the lawsuit was filed, one of the solutions to Carey Stanton's dilemma was striking a deal with The Nature Conservancy. The complex negotiations began in January of 1977. One of the key elements to the global solution was The Nature Conservancy independently negotiating a purchase of the Santa Cruz Island Company stock owned by Edwin III. Eventually, The Nature Conservancy paid $900,000 to Edwin III for his stock. The Nature Conservancy also agreed to pay $900,000 to Carey Stanton for half of his stock but gave him the proxy to vote the shares of stock acquired from Edwin III. In addition, The Conservancy paid Stanton substantial funds to pay estate taxes and expenses and the

---

[43]Diane Elfstrom Devine, a program manager for the island since 1981, states that The Nature Conservancy (TNC)'s mission is to preserve plants, animals and natural communities that represent the diversity of life on Earth by protecting the lands and waters they need to survive.

[44]Ehorn, "The Establishment of Channel Islands National Park," p. 6.

172 company to pay its obligations. In turn, Stanton agreed to leave the balance of his shares in the corporation to the Conservancy by his will.[45] The Santa Cruz Island Company then granted a fee interest in 42,300 acres to the Conservancy but reserved to the company "the full use, control, income and possession of the southerly portion of the island for a term of 30 years."[46] The Nature Conservancy took title to 12,200 acres of the northerly portion of the island and leased the acreage back to the Santa Cruz Island Company. Finally, Carey Stanton donated a Conservation Easement over the entire island owned by him. The solution was a pragmatic one for Stanton: he could retain control (or at least he thought so), preserve the island, pay the remaining estate taxes owed from his mother's estate and settle the lawsuit all at the same time. The Nature Conservancy paid a total of $2,524,000 to complete the deal.[47] The transaction between the Santa Cruz Island Company, The Nature Conservancy and Edwin III was finally completed on September 15, 1978. The settlement, however, did not resolve the animosity between Carey and his nephew, nor did it eliminate future discord.[48]

CONFLICT WITH THE NATURE CONSERVANCY

Carey Stanton, as president of the Santa Cruz Island Company, signed on September 13, 1978, the Conservation Easement which stated that ". . . feral animals inhabit the island and constitute an actual substantial degradation and impairment of the natural flora and the natural fauna and should be eliminated." Stanton in

---

[45]Bergen interview, p. 19.

[46]Forward to volume II, p. 4 and document entitled "Corporation Grant Deed" signed by Carey Stanton on September 15, 1978, No. 62. See also document entitled "Option For The Purchase Of Real Estate And A Conservation Easement," vol. 1, No. 6.

[47]David Watts letter to Alves, August 4, 1978. Watts stated that $564,000 was used to cover estate taxes and expenses owed in Evelyn Stanton's estate; $900,000 was paid directly to Carey; $900,000 was paid to Edwin III; and $160,000 paid to the Company for corporate expenses. The structure of the transactions also enabled Stanton to receive certain tax savings and tax planning opportunities.

[48]Telephone interview on September 13, 1994, with Robert Hansen, who was The Nature Conservancy's Santa Cruz Island Project Director from January 1980 through 1989. According to Hansen, neither Carey nor his nephew would speak to each other at the signing of the settlement documents.

the easement document clearly agreed that its purpose was "to preserve and protect in perpetuity and to enhance by restoration the natural ecological and aesthetic features and values of the island."[49] The document significantly stated that among the rights conveyed to The Nature Conservancy was the right:

> ... To enjoin any activity on, or use of, the Island which constitutes an actual or threatened substantial degradation or impairment of the natural flora, the natural fauna,[and] ... to enforce the restoration of such areas or features as may be damaged by such activities."[50]

The lease which covered the northern portion of the island (12,200 acres), however, specifically allowed the Santa Cruz Island Company to "undertake or allow to be undertaken selective reduction or elimination of feral animals." The Conservation Easement which covered the entire 54,500 acres also contained similar language which read that one of the "practices that was not to be precluded, prevented or limited" was the control of "feral animals by the use only of selective control techniques as heretofore conducted."[51] This easement language seemed to contradict the easement's overriding purpose to prevent ecological "degradation of the natural flora."

The extensive documentation of the parties' agreement is notable not only for what it says but also for what it omits, including any mention of the ramifications to the lucrative hunt club activities in the event that The Nature Conservancy decided to eliminate the feral animals to preserve the island flora. The parties avoided any mention of the hunt club and avoided defining such slippery terms as "selective control techniques."[52] These omissions, whether accidental or contrived, would be the grist which would later feed the island litigation fever.

[49]Deed of Conservation Easement contained in Santa Cruz Island Company, Sale of *Stock and Assets to The Nature Conservancy* (1978), vol. 2, No. 83.

[50]Ibid.

[51]See "Lease" which is document #89 in vol. II and "Deed of Conservation Easement" which is document #83 in vol. II in *Sale of Stock and Assets to The Nature Conservancy* (1978).

[52]Jaret Owens, who had extensive hunting experience and many years involvement with island hunting programs, never heard of the term. The term sounds like legalese.

174   The goals of the hunt club and the Conservation Easement clashed, and Stanton never advised the hunt club of the Conservation Easement before he signed it.[53] The purpose of the hunt club was to generate money for the Santa Cruz Island Company by killing the feral animals over time. Obviously, the purpose was not to eliminate the inventory of feral animals since this would put the hunt operation out of business.[54] On the other hand, the overriding purpose of the Conservation Easement was the total elimination of the feral animals from the island so that the island could be restored to its natural state.

The Nature Conservancy developed in 1979 a conservation plan which included the elimination of the feral sheep. The following year, not only did Stanton approve of the plan, but Frank Boren, a director of the Santa Cruz Island Company, reported that the Santa Cruz Island Hunt Club was not worried about the possible eradication efforts which might destroy many sheep.[55] The plan, as could be expected, raised new island controversy. The sheep contributed to soil erosion and reduction of native plants. The Santa Cruz Island Company had for years run a hunting club and derived substantial income from it. After Stanton entered an agreement with The Nature Conservancy, it had a legal obligation under the language of the conservation easement "to preserve and protect in perpetuity and to enhance the natural ecosystems."

Stanton disagreed. He felt that while the feral sheep were a problem, it was the Santa Cruz Island Company which had the right to control the sheep by use of "selective control techniques."[56] Stanton argued that he only agreed to the sheep

---

[53]Huffman interview.

[54]Owens interview, January 4, 1995. Jaret Owens worked for many years for the hunt club before establishing his own club, called Island Adventures, in the east end of the island. Owens observed that the club would never be able to eliminate the animals, but they could control the sheep and pig population and make money doing it.

[55]Minutes of the Santa Cruz Island Company Board of Directors meeting, September 10, 1980. Boren was the Conservancy's representative on the board which included Stanton and his attorney, David Watts.

[56]Schuyler, "Control of Feral Sheep," p. 444. Stanton admitted to Bill Huffman that The Nature Conservancy had the legal right to eliminate the sheep, but Stanton felt that they did not have the means or the ability to undertake such a project. Huffman interview.

removal program because Boren had verbally agreed to compensate the company to the tune of $20 per sheep. Considering that there were over 30,000 sheep to be removed, the cost would have been a staggering $600,000. Boren's denial of such an arrangement is consistent with the fact that the minutes of the meetings of the company's board of directors (Stanton, Boren and Watts) never mentioned such an understanding.[57] Even if the feral or wild sheep were assets of the Santa Cruz Island Company, Stanton's concept of a verbal arrangement made little practical sense since the Conservancy, as 80 percent shareholder of the company, would eventually reap the benefits.[58] It was undisputed that the company suffered economically as a result of the elimination of the sheep. Other factors, however, contributed to the financial woes of the company, such as the loss of $100,000 in income from the oil and gas properties owned by the company and the effects of the 1983-1984 drought which substantially reduced income from cattle operations.[59] Stanton obviously wanted the company to be financially viable so he could run it during his lifetime, and he was dismayed when he saw its financial underpinnings threatened. This heightened his adversarial attitude toward The Nature Conservancy. Nevertheless, Stanton's legal position was tenuous since there was little credible evidence supporting his contention of an oral agreement, and he had no leverage against The Nature Conservancy to force them to help the beleaguered company.

The control of the feral sheep by Stanton became an issue of money for the company which he ran rather than conservation. According to Robert Hansen, who was then the Santa Cruz Island Project Director for The Nature Conservancy, Stanton supported the eradication program until the program began to impact areas

[57]Interestingly, Douglas L. Thorpe, Stanton's attorney handling Stanton's disputes with The Nature Conservancy, never mentioned such an oral agreement in correspondence with The Nature Conservancy's counsel concerning the economic problems of the Santa Cruz Island Company. Letter from Douglas L. Thorpe to Quin Denvir, November 26, 1986.

[58]Letter from Douglas L. Thorpe to David D. Watts.

[59]Letter from Douglas L. Thorpe to Quin Denvir.

176   where the hunt club was flourishing.[60] The funding for the sheep removal came from a $2,037,544 grant to the Conservancy from The Max C. Fleischmann Foundation which in 1980 required Stanton's written approval of the immediate removal of the sheep.[61] The dispute concerning the removal of the sheep festered for several years and severely strained the relationship between Stanton and The Nature Conservancy. By 1983, Stanton had become an outspoken critic of The Nature Conservancy, and speculated that the future of the island would be better preserved by his long time nemesis, the National Park Service.[62] By this time, Stanton had made known his opposition to the Park Service's plan for developing visitor use on the east end of the island. The Nature Conservancy's elimination program not only financially impacted the Santa Cruz Island Company, but perhaps more importantly threatened Stanton's control of the island. Carey expressed his feelings in 1983 when he stated: "I just do not want to be pushed around . . . Let me alone and let me care for Santa Cruz Island."[63]

Stanton and The Nature Conservancy were prepared to file lawsuits over the eradication program and their respective rights under the Conservation Easement.[64] Eventually Stanton reluctantly capitulated and agreed in 1984 that all the feral sheep could be eliminated no later than June 1987. On the one hand, Stanton wanted the company to have the money from the hunt club, but on the other hand he wanted the Conservancy to conclude their

---

[60]Hansen interview, September 13, 1994. Hansen observed that the funding for the eradication program came in part from a grant from the Max Fleischmann Foundation, and Carey Stanton wrote a letter on March 18, 1980, in support of the grant. Hansen also recalled that before the eradication program took effect, representatives of The Nature Conservancy reviewed with Stanton their 1980 Preservation Plan which included the eradication program. According to Hansen, Stanton approved the Plan.

[61]Letter from F.R.Breen to Thomas T. Macy, February 13, 1980. The grant was to be allocated as follows: $663,000 for land acquisition; 5-year start-up operating cost of $884,100 which included the $240,000 cost for the sheep removal and $490,444 for capital expenditures.

[62]Stanton letter to Frank Boren, April 16, 1983.

[63]Stanton letter to David Watts, September 27, 1983.

[64]Telephone interview with Robert Hansen, September 13, 14, 1994. Hansen recalled that both The Nature Conservancy and Stanton had hired law firms and were ready to do battle.

elimination program so that their involvement with the island would be diminished.[65] He warned The Nature Conservancy, however, that there would be a "public outcry" for the massive sheep slaughter and possible litigation.[66] Shortly thereafter, The California Wildlife Federation threatened to seek an injunction against The Nature Conservancy in August 1984. The Federation argued that the control program ruined the finest recreational hunting opportunity in western North America. The Nature Conservancy and the Federation successfully negotiated a settlement, and a threatened lawsuit was never filed.[67] It was about this time that Stanton began seriously thinking about the formation of a non-profit foundation to help preserve the island's history.

From 1980 to 1985 the Santa Cruz Island Hunt Club flourished despite the sheep eradication program. For example, the company earned a net $429,616 for the three-year period between 1983 and 1985. Ironically, the hunt club went out of business after 1985 in part because of insurance problems.[68] After learning of the club's decision to shut down its hunting operation, the company advised The Nature Conservancy that it "has the authority to eliminate the sheep on the island as soon as possible" so that their "presence on Santa Cruz Island can be minimized until 2008."[69]

By June 1989, the sheep eradication program resulted in shooting a total of 31,871 sheep and cost the Conservancy at least $240,000.[70] The program has to date yielded tangible evidence of

---

[65]Thorpe letter to David D. Watts, June 29, 1984.

[66]Stanton letter to David D.Watts, July 27, 1984.

[67]Schuyler, "Control of Feral Sheep" p. 450. The article incorrectly states that a suit was filed. See also *Santa Barbara News-Press,* "Groups work out pact on island sheep killing," September 1, 1984, p. A-2.

[68]Bill Huffman related that their liability premiums increased ten-fold and as a result they stopped operating the hunt club until they could solve the insurance problem. By the time they resolved the insurance problem, there were no sheep to hunt because of the eradication program.

[69]David D. Watts letter to Frank D. Boren, January 10, 1986. In this letter, there also is no mention of an oral agreement to compensate the Santa Cruz Island Company for the sheep shot.

[70]Schuyler, "Control of Feral Sheep," pp. 446-448.

the gradual recovery of the island ecosystem. Naturally, the program produced paradoxical results. The rapid elimination of the sheep, the end of the 1991 drought, and the lack of competition from other plants on the island contributed to the dramatic increase in fennel growth.[71] As the natural vegetation thrives, risks of fires also increase, but arguably there are benefits to this natural cycle.[72]

END OF THE STANTON ERA

Carey Stanton died in his home on the island on December 8, 1987, sparing him any more island strife. Stanton was very distraught at the time, not only because of his poor relationship with The Nature Conservancy, but also because of the recent death of his long time friend and ranch manager, Henry Duffield (1921-1986) who died on the island the previous year.[73] Duffield came to the island as a ranch manager for Ed Stanton in 1960. Henry, a polio victim like Carey, managed the island for 26 years despite being paralyzed from the waist down.

As a result of Stanton's death, The Nature Conservancy became owners of the assets of the Santa Cruz Island Company which included 90 percent of Santa Cruz Island. The following year, The Nature Conservancy, as sole owner of the Santa Cruz Island Company, changed the company to a nonprofit public benefit corporation.[74]The Santa Cruz Island Company was dissolved for the last time on November 12, 1992.[75]

The 50 year Stanton era (1937-1987) ended leaving in its wake

---

[71]Diane Elfstrom Devine interview. Devine said that the abundant rainfall and the pleasant Mediterranean climate also contributed to revitalization of the island's flora.

[72]See *Santa Barbara News-Press,* "Controlled fire aids island's native plants" by Peter C. Howorth, November 19, 1995. The Nature Conservancy and the National Park Service attempt to carefully orchestrate control burns to eliminate the non-native species of grass. One such burn, however, got out of control in December of 1994 because of a gust of wind. *Santa Barbara News-Press,* December 9, 1994.

[73]Personal interview of William Ehorn by John Gherini, April of 1994.

[74]Restated Article of Incorporation filed with the office of the Secretary of State on April 8, 1988.

[75]Certificate of Dissolution filed in the office of Secretary of State on November 12, 1992.

two significant legacies: the preservation of the island by The
Nature Conservancy and the creation in 1986 of the Santa Cruz
Island Foundation.[76] The present challenge of the Foundation
will be to carry out its goal of island research and historic preservation free of the vestiges of Stanton's often petulant disputes
with the National Park Service and The Nature Conservancy.
Toward this end, the nonprofit foundation completely restored
the historic chapel in 1991.[77] Stanton, during his lifetime, initiated the tradition of a liturgical celebration at the chapel site on
the Feast of the Holy Cross. This celebration, on May 3rd of each
year, has been continued by the joint action of The Nature Conservancy and the Santa Cruz Island Foundation.

---

[76]The original Articles of Incorporation were filed on September 22, 1986, and restated
in 1990. As restated, the articles set forth the mission of the Foundation: "This corporation
is a nonprofit public benefit corporation and is not organized for the private gain of any
person. It is organized. . .to collect, maintain, and catalogue items of real and personal
property or interests therein regarding Santa Cruz Island, and the other California Channel Islands, unique island environments off the coast of Southern California, and to display for public benefit said items in cooperation with The Nature Conservancy, the
National Park Service, or otherwise, as well as to promote research and publications dealing with historical and cultural aspects of the California Channel Islands, to organize and
sponsor public exhibits and/or events dealing with California's Channel Islands, to organize and sponsor educational trips to Santa Cruz in conjunction with The Nature Conservancy, and the National Park Service, and otherwise, to organize and sponsor educational
trips to the other of California's Channel Islands, to present and sponsor Channel Islands
public lectures and slide shows, Channel Islands school presentations, to promote public
access to research materials, books, maps, art, artifacts, furniture etc., related to the California Channel Islands, and to preserve and restore for public benefit structures on California Channel Islands."

[77]Daily and Dewey, "Pictorial Restoration of The Chapel of the Holy Cross," p. 105.

Chapter 8

Gherini Family Era: 1926 to 1997

T he Gherini era, the longest lasting family period of Santa Cruz Island, stretched 71 years. After a court partitioned the island into seven parcels in 1925, the Gherini family began operating a ranch the following year on parcels 6 and 7, comprising 6,253.49 acres on the east end of the island. The era ended in February 1997 when the National Park Service legally acquired the fractional interest of Francis Gherini, the last descendent of Justinian Caire to have a fee interest in the island.

THE AFTERMATH OF THE CAIRE LITIGATION

The prolonged island litigation which started in 1912 and ended in 1932 strained the financial resources and emotional stamina of the Rossi and Capuccio families. Both P. C. Rossi, Amelie Caire's husband, and Goffredo Capuccio, Sr., Aglae Caire's husband, died near the inception of the litigation. Amelie Caire Rossi died on March 17, 1917, leaving ten children who succeeded to their mother's interest in the defunct Santa Cruz Island Company.[1]

---

[1]*In the Matter of the Estate of Amelie A. Rossi.* Title passed to Amelie's heirs through decrees of distribution in Amelie's estate. For estate and inheritance tax purposes, assets are valued as of date of death. The Internal Revenue Service determined that even though there was litigation involving the family company, Amelie's seven shares were worth $46,335 or $6,619 per share. This valuation was surprisingly close to the $6,000 per share value which the court appointed referees arrived at in the partition case in 1924. Letter from Deputy Commissioner of Internal Revenue Service J. Hagerman to Ambrose Gherini, June 28, 1919.

182   Aglae Caire Capuccio, widowed in 1915 when her husband, Goffredo Sr., suddenly died, experienced the hardship of raising two
minor children by herself.

After winning parcels 6 and 7 in the partition lawsuit, Capuccio
and the Rossi heirs faced in 1926 the difficult burden of managing an island ranch. The Santa Cruz Island Company had allowed
the ranch to deteriorate. The lack of interest in maintaining it
probably began in 1923-1924 when it became apparent that the
island would be physically divided and that the east end would
probably be awarded to Rossi and Capuccio. Immediate work
needed to be done on fences, trails, buildings, and the wells.
Equipment and supplies needed to be ordered and transported.
These projects seemed daunting since Capuccio and the Rossis
had no boat, and there was no pier facility at Scorpion Harbor.
Running an island ranch became a logistical nightmare since neither Capuccio nor the Rossi heirs had any experience in running
a ranch; that task fell on Ambrose Gherini who also was a novice
at this type of venture. Gherini recognized that the ranch was not
only in disrepair, but also the flock of sheep was too small for the
size of the property. He observed that "it is much like operating a
factory far short of its capacity."[2]

Shortly after the partition case, Aglae Caire Capuccio hired her
own attorney to negotiate a sale of her interest in the island to
Amelie's children. The agreement was entered into on October
18, 1926. The purchase price was $65,478, of which $15,478 was
paid upon signing of the agreement. The Amelie Caire Rossi
heirs signed a $50,000 note to Aglae Capuccio for the balance of
the purchase price.[3]

The Rossi heirs then agreed in October of 1926 to operate the
island ranch through the name of the National Trading Company.[4] This company had been incorporated on October 10, 1916,

---

[2]National Trading Company Financial Report, December 31, 1928.

[3]This amounted to 5 shares of stock since the other 2 shares were granted to Ambrose
Gherini and David Freidenrich, Sr., under the 1921 agreement. The note was for 5 years
with interest at 6% to be paid monthly.

[4]Minutes of National Trading Company, October 19, 1926.

and was formed primarily to conduct an import-export business unrelated to the island.[5] The company originally exported a large quantity of green coffee to Russia prior to the Revolution in 1917. For a while the business prospered until the political upheaval in Russia disrupted the trade. Ambrose Gherini eventually became the sole shareholder, but the company remained inactive from 1919 to 1926 when it was decided that the corporation would operate the island ranch on the east end. Parcels 6 and 7, however, were never transferred to the company.[6]

By the end of 1929, when the country reeled from the Great Stock Market Crash, the island sheep operations on the east end showed a net profit of $69.66. The National Trading Company reported livestock inventory of 4,047 sheep, 24 hogs, 12 horses and 12 chickens. The barns held 200 tons of hay and 16,544 pounds of unmarketable wool. The price for sheep achieved a record high, but there were few sheep in a condition to be sold because of the severe drought in 1929. Problems mounted and the responsibility for managing the ranch created tensions among the many Rossi heirs. Ambrose Gherini, having assumed the responsibility of operating the ranch, did so for two and a half years without compensation from the co-owners. Ambrose felt there was "absolutely no cooperation or assistance from the co-owners," and that the situation was unjust and needed immediate resolution.[7] Edmund Rossi resigned on March 10, 1930, as Vice-President of the National Trading Company and Esther A. Rossi resigned as Secretary.

---

[5]The original shareholders and directors were Clemente Zulberti, Harold C. Reyman and J. Edwin Lyons. Reyman, a couple months later, transferred his interest to Ambrose Gherini who was elected president in January 1917.

[6]Letter from Ambrose Gherini to Pier Gherini, January 21, 1952. The corporation was used only for convenience and all of the ranch income and disbursements were reported on the individual tax returns of Ambrose and Maria Gherini. Affidavit of Ambrose Gherini, April 7, 1938. The company name was amended on March 21, 1930, to read "National Trading Company Ltd." Thereafter the company remained in existence until it was dissolved in March 1963. The name continued to be used for the east end ranch operations until 1984. The abbreviation of the company name was NATCO which was used to name the boat, *Natco*. All the wool sacks shipped from the Gherini Ranch bore the name "Natco."

[7]National Trading Company Annual Report, December 31, 1929.

184   Maria Rossi Gherini acted quickly to prevent further family discord by agreeing to buy the fractional interests (95/100 of one
share) of her brothers and sisters in the island and of the Santa
Cruz Island Company for $35,555.[8] Attorney Henry E. Monroe
independently represented the Rossis, and they signed the agreement on March 18, 1930.[9] In addition, as further consideration
for the purchase, Maria assumed all liability for the payment of
the $50,000 note owed to Aglae Caire Capuccio under the Octo-
ber 18, 1926, agreement between the Rossis and her.[10] A deed to
Maria Gherini of parcels 6 and 7 of Santa Cruz Island was executed by her brothers and sisters on March 18, 1930, but was not
recorded until Maria paid off her aunt Aglae on June 28, 1932.

Maria now owned two-thirds of parcels 6 and 7 for which she
paid $85,555.[11] Her husband Ambrose owned one-third of those
parcels for which he worked for twenty years.[12] Parcels 6 and 7 of
the east end of Santa Cruz Island would hence be referred to as
the Gherini Ranch.

ISLAND RANCHING BY THE GHERINIS

The Gherini Ranch (parcels 6 and 7) involved an active sheep

---

[8]Maria Gherini had already purchased her sister Aimee Rossi's interest when Aimee
entered the religious order of the Religious of The Sacred Heart. The valuation of $40,000
meant that each fractional interest was valued at $4,444.44. Therefore, Maria Gherini actu-
ally paid $35,555 for each of the other 8 fractional interests of her brothers and sisters.

[9]The Rossis purchased Aglae's 5 shares in the Santa Cruz Island Company in 1926.
These 5 shares, plus the remaining 4.5 shares owned by Amelie Rossi's heirs, equal the 9.5
shares of the Santa Cruz Island Company which Maria Gherini was purchasing.

[10]Agreement between Maria Gherini and Edmund Rossi et al., dated March 18, 1930.

[11]Deed from the Rossis to Maria Gherini on March 18, 1930. By 1930, the heirs of Amelie
Caire Rossi had a combined total of 9.5 shares of stock of the defunct Santa Cruz Island
Company. Maria Rossi Gherini actually purchased 8.55 shares of stock since she was entitled to .95 of one share. Maria, therefore, paid $10,006 per share. This amount not only
exceeded the Internal Revenue Service's valuation of the shares (i.e., $6,619 per share) in
the *Estate of Amelie Rossi* in 1917, but also the $6,000 per share valuation set by the referees
in the partition litigation for parcels 6 and 7 located on the east end of Santa Cruz island.
The purchase did not include the 3.65 shares of stock which Amelie's heirs and Aglae
would each have been entitled to under the decree of distribution which was filed on May
1, 1931, in the *Matter of the Estate of Helene A. Caire*. This amount was probably paid when
the island was sold to Stanton in 1937.

[12]After all the purchases and transfers, Maria Gherini had what amounted to 9.5 shares
of the Santa Cruz Island Company and Ambrose Gherini had 4.5 shares.

Ambrose Gherini at Smugglers'
on Santa Cruz Island, early
1930s. *Photo courtesy of Ilda
Gherini McGinness.*

operation from 1926-1984. The ranching problems which Justinian Caire faced in the 1880s and 1890s knew no time barrier.
Caire's descendants experienced similar operational problems.
Ambrose Gherini ran the ranch and his wife, Maria, kept the
books. They relied on their children, particularly their sons, Pier
and Francis, to work on the island ranch in the summer months.
Initially, Ambrose Gherini consulted Clifford McElrath, a former
superintendent for the Caires, concerning a dual operation of cattle and sheep. Upon his advice, the Gherinis confined their operation to raising sheep for meat and wool.

Pier Gherini, who managed the Gherini Ranch with his father
from 1945-1952 and then later with his brother Francis, subsequently observed: "I wasn't raised on the island, but I might as
well have been. I spent almost all my spare time there."[13] He
recalled that his childhood was "governed by that case."[14] The liti-

---

[13]*Golden Coast News,* October 22, 1964. Ilda Gherini McGinness recalls that her mother,
Maria, planted the existing orange tree at Smugglers' because she thought her son, Pier,
would live there for a while. Pier decided otherwise and settled in Santa Barbara.

[14]*Santa Barbara News-Press,* "Legacy of Santa Cruz lives on–sheep, suits recalled by Pier
Gherini," August 19, 1986.

186 gation had taken its toll on Ambrose, too. "My dad was fed up," Pier Gherini confided. "He spent time on the island, but because of that case, it wasn't very satisfactory for him."[15] Ambrose suffered a severe stroke in 1936.[16]

The Gherinis soon learned the importance of reliable boat transportation. Because they had no boat during their first years of operation, they depended necessarily on unique arrangements for boat transportation to operate the island rancho. For routine supplies like groceries, gasoline, diesel, fencing, tools, engine parts, etc., the Gherinis relied on the Larco fish boats from Santa Barbara to carry needed goods to the ranch. In exchange for this transportation, the Gherinis granted the Larco Fish Company

[15]Ibid .
[16]Interview with Marie Gherini Ringrose, June 24, 1983, p. 17.

Six workers loading large wool sacks onto a boat called *Dawn* at the first wharf at Scorpion Harbor, 1933. *Photo courtesy of Ilda Gherini McGinness.*

Gherini Ranch at Scorpion Valley, approximately 1930.
Pier Gherini family collection.

the right to maintain fish camps at Potato Bay, Scorpion, San Pedro Point and Yellow Banks. These camps, each having its own lobster grounds, were occupied by an interesting array of rugged individuals such as Alex "Big Swede" Swanson, Sam Hageras, Ben Journeay, and Charley Gunderson. All these men were experienced fishermen who made their livelihood catching lobsters for the Larco Fish Company.[17]

Transporting livestock presented an even greater challenge and posed more headaches than the shipment of ordinary supplies. Prior to building a wharf, the animals had to be lightered to the boat. When the Gherinis took over the east end and began

---

[17]Pier Gherini, "Island Rancho," in *Anthology,* p. 74.

operating a sheep ranch in 1926, they not only lacked a boat, but there was no pier. The construction of one became the first priority in the early 1930s. The most logical place for a pier for the east end was Scorpion which is a natural deep water harbor. The heavy surf and shallow waters at Smugglers' Harbor make it impractical if not impossible to unload supplies there. The first pier, located in the center of the beach at Scorpion Harbor, consisted of thick trunks of eucalyptus trees acting as piers for the wharf. Pier Gherini and Goffredo Capuccio, Jr., helped construct a combination cement and wood wharf which was not completed until 1938.[18] Years later in 1966, William C. Peterson and Hersel

[18]Gherini, "Island Rancho," p. 73. Pier Gherini, because of an eye problem, took a year off from law school and spent most of that year on the island helping build the wharf.

Photo of the first wharf built at Scorpion Harbor in 1930s. Note rows of former vineyards which correspond to the Map of 1885. A Larco fishing camp (small shack) is on the hill to the right of the wharf. Insert shows a close-up of the wharf. The location was unsatisfactory because it could only be used at high tide. The large photo was taken by Mel Whitman in 1932-33. *Pier Gherini family collection.*

Wells erected a steel pier. Violent northeastern storms, usually during winter, destroyed the wharves, no matter what the design. Today, only the cement block at the west end of Scorpion Harbor remains as a reminder of the hard work at the long-gone wharf.

The Gherinis annually transported 1,000 to 1,500 sheep to the mainland to be sold.[19] With a pier in place, ranch hands herded the sheep onto the rickety wharf, through the wooden corrals and

---

[19]National Trading Company financial records.

Working at the Gherini Ranch: Marie Gherini Ringrose loading wool sacks in early 1940s; Pier Gherini sacking wool in 1977. *Pier Gherini family collection.*

into the loading chute which hung precariously over the side of the pier. The sheep often leaped from the chute onto the boat which frequently moved with the surging currents. The boat, loaded with sheep, sailed for Santa Barbara with deckhands moving among the packed sheep and lifting up the animals who had fallen to prevent them from suffocating. The trip ended at Stearns Wharf where the sheep were off-loaded. In later years, the boats cruised down channel to Port Hueneme in Ventura County which was better equipped to handle livestock. From the mainland ports, the sheep were moved into waiting trucks and driven to the livestock yards and then slaughtered for meat.

During the early years, the Gherinis relied upon Alvin Hyder, who owned a 65-foot boat called the *Nora*. Hyder, even though a skilled operator, became notorious for his botched time schedules.[20] Needless to say, the obvious solution to the transportation

[20]Gherini, "Island Rancho," p. 75.

The Ambrose and Maria Gherini Family at Scorpion Harbor, Santa Cruz Island in the early 1930s. Identified in the picture are from left to right: 1. Marie Gherini Ringrose ("Dini"); 2. Maria Rossi Gherini; 3. Pier Gherini; 4. Felix Mauri (the foreman); 5. Ilda Gherini McGinness; 6. Ambrose Gherini; and 7. Francis Gherini. *Photo courtesy of Ilda Gherini McGinness.*

dilemma was for the Gherinis to purchase their own boat which they did in 1932 when they bought a 42-foot Alaskan salmon troller. They named the vessel *Natco* (short for National Trading Company), and it was usually moored at Santa Barbara Harbor. Francis Gherini, an attorney like his father Ambrose and his brother Pier, ran the *Natco* except during the 1940s.[21]

---

[21]Francis Gherini had extensive maritime experience. During World War II he commanded a transport in the famous Battle of Leyte Gulf in October of 1944. Francis earned his undergraduate degree from the University of California at Berkeley and his law degree from Stanford University. He practiced law in the Ventura and Oxnard area for many years. After making myriad crossings of the unpredictable Santa Barbara Channel on the *Natco* and *Hodge*, Francis later obtained a pilot's license and logged many flights to the island. Letter from Francis Gherini to Tom Gherini, August 1, 1984.

From left to right, Ilda Gherini McGinness, an unidentified visitor, Maria Rossi
Gherini and Marie Gherini Ringrose at Scorpion on Santa Cruz Island, 1932
Photo courtesy of Marie Ringrose Gherini.

With the onset of World War II, Ambrose continued the task of
managing the ranch himself which was made onerous because of
rationed supplies, especially fuel. Additionally, it was difficult to
find good help, and he could not rely on his sons since they were
serving in the Armed Forces. At times he recruited his daughters,
Marie and Ilda, to help with general island operations including
shearing. Since Francis was in the Navy, Hal Proctor operated the
Natco, transporting supplies and livestock to and from Santa Barbara.[22]

After World War II, Ambrose Gherini explored other uses of
the island. In the late 1940s and early 1950s, the Gherinis considered raising between 500-1,000 head of cattle.[23] They also considered harvesting the olives at Smugglers', but the crop was too
small to be profitable.[24] While considering these other options,

[22]Gherini, "Island Rancho," p. 78.
[23]Letter from Ambrose Gherini to Robert Sudden, January 4, 1950.
[24]Letter from Ambrose Gherini to Pier Gherini, February 17, 1950.

the ongoing challenges of running the island ranch remained. From 1945-1950 when Francis was living in Guatemala and then in Louisiana, Henry Weber (and occasionally Hal Proctor and Joe Griggs) piloted the *Natco* which nearly sank in 1947 as it broke from its moorings at Scorpion Harbor and washed ashore. She was repaired and put back into service. Other problems confronted the Gherinis. For instance, because of the severity of the 1948 drought, the Gherinis shipped 2,240 sheep off the island from the ranch.[25] Despite these obstacles, the Gherini family restocked their ranch and continued raising sheep for another 36 years.

Upon his return to California, Francis took charge of the *Natco* and subsequently the *Hodge*. The *Natco* served the east end for 27 years until she was replaced in 1959 by the larger and more adaptable *Hodge* (61.4 feet). The *Hodge,* built in Sturgeon Bay, Wisconsin, in 1942, was used by the United States Army during World War II to transport supplies between the Aleutian Islands in Alaska. Like the *Natco,* the *Hodge* was moored at Santa Barbara Harbor. The 37-ton *Hodge,* a boat of similar size to the *Santa Cruz,* met a similar fate in January 1976 when she sank three miles outside Santa Barbara Harbor.[26] Thereafter, the *Vaquero II,* built in 1958 by Vail & Vickers for the cattle operation on Santa Rosa Island, was used to ship both cattle and sheep off Santa Cruz Island to the mainland. The *Vaquero* II could carry over 600 sheep.

Ambrose Gherini also dreamed of developing the ranch into a resort but quickly realized that no one was interested. "It is all nonsense to dwell on unrealizable potentialities," remarked

---

[25]Letter from Ambrose Gherini to Pier Gherini, April 7, 1948.

[26]*Santa Barbara News-Press,* January 10, page A-l, and January 11, 1976, page A-4. The weather was clear with seas of 4-6 feet and 10 mph winds. Upon leaving Santa Barbara Harbor, the *Hodge* scraped its bottom on the sandbar which had restricted the harbor's channel. A Marine Surveyor concluded that "latent defects in the vessel's plank fastenings in the area of the bow were the cause of the sinking . . ." The grounding may have contributed to the fastening failure but the speed of the vessel at 8-10 knots "created a pounding force and resulted in the complete loss of bow fastenings . . ." G.F. Swanson letter. The sinking occurred approximately three miles from the harbor and the Coast Guard cutter *Point Judith* commanded by Lt. Jeffrey Hibbits, rescued all on board including the author.

The *Natco* washed ashore at Scorpion Harbor in 1947 (top,left).
The *Hodge* tied up in Santa Barbara Harbor in 1974 (top, right).
The *Vaquero II* docking at Scorpion Harbor, 1977,
to take on a load of sheep (lower photo).
Pier Gherini family collection.

Ambrose and Maria Gherini relaxing at Scorpion Ranch in the early 1930s. Ambrose is petting "Jack" the bull collie sheepdog, and Maria is feeding an orphan lamb. *Photo courtesy of Ilda Gherini McGinness.*

Ambrose Gherini (1878-1952) and Maria Gherini (1883-1960) in August 1951. *Pier Gherini family collection.*

196 Ambrose, a pragmatic man. "We know they are there, but what is the good of anything until you realize on it."[27] He believed that if money could not be made from the agricultural use of the island ranch then "we had better give thought of selling the property." [28] He admitted to his son, Pier: ". . . Both Mama and I are getting on in years, and we do not want to leave any messes to our successors . . . And the main problem is the island."[29] Ambrose died on April 7, 1952, and his interest in the island which he acquired as a result of 20 years of legal work on the historic island cases passed to his wife, Maria.[30] There was now one owner of parcels 6 and 7.

Maria Gherini continued the island sheep ranching by relying on her two sons, Pier and Francis. She remained active by keeping meticulous records until a few months before she died on September 4, 1960. This was the same year of the sinking of the schooner *Santa Cruz*. Maria first traveled to the island on the vessel's maiden voyage in 1893. Upon Maria's death her interest in the island passed to her four children: Marie Gherini Ringrose (b.1907-), Ilda Gherini McGinness (b.1910-), Pier Gherini (1912-1989), and Francis Gherini (b.1914-). Justinian Caire's great-grandchildren each had an undivided quarter interest in parcels 6 and 7 of the island.[31] Despite Maria's passing, the family carried on the demanding tradition of running an island sheep ranch.

The breed of sheep in the Gherini era, as in the Caire era, was predominantly Rambouillet-Merino although other breeds were used. The wool was of a fine quality. The sheep were smaller, quicker and more of a range animal than their mainland counterparts. Round-up and shearing usually occurred once a year in May and June.[32] The sheep inventory varied from year to year as did the number of animals shorn and wool sacks produced. Ranch

---

[27]Letter from Ambrose Gherini to Pier Gherini, April 28, 1950.

[28]Letter from Ambrose Gherini to Pier Gherini, January 20, 1950.

[29]Letter from Ambrose Gherini to Pier Gherini, January 9, 1950.

[30]Judgment of Final Distribution filed on February 14, 1956 *In the Matter of the Estate of Ambrose Gherini.*

[31]Judgment of Final Distribution filed on July 23, 1962 *In the Matter of the Estate of Maria Gherini.*

[32]Pier Gherini radio logs. See also, Gherini, "Island Rancho," in *Anthology*, pp. 71-78 . See also Warren, Jr., 114: 267-270.

records reveal that 5,182 head in January of 1932 represented the highest sheep count on the Gherini Ranch. By the end of 1933, the flock numbered 3,730 head of sheep and during that year the family sold 71,589 pounds of wool which included several years of wool clip.[33] In 1946, the animals shorn totaled 4,373, producing 23,529 pounds of wool.[34] In 1958, shearing occurred at three different times of the year which was unusual, and the shearers shaved the fleeces off 3,265 sheep. Shearers then clipped 3,514 sheep and workers packed 37 sacks of wool in 1965, and in 1972 the shearers trimmed 2,769 sheep producing 41 sacks of wool. [35] After the wool was sacked, market conditions often dictated when the heavy and cumbersome burlap wool sacks weighing between 300-400 pounds would be loaded onto the boat for shipment to the mainland. This job usually occurred without incident except in January of 1959 when the wharf collapsed and 30 sacks, waiting to be loaded onto the boat, dropped to the ocean. Only 10 sacks could be retrieved.[36]

Over the years, sheep ranching also changed little except that the Gherinis built a better fence system than their predecessors. Ambrose Gherini felt that "good fences are a main ally on the ranch."[37] "It is not enough to put up good fences," Ambrose explained, "but we have to see that they are kept up. That is something that can only be brought about if we have a good man on the place."[38] The purpose of the extensive fence system was to have greater control of the animals and to permit conservation of the range lands by closing certain fields to permit reseeding and regrowth.[39] More fences, however, meant more work. The Gherinis created at least seventeen different pastures and utilized almost all of the 6,200 acres of parcels 6 and 7. As in prior years, round-ups and shearing became an annual ritual in the late

---

[33]Profit and Loss Statement for National Trading Co., December 31, 1933.
[34]Letter from Ambrose Gherini to Pier Gherini, April 29, 1947.
[35]Pier Gherini radio logs.
[36]Ibid.
[37]Letter from Ambrose Gherini to Pier Gherini, May 19, 1947.
[38]Letter from Ambrose Gherini to Pier Gherini, May 27, 1947.
[39]Gherini, "Island Rancho," in Anthology, p. 73.

198 spring, and the Gherinis often recruited family members and friends to do island work. Pier relied on the expertise and common sense of men like Joe Bosio to obtain needed equipment and supplies. Pier also made sure his sons, Pier Jr., John, and Tom, who were Justinian Caire's great-great-grandchildren, routinely experienced the island work ethic particularly during the summer months. Francis gave his daughter, Andrea, the same experience. Not only was time served in building and repairing fences and riding on early morning roundups, but time was also spent in the wool sacks and in the corrals. Island work also meant maritime duty on the *Natco, Hodge,* and *Vaquero II* which often rocked and rolled in the heavy seas of Santa Barbara Channel. Times changed, but the hard work did not. Although no *fichas* were given as in previous years, there was pride in working on an island rancho.

"The story of the island ranch is largely the story of people," observed Pier Gherini. "All of these people had one common characteristic. They knew and loved the island. Each in his own way was rugged and self-reliant. They took its beauties and hardships in stride."[40]

Life on the island was lonely. The work was hard, and there was no shortage of things to do. The ranch hands routinely installed and fixed fence lines, maintained machinery, repaired the wharf, graded the roads, herded the sheep, operated the water pumps, cleaned the wells and cut the hay fields.[41] Usually two or three permanent employees ran the ranch. During shearing season additional crews came to work at the east end where Scorpion Ranch was the headquarters and Smugglers' Ranch was used sparingly. Many employees left vivid memories. Zulberto Zulberti was a long time worker for the Gherinis. Felix Mauri, an able iron worker, started each day with a "rosetta," consisting of four raw eggs and a glass of wine mixed together. Jim Perla worked on the island for 50 years.[42] Tony Hernandez and Manuel Garza and their crew of two or three men religiously came to the island to do the shearing. The roster, by no means complete, included other

[40]Gherini, "Island Rancho," p. 78.   [41]Pier Gherini radio logs.
[42]Gherini, "Island Rancho," in *Anthology,* p. 76.

colorful ranch hands such as Rudy Nilsby, Joe Griggs, Benny Arata, Ed Plimer, Joe Romero, Andy Lucerio, Serafino Servilla, Fidel Huerra, Hersel Wells and Bruce Cousins. The workers invariably had lasting relationships with island dogs such as Jack, a bull-collie, Sam, a 140 pound red-boned hound, Chico, a "Heinz-hound," and Bozo, a lovable mutt.[43] These dogs had a common trait of savoring a hunt for the island pigs.

The island workers had varied backgrounds. For example, Joe Griggs, who worked on the Gherini Ranch from 1944-1956, came from Oklahoma. He was one of the island's most skillful workers even though he had little formal education. "I havent got much of a education as you no," Griggs confessed to Ambrose Gherini in a short note. "And dont claim to no as much as Penny (the foreman in 1948) but I no how to work and get work don . . ."[44] "The best education a man can have is to be honest, and do good work," Ambrose replied. "All the rest does not amount to much."[45] Griggs educated himself by reading the magazine, *Popular Mechanics,* and there were few jobs that he could not do. He later became the ranch foreman and built the foreman's house in 1955.

Island laborers naturally looked forward to mainland shore excursions, but they, at times, became overzealous. The pre-dictable result was that some workers had to appear in police court only to face Justinian Caire's great grandson, Pier Gherini, who was police judge from 1946 through 1951.[46] Judge Gherini promptly sentenced them back to the island for an extended tour.

The task of unloading at Scorpion Harbor could be difficult and potentially dangerous especially when unloading heavy equipment. For example, in 1975, a pick-up truck was being off

---

[43]Ibid., 78.

[44]Letter from Joe Griggs to Ambrose Gherini, December 12, 1948.

[45]Letter from Ambrose Gherini to Joe Griggs, December 15, 1948.

[46]*Santa Barbara News-Press,* January 16, 1949, p. A-10. Pier Gherini was graduated from the University of California, Berkeley in 1934 and from its Boalt School of Law in 1938. He practiced law in the Santa Barbara area for over forty years. After serving in the Army Air Corps in World War II, he was elected Police Court Judge from 1946-1951. For ten years (1967-1977) he served on the California Fair Employment Practice Commission. He also chaired the Board of Freeholders which drafted the City Charter for Santa Barbara and served as Italian Vice-Consul for many years.

200 loaded from the *Hodge*. The ocean surged around the cement pier, and as the boat's boom lifted the truck from the deck and swung it over to the pier, the boom snapped like a toothpick. The truck dropped into the ocean and became another island relic. The splintered boom crashed to the deck and narrowly missed Tom Gherini moments after his brother John told him "let's get out of the way."

Losing equipment when off-loading was the exception and not the rule. Most equipment safely made it to the island, but because of the difficulty in getting equipment there, ingenuity played an important part in its use. For instance, the Waterloo Boy tractor lightered ashore in the early 1920s saw a variety of uses. Years after it became obsolete, Joe Griggs used parts of the Waterloo Boy to make a sawmill in 1955. The lumber, cut from eucalyptus trees, warped and hardened when it dried and was of little practical use. "The fact that we didn't need a mill in no way detracted from the ingenuity and skill that went into its making,"[47] Pier Gherini commented. When the sawmill fell into island disuse, the owners dumped the tractor's heavy metal wheels at the pier to act as a revetment against the waves.

The weather dominated island life and transportation schedules. It not only plagued island wharves but also wreaked havoc on other island projects such as the earthen dam built in a ravine located near the eastern tip of the island and a long dirt road graded along steep ridges of the Aguaje field. Workers used a small bulldozer (30 Caterpillar) to complete the projects in the early 1950s. Heavy rains in 1954 filled the dam but exploded through the spillway leaving the dam in ruins. The rains also washed out huge sections of the Aguaje road making it impassable. Such frustrations are a way of life on the island. The 1995 torrential winter rains, which inundated the entire Scorpion Valley, destroyed a large portion of the historic rock wall built over a century earlier in 1892 at the Scorpion Ranch. The National Park Service repaired the wall in November 1995.

---

[47]Pier Gherini, "Island Rancho," in *Anthology,* p. 78.

Sawmill at Gherini Ranch, 1955. Joe Griggs designed and built it.
"The fact that we didn't need a mill in no way detracted from the
ingenuity and skill that went into its making." Pier Gherini.
Pier Gherini family collection.

Communication also proved to be a difficult problem for an
island rancho. In the early years, infrequent boat trips were the
primary means of communication. This situation improved in
1935 when the Gherinis obtained a license from the Federal Communication Commission (FCC) to permit a 5 "watter" on the
island. By maintaining a communication schedule with Anacapa
Light Station, messages could be relayed to the mainland in case
of emergency. In later years, communications improved with the
approval by the FCC of a radio transmitter at Pier Gherini's house
and one on the island.[48] A morning and evening call schedule
became routine in his family, and the call letters of "KMD83 to
KMC83" were indelibly marked into their memories.[49]

---

[48]Ibid., p. 77.   [49]Pier Gherini kept a radio log for 33 years.

PLANS OF AN ISLAND RESORT RAISE NEW CONFLICTS

While the Gherinis worked a sheep ranch, they dreamed, perhaps unrealistically, of an island resort. The initial planning for a resort took place in the early 1960s. The Gherinis spent $20,000 to undertake the preparation of a conceptual master plan for recreational development of their property. The idea of a recreational island resort was nothing new. Ira Eaton leased a portion of the island from the Santa Cruz Island Company from 1913 to 1937 and operated a rustic resort which attracted many celebrities.[50] Ambrose Gherini envisioned a "Bermuda-type of recreational development."[51] He even attempted, albeit unsuccessfully, to solicit interest from Howard Hughes, United Airlines, TWA, and John Hancock Mutual Life Insurance Company to develop the island.[52] Ed Stanton also advertised the idea of an island "colony or subdivision" when he listed his property for sale in the early 1950s.

The dream of an island development continued when the Gherini family hired George Vernon Russell in 1963 to commence preparation of an island development plan. Russell, a fellow of the American Institute of Architects and a recipient of fifteen national and regional awards, was highly qualified. The preparation took a couple of years. The conceptual plan outlined a combination recreational, commercial, and residential development. A marina with slips for about 150 boats was planned for Scorpion Anchorage, while only a modest pier would be located at Smugglers' Cove. The plan also envisioned dams, a golf course, an airstrip, equestrian trails, and hunting lodges, in addition to

---

[50] See Eaton, *Diary Of A Sea Captain's Wife*, pp. 169-250.

[51] Interview of Ambrose Gherini by Chet Holcombe in "In Town Today" section of *Santa Barbara News-Press*, August, 1951. Gherini explained in a letter to Hughes Tool Company that what he owned was "at least one of the most paradisical places in this world," and that he wasn't interested in a "Coney Island development" but rather a plan which resulted in "a Beverly Hills supplemented by a resort similar to the Royal Hawaiian at Honolulu." Letter from Gherini to Malcolm Smith of Hughes Tool Co, June 22, 1949.

[52] Universally, the large companies contacted were not interested in such a project. Lucius T. Hill of John Hancock Mutual Life Insurance Company was prescient when he wrote that "the development of such a property would have to be on a very high scale and probably quite beyond the bounds or present possibilities under governmental limitations." Letter from Hill to Gherini, April 21, 1947.

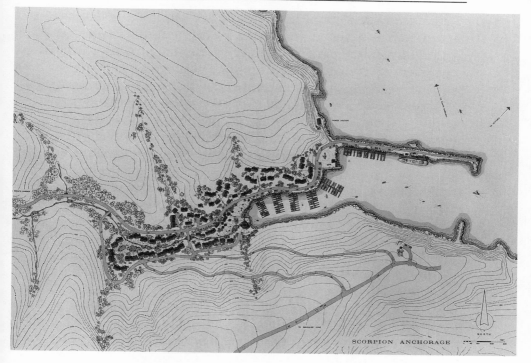

Conceptual drawing of Scorpion Ranch from the 1963 Gherini development plan.

the 500 residential lots varying from 1-5 acres. The plan forecast a population of 3,000 people.[53]

Pier Gherini, representing the Gherini family, presented the plan to the Santa Barbara County Planning Commission in October 1965 for approval as an amendment to the County General Plan. At this time the General Plan designated the island as agricultural and open space. The Planning Commission held four public hearings and heard varying viewpoints which revealed the friction between property rights and environmental protection.[54]

[53]Russell, "A Master Plan," p. 5.
[54]The hearings were held on October 20, 1965; December 1, 1965; January 5 and 12, 1966.

204   Architect Russell, in describing the project, said the development would rival the charm of the French and Italian Mediterranean coasts. Scorpion and Smugglers' would be small villages connected by roads. The nineteenth century adobe buildings at both locations which were constructed by Justinian Caire would be preserved and serve as cafes. The eucalyptus, cypress, and other trees would not be disturbed. Russell emphasized that approximately 4,000 acres would remain in open space.[55]

The testimony and questioning at the hearing immediately began to focus on the conflicts. Fred Eissler, representing the Los Padres Chapter of the Sierra Club, urged that the island's agricultural and open space designation remain unchanged because there has been in recent times ". . . a persistent interest in the possibility of having the Channel Islands included in the National Park System."[56] Commissioner Bonebaker countered that he ". . . can't see how somebody that owns land has to sit and wait for the federal government to come around to make up its mind to buy it . . . If they want to buy it, they can get off the dime and do it."[57]

As the Planning Commission hearings continued, the debate about the Gherini master plan reached a flash point. The commission received numerous letters urging that the island be made into a park and that a decision be deferred until the National Park Service could make a study. Others stated that approval of the plan would only drive up the price the government would have to pay for the island in the event they ever decided to acquire it. Even William P. Clark, Jr., who would later become Secretary of Interior, weighed in by urging the Planning Commission to approve the Gherini development plan.[58] The Park Service requested a delay. Herley Gayman of The Nature Conservancy testified that "we are shocked and deeply hurt at the thought that private development will just run in ahead of the acquisition of the Channel Islands as a national park."[59]

---

[55]Planning Commission transcript, October 20, 1965, pp. 8-19.
[56]Ibid., pp. 29-31.   [57]Ibid., p. 33.
[58]Letter from William P. Clark, Jr., to County of Santa Barbara, January 5, 1966.
[59]Planning Commission transcript, January 5, 1966, p. 54.

"Any time the federal government wants something, the federal government has the machinery to take it," Pier Gherini responded. "They can take anything at any time they want. We know and accept that, and we understand it."[60] As to the charge that the owners were trying to inflate the value of the land in case of governmental acquisition, Pier Gherini answered that it was "morally reprehensible and legally wrong . . . to freeze property in a particular category."[61]

The National Park Service also sent a representative, Leo Diederich, Assistant Regional Director of the National Park Service, to one of the hearings. He advised the commission that the Department of Interior ". . . has for some time been vitally interested in a Channel Islands National Park."[62] He began his remarks by noting the excellent detailed planning study prepared by the Gherini family. He mentioned that the National Park Service would have to do the same kind of thing in depth in the event a national park were authorized.[63]

Diederich's testimony gave a snapshot of what the future Channel Islands National Park might look like. He stated that Santa Cruz Island "would be the core of a superb national park which would offer a combination of island, seashore and marine values unmatched in any existing national park."[64] He pointed out that ". . . the harbor development and public service facilities to serve the general public would be no doubt quite similar and very probably in the same or similar locations" as envisioned in the Gherini plan.[65] There would, however, be no residential development allowed in the park and this is where the Gherini master plan contrasted with the park plans.[66] He also envisioned overnight lodging, horseback riding and nature trails.[67] Diederich, when asked if approval of the Gherini project would impede or in any way compromise or delay the acquisition of the park, said he did not know the answer except that "it would be a

---

[60]Planning Commission transcript, December 1, 1965, p. 16.
[61]Ibid., p. 19.
[62]Planning Commission transcript, January 5, 1966, p. 12.
[63]Ibid., p. 15.   [64]Ibid., p. 14.
[65]Ibid., p. 22.   [66]Ibid.   [67]Ibid., pp. 14-16.

206 much finer national park if it were all in the public ownership."[68]California Assemblyman Winfield Shoemaker of the 36th Assembly District also appeared before the Planning Commission and put the controversy in perspective:

> . . . The decision which you have to make is one that not only affects the Gherini family and Santa Barbara County and the State of California, but the entire nation. The question of these Channel Islands is one that is not purely local. The very nature of the islands make themselves a national interest.[69]

The Planning Commission on January 12, 1966, approved the plan by a 6 to 2 vote.[70] In March 1966, the County Board of Supervisors by a 3 to 2 vote affirmed the plan by upholding an amendment to the Santa Barbara County General Plan to allow such a development.[71] The victory was fleeting. The cost to undertake such a project on an island was daunting and the plan was never implemented. This was, in effect, the last hurrah for any private development of the island.

The Gherini master plan received a lot of publicity. The *Santa Barbara News-Press* editorial noted that the Board of Supervisors recognized the use of the island both as a potential resort and also as a national park. The editorial stated: ". . . It would seem that the ideal use for this island might be a combination of these two, if it could be determined that they are not in conflict . . ."[72] Such a determination, however, would never be made and conflict would continue.

PETERSON YEARS: 1979-1984

A new era began in 1979 when the Gherinis, wanting to extricate themselves from the burden of running an island sheepranch, entered into an agreement with William C. Peterson to operate the ranch.[73] Peterson (or Pete as he was known), a versa-

---

[68]Ibid., pp. 19-20. [69]Ibid., p. 30.

[70]Planning Commission transcript, January 12, 1966, p. 33.

[71]County of Santa Barbara Board of Supervisor Resolution 66-108, March 8, 1966.

[72]*Santa Barbara News Press*, March 10, 1966.

[73]The agreement required Peterson to pay the Gherinis $7,500 per year and one third of the gross proceeds in excess of $30,000.

tile individual who worked on the island in the 1960s, managed the ranch from 1979 to 1984.[74] Peterson, however, was not an experienced sheep rancher. "I knew absolutely nothing about sheep ranching," recalled Peterson.[75] He originally hired Michel, a 24-year woman from England, as ranch cook. Michel thought she would be working in Santa Cruz, California, but soon learned the ranch was on a coastal island. She proved that she could work as hard as her male counterparts, and she eventually assumed the responsibility for the flock as the chief shepherdess.[76] She and the rugged Peterson, 32 years her senior, later married.

Like Joe Griggs who worked on the island from 1944-1956, there didn't seem to be anything that Peterson could not build or fix. He adopted creative methods to load and ship the sheep and wool. For instance, he used a barge which could hold 1,000 sheep and later built a small landing craft called the *Double Eagle* which measured 65 feet and could hold 350 sheep. He even devised an idea of using a 4-foot wide conveyor belt, stretching 150 feet and operated by a 4-cylinder diesel engine, to off load sheep from the island.[77] Although he never actually installed the conveyor belt, he did develop a couple of unique ways of loading the sheep onto the vessels. One method involved a 22-foot floating corral built on top of 55-gallon barrels welded together. Approximately 50 sheep were loaded at a time. The amphibious corral, equipped with a loading chute, was pushed into the ocean by a specially rigged bulldozer. The crew on the waiting boat used a tow line to pull the corral to it. Peterson also built a mobile pier, resembling a flat bed trailer. Again he used the bulldozer to push the pier into the water from the shore. The *Double Eagle* then came up to the temporary dock, lowered its bow ramp onto the pier and the sheep were herded onto the vessel. After the procedure was completed, the bulldozer pulled the dock out of the water.

---

[74]Peterson spent nearly 10 years on the Gherini Ranch. In the 1960s he worked on the "wild cat drilling" operation for 3-4 years.

[75]William Peterson interview, February 22, 1996.

[76]Michelle Peterson interview, March 15, 1996.

[77]Letter from Francis Gherini to Pier Gherini, May 13, 1981.

208   The Petersons toiled to make the operation profitable, but they soon learned that nothing was simple about the island life which captivated them like so many others before them. Their island experiences with people, animals and events left lasting impressions. For instance, Michel recalled discovering a massive Chumash grave site which was exposed in January 1981 by grading work her husband was doing. Peterson quickly covered the site.[78] Pete remembered witnessing in early 1983 a savage winter storm that demolished the metal pier he built in the 1960s and sent gigantic waves into Scorpion Valley that nearly reached the ranch houses.

Nevertheless, the economics of running an island sheep ranch overwhelmed Peterson. By the end of his first year, the count of shorn animals dropped dramatically to 1,044 sheep producing only 8,775 pounds of wool. To meet expenses, he sold 1,555 animals in 1979 and 1,822 in 1980.[79] The inflationary years of the early 1980s and the subsequent economic downturn contributed to Peterson's problems, as expenses increased and the price of sheep and wool decreased. The Nature Conservancy sheep elimination program also added to his woes since there were fewer sheep migrating to the east end of the island. As a result it was difficult to build up the flock and the "factory was operating far short of its capacity."[80] Peterson even attempted to raise additional capital by salvaging the semi-precious metals such as brass off a Navy coastal mine sweeper which he towed in early 1980 from Los Angeles and beached at Scorpion Harbor.[81] Just about the time he

[78]Michel Peterson unpublished manuscript, chapter 12.

[79]Letters from Pier Gherini to Graydon B. Hall, County of Santa Barbara Agricultural Commissioner, February 14, 1980 and February 18, 1981.

[80]In 1980, the shearers clipped 1,100 sheep for a total of 5,500 pounds of wool. The production improved slightly in 1982 to 1,608 animals shorn for a total of 11,100 pounds of wool.

[81]The vessel, of the Bluebird class, was 133 feet long with a 28 foot beam. Another minesweeper, called the *Peacock,* lies at the bottom of Scorpion Harbor near Little Scorpion in sixty feet of water. Peterson related that someone towed the vessel to Scorpion in the summer of 1979 and it broke loose from its moorings. A third minesweeper was moored at Scorpion. It also broke free from its mooring and was drifting down channel when the Navy took it under tow to the mainland. The Coast Guard then towed it back to Santa Cruz Island and beached it at Smugglers' where Peterson eventually set it ablaze. All island shipwrecks are protected by the National Park Service.

The Petersons used a floating corral (top photo) and also a mobile pier to load sheep onto boats such as the *Double Eagle* at Scorpion Harbor in 1983 (bottom photo). Remnants of the minesweeper, salvaged by Peterson, lie on the beach.
Photos by Donna Lea.

thought his sheep business was turning the corner, Peterson suffered serious injuries in January 1984 from an airplane crash on the island. Within three days of the accident, Francis Gherini gave permission to Jaret Owens, a seasoned outdoorsman, to start a hunt club, thus setting the stage for conflicts between hunters and the herders. Michel, having married Peterson three weeks before the near fatal crash, was determined not to let the hunters disturb her flock. She loathed the senseless killing of tame sheep for the sake of "big game trophies" and "big bucks."

The last round-up, however, was yet to come. In May of 1984, a group of heavily armed hunters, headed by Owens, confronted Michel while she was herding the flock. "We are crossing this pasture on our way to hunt for hogs on the wild side," Owens explained. "Turn around and get to hell away from here if you know what's good for you," she screamed. The hunters decided to call her bluff and moved toward her. Michel, putting her hand on her side-arm, stood her ground. The tense standoff ended when the hunters retreated. Michel, along with her other riders, drove the flock of sheep to Scorpion Valley for shipment from Santa Cruz Island. There she was met by Peterson who was on the island for the first time since the accident. "That's the last round-up," he told his 29-year old bride of a few months. "Time to put your gun away and settle down." "Not bloody likely," she replied. "I've grown to love this way of life."[82] The agreement terminated, and the Gherinis were out of the sheep business.[83]

THE ISLAND ADVENTURES CLUB: HUNTING AND RECREATION

With the termination of the sheep business, the Gherini family for the first time embarked on another island enterprise when they signed an agreement in December 1984 with Jaret Owens to run a "business involving hunting and . . . certain public recreational activities . . ." which was known as "The Island Adventures Club." Jaret had previously worked for the Santa Cruz Island

---

[82]Michel Peterson, unpublished manuscript, pp. 17-1-17-11.
[83]Peterson by this time was nearly $14,000 in arrears under the agreement.

Hunt Club on the Stanton Ranch for many years in addition to his years of hunting in Alaska. He immediately engaged the services of his parents, Doris and Duane Owens, to help renovate the ranch for the new use. The back-breaking effort took several years. Like Margaret Eaton, the lure of the island mesmerized the Owens, particularly Duane, a retired principal of Nordoff High School in Ojai. Doris and Duane devoted many years to the island, overseeing the Scorpion Ranch. They retired in 1991 and left the island.

The hard work paid off. In his first year of operation, Owens' hunt/recreation club grossed nearly $53,000. Thereafter, the scope and intensity significantly increased as did the club's income. From 1984 through 1990, Owens' "Island Adventures" grossed over $1 million in revenues from the hunting and recreational programs.[84] The lucrative business continued into 1997. Hunters, often wearing camouflage uniforms, created a surreal environment by trekking over the landscape to kill the wild pigs and the docile sheep by using high powered rifles and bows and arrows. Owens had expanded the business to include bed and breakfast lodging at Smugglers' and Scorpion where there are numerous rustic campgrounds. Some visitors, using brightly colored kayaks, explore the island's volcanic caves and the secluded beaches and coves. There were even helicopter excursions run by PHi Heli-Tours of Santa Barbara in addition to the weekly invasion by day boat trips (particularly during the summer months) provided by Island Packers Corporation at Ventura Harbor.

The island recreation business, however, quickly led to more factious family disputes as to how it should be operated. With his older brother ailing, Francis Gherini insisted that he manage all the bookkeeping chores for the new recreation business. "I spend many hours with Jaret and I know precisely and specifically what is going on," Francis responded when questioned about certain aspects of the new business. "I intend to continue that operation over there in the same manner as I started it and

---

[84]Island Adventures Financial Statements prepared by Francis Gherini.

212 brought it to its present status, and will continue to operate it in the same way without, hopefully, any interference . . . "[85] This attitude strained family relations with more problems looming on the horizon.

ENVIRONMENTAL LEGAL CHALLENGES

In the late 1960s, Justinian Caire's descendants encountered new obstacles in the form of the environmental movement. One of the catalysts for the movement was the nationally publicized offshore Union Oil spill in January 1969. The oil-tarnished Santa Barbara Channel forever etched environmental consciousness into the minds of the public.

Historically, oil companies made several exploratory oil drillings on the island.[86] As early as 1929, the Santa Cruz Island Company leased a drilling site to Standard Oil Company of California.[87] In 1969, the Gherinis entered into a lease with Union Oil. After Union Oil obtained the necessary county permits, the Sierra Club filed suit in October 1969 against the Santa Barbara County Board of Supervisors for issuing the drilling permit.[88] The Sierra Club sought injunctive relief. After hearing the matter, Superior Court Judge C. Douglas Smith, on October 27, 1969, denied any injunctive relief on the technical ground that the environmental organization was not entitled to a hearing under the local drilling ordinance. The denial was actually only the beginning of environmental pressure to restrict or prohibit many uses on the island.

The 1970s brought more challenges for the Gherinis. In 1970,

---

[85]Letter from Francis Gherini to John Gherini, July 29, 1986.

[86]Stantons entered into a lease with Richfield Oil Company in 1954, and two wells were drilled on the west end. In 1964, Humble Oil drilled an exploratory well in Chinese Harbor. In 1964, the Gherini interest entered into a lease with a limited partnership called Santa Cruz Exploration Company. This operation was later taken over by Epsilon Oil Company which drilled one well. In 1966, Atlantic Richfield assumed the drilling. Other major companies contributed to the effort and even though no oil was found, potable water was discovered.

[87]The lease was recorded on January 9, 1930 at Book 203, p. 358 of the Official Records of Santa Barbara County.

[88]*Sierra Club et al. v. Beattie, et al.*

the California Legislature enacted the California Environmental Quality Act (CEQA)[89]. In the November 1972 general election, the voters of California passed an initiative measure called Proposition 20, which established the California Coastal Zone Conservation Act of 1972 and created the powerful Coastal Commission.[90] The enactment of these two state environmental laws dramatically changed land use planning for environmentally sensitive areas such as Santa Cruz Island and continued to make any development on it difficult, if not impossible.

In the late 1970s, the California Coastal Commission exercised its jurisdiction over the island in reviewing the County of Santa Barbara's Local Coastal Plan mandated by the Coastal Act. Coincidentally, this was in the same time period that legislation was being introduced in Congress to establish a Channel Islands National Park. Over the protest of the owners, the California Coastal Commission substantially reduced the zoning of the island from ten-acre zoning to 320-acre zoning. As it applied to the Gherini ranch this would only allow for 21 dwelling units. This was a far cry from the 500 units envisioned in the master plan in 1966. In addition, the Coastal Commission prohibited any oil development of the island. The process, in completing the Local Coastal Plan for the island, took nearly ten years and involved more litigation, this time with the California Coastal Commission. These events led Francis Gherini in 1985 to observe that: ". . . it's unclear that anyone could ever develop Santa Cruz commercially."[91]

The Coastal Commission matter was finally resolved in 1988 when the State Court of Appeal upheld the actions of the Coastal Commission.[92] The Court noted that ". . . the biological significance and ecological sensitivity of the area was fully documented by its national park and sanctuary designations by state and fed-

---

[89]Public Resource Section 21000 et seq.

[90]Public Resources Code section 27000. This act was subsequently replaced by the California Coastal Act of 1976. Public Resources Code section 30000.

[91]Karasik, "Islanders," p. 16.

[92]*Pier Gherini, et al., v. California Coastal Comm.* (1988) 204 Cal.App.3d 699.

214   eral agencies."[93] The Court also rejected the owners' claim that the action of the Coastal Commission amounted to inverse condemnation. The appellate court pointed out that there can be neither an inverse taking for mere land use regulation nor a monetary claim for diminution of land value caused by the regulation.[94]

The decision in the Coastal Commission case was perhaps the last straw. After he had carefully reviewed the decision, Pier Gherini, who at the time was in failing health, said "It's over." He died on June 29, 1989, still owning his interest in the island. It was time to sell parcels 6 and 7!

---

[93]Ibid., p. 708.
[94]Ibid., p. 714.

Chapter 9

Creation of the Channel Islands National Park

PRELUDE TO A PARK

The idea of preserving the natural wonders of the United States for its citizens started when Congress established Yellowstone as the nation's first national park in 1872; however, creating a mechanism to manage these wonderlands would take many years. In 1891, Congress enacted the Forest Reserve Act which separated the idea of forest conservation from national parks. The legislation allowed the President to create, by proclamation, permanent forests, and Congress retained the authority to establish the national parks. Later, Congress expanded the presidential authority by passing the 1906 Lacey Antiquities Act allowing the President to create, by proclamation, national monuments. In 1910, President William Howard Taft urged the creation of a National Park Service to manage the park system. Congress did not heed this request until August 25, 1916, when it passed the Kent-Smoot Bill. President Woodrow Wilson quickly signed the bill that created the National Park Service.[1] Stephen Tying Mather, the first director of the Park Service, was succeeded by Horace M. Albright and together these men were instrumental in not only spearheading the drive to create the Park Service but

---

[1]Albright, Dickenson, and Mott, Jr., *The National Park Service*, pp. 6-14.

216   also in establishing the preservation philosophy to guide the management of sites within the national park system.

In January 1933, Albright directed Roger W. Toll of the National Park Service to undertake the first assessment of the eight Channel Islands for national park status. Toll completed the work in March 1933. In his report to Albright, Toll concluded that the privately held islands of Santa Catalina, Santa Cruz and Santa Rosa had many attractive features and that the group of islands taken as a whole presented possibilities for an oceanic or marine park of national character and importance. Toll recommended national park status, not on the basis of land features but upon the islands' marine features. The report concluded that legislation establishing the Channel Islands National Park be deferred until suitable tracts on the privately held islands had been donated to the government.[2] At this time, the twenty-year Caire litigation involving Santa Cruz Island had just ended in 1932, and the owners showed little interest in giving the government any portion of the island. One writer reported, however, that the Caire family considered selling for $750,000 their interest to the Government for a state or federal park.[3]

Albright retired as director in 1933 urging the service to "keep large sections of primitive country from the influence of destructive civilization . . . to detect and defeat attempts to exploit commercially the resources of the national parks."[4] While there was no further action in creating a Channel Islands National Park during Albright's tenure as director, his nephew, Stanley T. Albright, the Field Director for the Pacific West Field Area of the National Park Service in the 1990s, would be given the task of carrying out his uncle's philosophy for managing and preserving the Channel Islands.

Other events set the stage for the creation of the Channel Islands National Park. President Franklin Roosevelt, by Presidential Proclamation on August 22, 1938, created the Channel

---

[2]Toll, "Report on the Channel Island Survey," January 1933.

[3]Hillinger, *The California Islands,* p. 96.

[4]Albright, Dickenson, and Mott, Jr., *The National Park Service,* p. 51.

Islands National Monument, which incorporated the islands of Anacapa and Santa Barbara. President Harry Truman expanded the monument in 1949 to include an area of one nautical mile of water around the two islands.

Over time, interest increased to preserve the Channel Islands in their natural state and to prevent any type of extensive development. "As the mainland population increases, so will the pressure on the islands' resources," Jean-Michel Cousteau noted. "If we can learn to properly manage these rugged isles, perhaps we can apply this knowledge toward improving resource management on a global scale."[5]

THE CREATION OF THE PARK

In the early 1960s, Thomas Storke, the influential and politically powerful editor of the *Santa Barbara News-Press,* spearheaded an intense lobbying effort to create a Channel Islands National Park. He contacted both United States Senators from California, Republican Thomas H. Kuchel and Democrat Claire Engle and urged their support.[6] As a result, in January 1961, Senate Bill 543 was introduced to study the feasibility of the creation of certain national park proposals which generated increased interest in the island. Local historian, Walker A. Tompkins, wrote in the *Santa Barbara News-Press* in March 1961: "Viva los Channel Islands! God speed the day when the National Park Service plants its flag on island soil."[7]

In April 1963, Engle introduced Senate Bill 1303, entitled "The Channel Islands National Seashore Act." The island owners opposed this bill and Senate Bill 543. They felt that any development of the island for recreational purposes should be done by private enterprise and not by the federal government which already had substantial acreage to manage.[8] Senator Engle,

[5]Forward by Jean-Michel Cousteau in "The Channel Islands National Park" written principally by Nancy Ehorn.

[6]Roberts, *San Miguel Island,* pp. 132-135.

[7]*Santa Barbara News-Press,* March 26, 1961 (Sunday edition).

[8]Letter from Pier Gherini to Senator Kuchel, June 7, 1961. The owners also opposed a State resolution recommending the creation of a Channel Islands National Park. Telegram to State Senator John J. Hollister, Jr., May 30, 1961.

218   although sensitive to the concerns of the private owners, stated that the purpose of his legislation was ". . . long range, transcending current circumstances of ownership and management."[9]

The public debate about the future use of the island was in full swing. Phil C. Orr, curator for the Santa Barbara Museum of Natural History, wrote to Senator Kuchel stating that the islands were not suitable both for recreation and conservation at the same time.[10] The arguments concerning public and private rights, as well as the conflicts between conservationist and recreationalist, reached a boiling point.

The debate became highly partisan and entered the political arena in the 1964 Congressional campaign between Republican Congressman Charles Teague and his Democratic challenger, George Taylor. Teague opposed the idea of a Channel Islands National Park because of its expense. Taylor stated his first legislative priority would be to create a park out of Santa Cruz and Santa Rosa Islands.[11] The Gherini family, as owners of the east end of Santa Cruz Island, added fuel to the fire by announcing conceptual plans to develop their island property.

Candidate Taylor solicited the help of then Secretary of Interior Stewart L. Udall. Udall, who predicted passage of legislation creating a Channel Islands National Park, joined the fray by accusing the island owners of a lack of cooperation in refusing to allow the National Park Service to visit the islands in order to make a study. Before making a flight over the islands with candidate Taylor, Secretary Udall quipped that he would have to ". . . watch out for anti-aircraft fire" when flying over the "forbidden" Channel Islands.[12]

Secretary Udall's remarks drew a quick rebuke from the island owners. Pier Gherini, in writing to Secretary Udall, stated a working ranch is not an arsenal and that the late Senator Engle had assured the owners that there would be no conflict between the

---

[9]Letter from Senator Engle to Pier Gherini, April 10, 1963.

[10]*Oakland Tribune*, "Foes Zero in on Seashore Proposal," April 4, 1965.

[11]*Santa Barbara News-Press* articles: "Teague Hits at Channel Bill, Why?," April 17, 1963; "Teague Lists Island Park Bill Objections," April 20, 1963; "Island Development Project Seen Boosting Park Cost," October 14, 1964.

[12]*Santa Barbara News-Press*, "Channel Isles Park Bill OK Forecast," October 29, 1964 .

long range development proposals initiated by the Gherinis and his proposals for legislation for national seashore installations.[13] Dr. Carey Stanton, representing the Santa Cruz Island Company, also opposed Udall's statements and objected to a Department of Interior survey which he felt would not be an "unprejudiced survey."[14] Though the initial bills proposed to create a Channel Islands National Park never became law as boldly predicted by Secretary Udall, the debate continued. Despite Udall's support of Taylor's candidacy, Teague won the election.

New impetus for a Channel Islands National Park occurred in 1974 when the Park Service assigned William H. Ehorn as superintendent of the Channel Islands National Monument. During his fifteen years as superintendent, the Channel Islands National Park became a reality, with Ehorn working closely with Congressman Robert J. Lagomarsino (Rep., Cal.), not only assisting in the passage of the legislation, but also in administering a growing park. Ehorn's staff of seven in 1974 grew to seventy by the time he left in 1989. His 1974 budget of $164,000 increased to two million by 1989. After his arrival in 1974, Ehorn supervised the planning and construction of the present park headquarters and visitor center which was completed in 1981.[15] The *Ventura Star Free Press* described Ehorn as "the guardian of the islands," "the quintessential park ranger."[16]

Renewed interest in creating a Channel Islands National Park surfaced in the 1970s, and the time appeared ripe for its passage. In 1977, legislation was again introduced to establish a park for the islands but was not enacted.[17] Within the Gherini family, con-

[13]Letter from Pier Gherini to Stuart Udall, December 10, 1964. ". . . I resent the implications from that kind of joke," Pier Gherini responded. "The Gherini family has been here for many, many years, and we are responsible members of the community." *Santa Barbara News-Press*, "Udall Chided Over Santa Cruz, " November 1, 1964 .

[14]A letter from Dr. Carey Stanton to Congressman Charles M. Teague, June 9, 1966.

[15]Ehorn, "The Establishment of Channel Islands National Park," p. 2.

[16]*Ventura Star Free Press,* "The Guardian of the Islands," July 7, 1989.

[17]Senate Bill 1906 introduced July 19, 1977 by Senator Alan Cranston, and House Bill H.R. 7264 was introduced May 18, 1977 by Congressman Anthony Beilenson. Both bills sought to establish a combined Channel Islands and Santa Monica Mountains National Park. Bill Ehorn met with Beilenson and recommended that the islands should be separate from the Santa Monica Mountains. Neither bill was enacted.

220 siderable discussion took place about the island's future because of the advancing age of the owners. Pier Gherini had already suffered two strokes, and was worrying about enormous estate tax consequences if nothing was done. Francis Gherini, however, spelled out his opposition to the legislation. "Neither I nor anyone in my family have or ever did have any interest or desire that my portion in Santa Cruz Island be sold to the government or anyone else," Francis wrote his brother, Pier. "However, I am appreciative that all of us are differently situated and diversely motivated," he explained to Pier, "and that . . . others might well desire to dispose of their interests in the island."[18]

In general, Francis appeared to view cynically the legislative process to make Santa Cruz Island a part of the Channel Islands National Park and in particular, he seemed to distrust the motivations of Congressman Lagomarsino, one of the chief sponsors of the legislative movement. In a letter in February of 1979 to his brother, Pier, Francis stated he felt that Lagomarsino had "a very definite conflict of interests" since Lagomarsino's brother, Rick, was involved with the Santa Cruz Island Hunt Club which had the hunting contract with the Santa Cruz Island Company. Francis speculated that Lagomarsino was pushing for national monument status rather than national park status to help his brother, Rick, who, Francis concluded, "would definitely be interested in a national monument with its little or no visitation since that would only enhance his business and remove all competition such as the visitors coming to visit a national park."[19]

Francis's charge, however, lacks merit since the long term goals of preserving the Channel Islands, whether as a national park or as a national monument, are the same. A national park and national monument are administered in a similar fashion, and the Park Service usually prohibits hunting and grazing in both as a matter of policy, irrespective of park or monument status. Events to make a Channel Islands National Park moved quickly. A little over a month later, on March 14, 1979, Congressman Robert J. Lagomarsino introduced the Channel Islands Marine National

---

[18]Letter from Francis Gherini to Pier Gherini, January 10, 1978.

[19]Letter from Francis Gherini to Pier Gherini, February 1, 1979.

Park Bill.[20] Congressman Lagomarsino shared Senator Claire Engle's vision of environmental preservation of the Channel Islands, as well as his sensitivity to the rights of the owners. Ehorn worked closely with Lagomarsino's staff, particularly his Legislative Assistant, Michael Wootton, in drafting the legislation and providing the necessary information to present to the House Subcommittee on Interior and Insular Affairs. Once introduced, the legislation moved swiftly through the House, primarily through the efforts of the popular Lagomarsino and the powerful Phillip Burton, a congressman from San Francisco who was chairman of the subcommittee responsible for national parks. Congressman Burton, a Democrat, praised Republican Lagomarsino's "exceptional leadership and initiative" and observed that ". . . the Channel Islands are a remarkable American resource, unique and little altered by man's imprint."[21]

Bipartisan support propelled the legislation through Congress. Once the House passed the measure in the summer of 1979, it was sent to the Senate where Senator Alan Cranston of California used his influence to guide the legislation. The bill was referred to the Senate Committee on Energy and Natural Resources, and the director of the National Parks Service summoned Ehorn to testify in support of the enactment. Ehorn's testimony was persuasive and support for the legislation was widespread. The Senate approved the bill in October of 1979, and after conference committee it was sent to President Jimmy Carter.[22] President Carter, on March 5, 1980, signed Public Law 96-199 that established Channel Islands National Park as the 40th National Park which included five of the eight channel islands: San Miguel, Santa Rosa, Santa Cruz, Anacapa and Santa Barbara Islands.[23]Congressman Lagomarsino considered the creation of the Channel Islands National Park one of his most important leg-

---

[20]Lagomarsino, whose Congressional district included portions of Santa Barbara and Ventura Counties, introduced Bill H.R. 2975 on March 14, 1979. This bill was eventually incorporated into H.R. 3757, an omnibus Interior Bill. Senator Cranston introduced S. 1104 on May 9, 1979, as his own version of a Channel Islands National Park Bill.

[21]*House Congressional Record*, 96 Cong., 1st. Sess., May 7, 1979.

[22]Ehorn, "The Establishment of Channel Islands National Park," unpublished article, 1993, pp. 7-9.   [23]Public Law 96-199, 16 United States Code (U.S.C.) 410 ff-1.

222 islative accomplishments.[24] On October 4, 1996, the 104th Congress honored Lagomarsino by naming the Channel Islands National Park Visitor Center after him.[25] "Lagomarsino successfully guided the legislation through Congress establishing the Channel Islands National Park," noted Congressman Elton Gallegly (R. Cal.), who co-sponsored the resolution naming the visitor center after Lagomarsino. "Because of his efforts, virtually all of the islands are now protected, ensuring that they will remain free of development and in their pristine state which will be open to the public for generations to come."[26]

THE ANATOMY OF ACQUISITION

The Channel Islands' legislation created the park and *authorized* the acquisition of the remaining private property interest, except those lands held by The Nature Conservancy, which owned 90 percent of Santa Cruz Island, or any other national non-profit conservation organization.[27] The park bill mandated that Santa Rosa Island be purchased first, and this was accomplished in 1986. The law, however, did not provide for the funding of the park lands. The actual acquisitions would take many years and would be complicated by the fact that Pier Gherini, Marie Gherini Ringrose, Ilda Gherini McGinness and Francis Gherini each owned an undivided quarter interest in the Gherini Ranch (parcels 6 and 7). The process of purchasing these fractional interests led to new disputes among the owners as to how, when and for how much to sell.[28]

Early on, Francis Gherini contacted his personal friend, William P. Clark, Jr., who was Secretary of Interior in the Reagan

---

[24]*Santa Barbara News Press*, "Grazing Won't Hurt Channel Islands," November 14, 1993.

[25]*Ventura Star*, October 4, 1996. House Joint Resolution 50 sponsored by Congressman Elton Gallegly (R. Cal.).

[26]Remarks by Congressman Gallegly in the House of Representatives, January 11, 1995.

[27]Public Law 96-199, section 202 (b), required the consent of any national conservation organization unless the Secretary determined that the uses of the property were inconsistent with the purposes of the Act. As of today, The Nature Conservancy owns 90 percent of the island.

[28]The author was personally involved in the acquisition process from the inception of the legislation creating the park in 1980 through 1992.

Administration from 1983 to 1985. Clark was familiar with the island property since he supported the Gherini development plan in 1966, and Francis felt his association with Clark would lead to an early resolution of the acquisition. This expectation is evident in the note Francis wrote his sister, Marie, in early 1984: "There should be exciting things happening with reference to the island in 1984-1985. When the Sec[retary]. of Interior calls you on the phone from Wash. as Bill Clark did me and asks what we want and we discuss things in confidence—you can bet we are going to get a fair shake."[29] Francis then wrote Clark in June 1984 that of particular concern to the owners was the continued lack of appropriations to purchase the island interest and the devastating estate tax consequences to the owners in the event of their death.[30] Within a month, the acting director of the National Park Service rather than Clark replied to Francis that "budgetary constraints and the need to reduce the Federal deficit precluded . . . seeking funds for the park . . ."[31]

Despite the budget problems, it was through Ehorn's leadership that the National Park Service commenced the difficult process of acquiring the Gherini Ranch. He was sensitive to the advanced ages of the owners and to the difficult predicament which they faced, particularly with regard to estate taxes.[32] Ehorn already negotiated the purchase of Santa Rosa Island in 1986, and in 1989 he led the way for the National Park Service to acquire the first of four fractional interests of the Gherini Ranch.

After Pier Gherini died on June 29, 1989, his children decided to sell their father's undivided fractional interest in the east end of the island to pay $3,122,396 in estate taxes due nine months from date of death. The National Park Service demonstrated its good faith by agreeing to purchase Pier Gherini's fractional interest in an extraordinary effort to avoid more island litigation, not only between the owners themselves but also with the United

---

[29]Letter from Francis Gherini to Marie (Dini) Ringrose, January 1, 1984.

[30]Letter from Francis Gherini to William Clark Jr., June 18, 1984.

[31]Letter from M.L. Grier to Francis Gherini, July 13, 1984.

[32]*Santa Barbara News-Press*, "Bill Ehorn is the man who linked up the Channel Islands." by Peter C. Horworth, July 8, 1989.

States Government.[33] Even this effort, however, failed to abate island family strife. Francis Gherini wrote Stanley T. Albright, Regional Director of Western Region of National Park Service, on August 14, 1989, "strenuously" objecting to the sale of his brother's interest since there was only enough money available for the purchase of a single fractional interest.[34] At the time, the Park Service offered $4.5 million for each fractional interest, but they only had sufficient funds to buy one fractional interest.[35] Marie Gherini Ringrose and Ilda Gherini McGinness, the other two owners, had also accepted the Park Service offer to purchase and agreed that the undivided one quarter interest of parcels 6 and 7 owned by Pier Gherini's estate could be sold first. Francis wanted $5 million for his fractional interest and therefore rejected the National Park Service's offer.[36]

Francis Gherini then hired in September 1989, his long-time personal friend and former Secretary of Interior, William P. Clark, Jr., to represent him in his negotiations with the National Park Service. As reported by the *Los Angeles Times*, "Five years after leaving the post of U.S. Secretary of the Interior, William P. Clark, Jr., is again working on department business—but now he is helping an old friend fight for more money in a real estate deal with Clark's old agency."[37] Clark reportedly denied that he represented Francis, although public documents show otherwise.[38]

---

[33]In addition to William Ehorn, this cooperation was in large part due to the individual efforts of people such as Stanley Albright, Regional Director of the Western Region; Will Kriz, Director of Land Resources Division (Washington D.C); and Edward Haberlin, Chief of Division of Land Resources (San Francisco).

[34]Letter from Francis Gherini to Stanley Albright, August 14, 1989.

[35]The National Park Service hired Robert L. Foreman to appraise the Gherini Ranch. He determined that the ranch had a value of $16,600,000 as of March 1, 1988. A previous appraisal by E. A. Tharpe showed a value of $12,571,000 as of April 1, 1985. The Park Service rejected this appraisal. Ronald D. Grant and F. Byron Grant appraised the Gherini Ranch for the owners at $25,000,000 as of September 1, 1982.

[36]Letter from Roger M. Sullivan to Stanley Albright, August 16, 1989.

[37]*Los Angeles Times*, "Displeasure Island-Useful Friends," Thursday, May 24, 1990.

[38]See verified Further Response filed by Francis Gherini in April 1990 in the *Estate of Pier Gherini*, p.2, ln. 8-11. The response, signed by Francis Gherini under penalty of perjury, states: "In late September, 1989, respondent employed the Honorable William P. Clark, Jr. to represent respondent [Francis] in negotiations with the National Park Service for the sale of the respondent's interest in the property."

After having accused Lagomarsino of a conflict of interest, Francis ironically created a situation which raised the same issue. Some people now questioned whether Clark's association with Francis raised public policy issues concerning conflict of interest or the appearance of a conflict of interest by former public officials like Clark.[39] How these issues are resolved may dictate the future of the Channel Islands National Park and dictate the future acquisition methods employed by the federal government.

In the meantime, controversy swirled in the Caire tradition. While still retaining Clark, Francis Gherini hired yet another attorney and on March 22, 1990, sued his nephew, Thomas Gherini, as executor of the estate of Pier Gherini. In the lawsuit Francis claimed that he was entitled to attorneys' fees as a result of the sale of his brother's interest notwithstanding the fact that he opposed the sale in the first place.[40] The fee issue arose from a 1984 attorney fee contract, whereby the owners of the east end had set forth the compensation to the attorneys representing the owners in the event the Gherini Ranch was sold to the federal government.[41] The lawsuit with the estate was finally settled with the approval of the probate court, Francis withdrew his claim for fees and the action was dismissed on January 14, 1991.[42]

Even though Thomas Gherini, as executor of the estate of Pier Gherini, agreed with the Park Service to sell his father's one-quarter interest in the Gherini Ranch for $4.5 million, Congress still needed to approve the agreement and appropriate the necessary funds. There was, however, bipartisan opposition to the price being paid for the island land, particularly for a fractional interest.[43] The estate therefore agreed to a modification of the pur-

---

[39]*Los Angeles Times*, "Displeasure Island-Useful Friends," Thursday, May 24, 1990.

[40]*Francis Gherini v. Thomas Gherini as executor of the Will of Pier Gherini.*

[41]Roger Sullivan and Henry Workman of the Los Angeles law firm of Sullivan, Workman and Dee, Francis Gherini and his nephew John Gherini were the attorneys whose compensation was determined under the 1984 agreement.

[42]Order approving the settlement was entered on January 22, 1991. *Estate of Pier Gherini.*

[43]This opposition came primarily from Congressman Sidney Yates (Dem., Illinois.) who was chairman of the Interior and Related Agencies Subcommittee of the House Appropriation Subcommittee and Congressman Ralph Regula (Rep., Ohio.) who was the ranking minority member of same committee. Letter from Regula and Yates to Secretary Manuel Lujan, Jr., March 30, 1990.

226 chase agreement to $3.8 million, and the sale was completed on April 25, 1990.[44] For the first time since California became a state, the United States government had an interest in the island for purposes other than a lighthouse.

The purchase of this fractional interest by the federal government significantly raised an issue of public policy which usually dictated that the purchase of such interests be avoided. As the history of the island amply demonstrated, fractional interest in property usually leads to conflicts. In this case, the Park Service purchased perhaps its largest fractional interest.[45] The Justice Department, however, approved the acquisition of the fractional interest. Lewis M. Baylor, Chief of the Title Unit for the Department of Justice, explained:

> . . . it is felt that the United States should not lightly enter into the acquisition of an undivided interest in land if any other options are available. The unique aspects of this transaction, including the size and location of the land, its great cost, the intended use to be made of the land, and the untimely death of one of the owners, have combined to create special circumstances which it is believed justify special consideration.[46]

Senator Robert C. Byrd (Dem., West Virginia), as chairman of the subcommittee on the Department of the Interior and Related Agencies, initially opposed the acquisition of a fractional interest based on public policy grounds. Senator James McClure (Rep., Idaho), then the ranking Republican member of the Interior Appropriations Subcommittee, supported the acquisition. At the urging of Congressman Lagomarsino, Senator McClure personally met with Senator Byrd and persuaded him to change his position. Senator Byrd, in a letter dated April 20, 1990, to Lou Gallegos, the Department of Interior's Assistant Secretary for Policy, Management and Budget, wrote:

---

[44]Warranty Deed from Thomas Gherini to United States of America. The purchase price was $3,874,750 for the undivided quarter interest. The heirs of Pier Gherini retained a reservation of right to use for 25 years the Scorpion Ranch facility and other small areas for "non-commercial purposes." This right was authorized by the enabling legislation and is spelled out in the warranty deed.

[45]Conversations by the author with Will Kriz, Director of Land Resources Division.

[46]Letter from Lewis M. Baylor to David A. Watts, March 12, 1990.

... Given the importance of the Gherini Ranch acquisition to the protection of the Channel Islands National Park and the need to alleviate the financial hardship presently being experienced by the heirs of Pier Gherini ... the committee has no objection to the reprogramming ... to permit the proposed purchase.[47]

The National Park Service then had the Gherini Ranch reappraised, and in 1992 Congress was willing to appropriate an additional $12 million to purchase the remaining three fractional interests of the Gherini Ranch.[48] Marie Gherini Ringrose and Ilda Gherini McGinness consistently wanted the island acquisition resolved amicably and felt that the appraisal was fair. They, therefore, sold, in December of 1992, their interest in the island to the National Park Service for $4 million each.[49] This sale left their brother, Francis, who rejected the government's offer, owning an undivided 25 percent interest and the National Park Service owning an undivided 75 percent interest. The tenancy in common created an awkward marriage of public and private ownership. Under California law, each co-tenant is equally entitled to share in the possession of the entire property regardless of their percentage interest. However, neither co-tenant can exclude the other from possession or profits nor can a co-tenant commit waste on the property.[50] This unique arrangement seemed destined for more island conflict, particularly since real estate values had declined, and government condemnation appeared inevitable.[51] The fourth government appraisal showed a value of $2.9 million for Francis' interest in 1995.

---

[47]Senator Robert C. Byrd in a letter to Lou Gallegos, April 20, 1990.

[48]Robert L. Foreman valued the island ranch property at $16,130,000 as of October 1, 1990. This was the third appraisal paid for by the National Park Service. This report was the basis for the value of $4 million for each fractional interest.

[49]William C. Kelly, Jr. of the Washington, D.C. law firm of Latham and Watkins was instrumental in working with John Gherini in securing the necessary appropriations for the acquisition of three of the four interests of the Gherini Ranch on Santa Cruz Island.

Francis Gherini would years later claim that the government stole the property and that his sisters did not get fair market value for their interests. He made these statements despite the fact that he was one of four attorneys representing his sisters and was paid $161,000 in fees for his role in the transaction. (*Los Angeles Times*, February 8, 1997).

[50]Witkin, *Summary of California Law*, vol 4 pp. 465-466.

[51]*Los Angeles Times*, February 21, 1995.

PROBLEMS IN THE PARK: 1990-1996

In the interim, Francis Gherini, who turned eighty-two years old on July 4, 1996, was the last descendant of Justinian Caire to own a fee interest in the island. As a 25 percent owner of the Gherini Ranch, Francis continued, over the objection of the National Park Service, to contract with the privately operated "Island Adventures," the commercial hunting and recreational business operated since 1984 by Jaret Owens of Ojai, California.[52] In 1995, Jaret's operation grossed $188,120 of which the Park Service received $35,272 and Francis Gherini received $11,757 as their 25 percent share of the gross proceeds as co-owners.[53]

The commercial use of Santa Cruz Island, however, raised new policy issues and posed the question of who was guarding the public's interest. The Park Service wanted to limit commercial use of the Gherini Ranch since it owned an undivided 75 percent interest for which it paid nearly $12 million. The primary authority and jurisdiction of land use policy, however, at that time still fell on the County since The Nature Conservancy owned 90 percent of the island and Francis Gherini still owned an undivided fractional interest in the Gherini Ranch. Unfortunately, the National Park Service and the County of Santa Barbara were unable to coordinate a plan to manage the island's resources.

The Park Service's goal to curb the commercial activity was frustrated by the inconsistent positions taken by the County of Santa Barbara regarding regulation of commercial activities on the island. For instance in 1990, both the County and the California Coastal Commission approved a major conditional use permit after public hearings for a recreational camp site proposed by The Nature Conservancy at Prisoners' Harbor. The plan entailed building 15 tent platforms, a cook house and bathroom facility on

---

[52]During the administration of the *Estate of Pier Gherini*, the recreational business also led to disputes concerning the distribution of funds owed to the owners. On September 10, 1990, the Probate Court ruled that Francis Gherini unlawfully withheld funds from the estate and ordered him to pay the funds back to the estate. See Probate Order filed September 10, 1990, Santa Barbara Superior Court No. 177668.

[53]Setnicka interview, February 13, 1996. Jaret pays 25 percent of the gross proceeds to the co-owners who in turn split the proceeds in proportion to their ownership interest. This method of distribution has been the arrangement since 1984.

a three-acre parcel. While recognizing that the islands' national park designation does not curtail state or local authority to exercise their police power jurisdiction, the County approved the camp site project for only six years and imposed 27 conditions.[54] The County justified the stringent conditions by noting that this was the first commercial use the County had permitted on the island and that the island is a unique and sensitive habitat.[55] The Nature Conservancy elected not to proceed with the project.

The following year, the County dealt with the commercial use of the entire 6,200 acre Gherini Ranch where hunting, camping and bed and breakfast facilities were established in 1984 and thereafter. The National Park Service advised the County of Santa Barbara that it "has no interest in having the commercial activities" on the Gherini Ranch.[56] Initially, the County, well known for its environmental protectionism, had determined that a major conditional use permit was required but later reversed its position.[57] The reversal appeared directly contrary to the policy actions taken on The Nature Conservancy's proposal for the Prisoners' Harbor camp site. The Nature Conservancy Project did not qualify for an exemption under Policy 5 of the Santa Barbara Local Coastal Program because the new project was more extensive than the previous recreational activities at Prisoners' Harbor.[58]

In order to defend its reversal, the County's Resource Management Department determined that Jaret Owens' hunt club at the

---

[54]Letter concerning 89-CP-103(cz) from John Patton of Resource Management Department to The Nature Conservancy, June 26, 1990. Staff Report of California Coastal Commission for application No. 4090-32, September 20, 1990. Santa Barbara County Planning Commission Staff Report and Recommendations, March 22, 1990.

[55]County Counsel memo by Colleen Beall to The Planning Commission, April 3, 1990.

[56]Letter from C. Mack Shaver to Veronica L. Lanz, County Zoning Compliance Officer, July 18, 1991.

[57]Letter from Veronica L. Lanz to C. Mack Shaver, July 10, 1991.

[58]Langle telephone interview, March 5, 1996. Policy 5 states: "Light recreational uses, both public and private, may be allowed with a conditional use permit provided that the kinds, intensity, and location of uses are managed to avoid impacts to all habitat, archaeological, and historical resources. The existing hunt clubs and landing permit systems which are operated by the property owners shall be allowed to continue at their current levels without permit requirements." The intent of Policy 5 was to grandfather the existing commercial hunt clubs operated in March of 1981 by the Santa Cruz Island Company on the Stanton portion of the island and by the Vail/Vickers family on Santa Rosa Island. There was no commercial hunt club on the Gherini Ranch at this time.

230 Gherini Ranch was exempt under Policy 5. Noel Langle, Director of the Resource Management Department, explained that the critical date is March 1981 when the certification of the County's Local Coastal Program took effect. "The hunt clubs and landing permit systems in operation at the time of adoption of the County's Local Coastal Program may continue *at the level of operation* in existence at that time," Langle pointed out to Park Superintendent C. Mack Shaver.[59]

As for Owens' hunt club at the Gherini Ranch, the issue was whether there was a commercial hunt club existing as of March 1981. Francis Gherini wrote in support of Jaret Owens' application for exemption from the conditional use process. In his letter to the County in 1992, Gherini represented that "hunting on the east end of Santa Cruz Island has been ongoing for many years" and that "Mr. William Peterson, who had a 5-year Operational Agreement immediately prior to Jaret Owens' presence on the Island engaged in a hunting operation in addition to his sheep activities."[60] This statement, however, appeared to conflict with Francis' statement in 1982 to William Ehorn, then superintendent of Channel Islands National Park, that "the owners of the east end of Santa Cruz Island have never desired to have a hunt club and do not now."[61] The historical evidence clearly shows that prior to 1984, there was no commercial hunt club or recreational activity on the Gherini Ranch, and the County should have invoked the conditional use procedure.[62]

---

[59]Letter from Noel Langle to C. Mack Shaver, July 15, 1992. Emphasis added.

[60]Letter from Francis Gherini to Veronica L Lanz, March 12, 1992. Francis states that Peterson had a hunting operation to protect fences and augment his income. Peterson denied any such activity. Peterson telephone interview, February 22, 1996.

[61]Letter from Francis Gherini to William H. Ehorn, July, 1, 1982.

[62]The staff reports of the County and California Coastal Commission indicate that the Channel Islands remain one of a few areas of the County where the California Coastal Commission has not given final certification of the coastal land use plan of the Local Coastal Program. Because of the lack of certification, these areas are called "white holes"; and require permits for any development from both the County and the California Coastal Commission. This would seem to indicate that a permit would automatically be required for any development irrespective of the applicability of Policy 5. The County did not rely on Policy 5 in reviewing and requiring a conditional use permit for The Nature Conservancy's Prisoners' Harbor campsite project. See County of Santa Barbara Staff Report for

The County, however, never verified the information submitted on behalf of Owens' hunt club project nor had it monitored it.[63] Even though the burden of proof is on the applicant, the County had allowed the commercial activity to expand beyond its orginial scope since 1984 because it did not appear from its "records that there was any documentation as to what that level of activity was at that time."[64] Instead the County argued that it must "rely on historical records from a variety of sources including Mr. Owens."[65] More importantly, the County stated that "the types of recreational activities currently enjoyed by the guests of Santa Cruz Island implement one of the basic purposes of the County's Local Coastal Plan which is to maximize public access and public recreational opportunites in the Coastal Zone."[66] This broad statement not only conflicted with the mandate of the enabling legislation that entry to the Park be "limited" but also did not legally justify the County's disparate and inconsistent treatment between The Nature Conservancy Project and hunt club on the Gherini Ranch.

As a result of the Park Service and County's failure to coordinate with one another in managing and protecting the island's resources, commercial activity on the Gherini Ranch continued unabated and unregulated. There had been no conditional use permit issued and no public review on how this activity affected the fragile resources of the island. "Meanwhile, thousands of feral sheep are eating the landscape down to the nub, wild pigs are rooting up the place, hunters are trashing it and erosion from overgrazing is wreaking havoc," local columnist Barney Brantingham observed while noting that public funds have been used to purchase three-quarters of the island's east end (the Gherini Ranch). "The situation is ridiculous . . . and it's a disaster growing worse by the hour."[67] Francis Gherini, however, offered a different

---

project 89-CP-103 (cx), March 22, 1990, and California Coastal Commission staff report for application #4-90–32, September 20, 1990.

[63]The County's investigation of the facts seemed negligible. It could have easily requested financial statements, pictures, etc. of the activities in existence in March of 1981.

[64]Letter from Langle to Shaver, July 15, 1992.

[65]Ibid.

[66]Ibid.   [67]*Santa Barbara News-Press,* February 24, 1995.

232 perspective by stating: "If they bought me out, they could get rid of the sheep in two weeks. There has been a lot of talk, but I haven't seen the color of anybody's money yet."[68]

The dispute over the land use control of Santa Cruz Island was a controversial subject generating conflicting positions even among interested nonprofit organizations. Brian Huse, Pacific Region Director of the nonprofit National Parks and Conservation Association, felt that the land use dispute prevented the Park Service from "providing service to the public." Marla Daily, the president of the nonprofit Santa Cruz Island Foundation, countered by stating that "Everything Island Adventure does is to the benefit of the public." It would seem, however, that the determination of whether the unregulated commercial activity was in the public interest should have been made only after having public hearings contemplated by the conditional use permit process.[69]

The public polemic concerning the commercial use on the Gherini Ranch (some would say it was intense; others would say it was minimal) not only underscored the admonition given by Horace Albright in 1933 but also highlighted yet another island controversy between the preservation of the island resources and the visitor use of the property which the legislation mandated would be "free" but "limited." Furthermore, unregulated commercial activity clashes with the intent of the enabling legislation that created the Channel Islands National Park. The legislation (Public Law 96-119) states in section 201 that the act was "intended to protect the nationally significant natural, scenic, wildlife, marine, ecological, archaeological, cultural, and scientific values of the Channel Islands." Until these conflicts were resolved, a meaningful attempt to prepare a management plan for administering the park on Santa Cruz Island's east end could not move forward despite the Park Service's significant investment in the property. Because of this situation, the salutary purposes of the legislation remained in question.

---

[68]*Los Angeles Times*, February 21, 1995.

[69]*Santa Barbara News-Press*, July 6, 1996, A-1, A-14; see also *Venture Star*, June 19, 1996.

PROTECTING THE PARK

With a defiant land owner allowing unregulated commercial use and a County permitting the use to continue, the Park Service faced difficult decisions. Acting Superintendent Tim Setnicka immediately set out a plan to demonstrate to Congresswoman Andrea Seastrand (Rep., Cal.) the urgency of protecting the island's valuable resources. Several visits to the island convinced Seastrand of the urgency.

In an attempt to bring closure to the ongoing saga of private ownership of the Gherini Ranch and to the continued decimation of the land on the east end of Santa Cruz Island, Seastrand introduced H.R. 4059 on September 11, 1996, to provide a rare legislative taking of the remaining fractional ownership interest in the Gherini Ranch. "We on the Central Coast, who care deeply about this park, have waited patiently for this agreement to be successfully negotiated so that the last piece of this national treasure can be finally put into place," Seastrand said.[70]

Francis Gherini, however, immediately devised a scheme to circumvent the legislation by signing a "gift deed" of one percent of his island interest to the Santa Cruz Island Foundation on September 23, 1996. The "gift deed" had a catch. It reserved to Francis Gherini and "his heirs a nonexclusive easement in gross, with the unrestricted right of use and occupancy for all recreational purposes over, under, through and across the entirety of said property."[71]

Like many pending bills, H.R. 4059 became a part of a larger bill called the Omnibus Parks Bill (H.R. 4236). The omnibus bill sailed quickly through the House by winning passage on a vote of 404-4 on September 28, 1996, but ran into opposition in the Senate. In the chaotic and waning days of the 104th Congress, other issues, unrelated to the Channel Islands, controlled events. The fate of H.R. 4059, like many other park bills, remained in doubt until the last minutes of the session. After intense wrangling, the

---

[70]*Santa Barbara News-Press,* October 4, 1996, A-1; *Los Angeles Times,* October 4, 1996, A-33. Seastrand news release.

[71]Francis Gherini Gift Deed to Santa Cruz Island Foundation was recorded in the Official Records of Santa Barbara County on December 3, 1996. The gift raises interesting valuation issues.

234 Senate resolved those issues and passed the Omnibus Parks Bill (including H.R. 4059) on October 3, 1996. It was the last major piece of legislation to clear the 104th Congress and the largest parks bill in more than a decade.[72] President Bill Clinton signed the legislation on November 12, 1996 (Public Law 104-333).

Under H.R. 4059 Congress amended section 202 of the original Channel Islands National Park legislation (Public Law 96-199; 16 U.S.C. 410ff-1) by authorizing a taking of the remaining ownership interest of Gherini Ranch. The legislation became effective on February 10, 1997, 90 days after the signing of the bill by the President. The legislation further acknowledged that the government will be required to pay just compensation for the interests taken and provided a special procedure for ascertaining the fair market value.

With the deadline of February 10th fast approaching, a flurry of events occurred. On January 14, 1997, after obtaining three search and arrest warrants, nineteen heavily armed federal and local law enforcement officers, using a Blackhawk helicopter, descended upon the Scorpion and Smugglers' ranches in order to serve the warrants. The officers arrested three members of Island Adventures. The most serious offense involved the alleged excavation of Native American island gravesites.[73] The Park Service justified the surprise commando type raid because the hunters were armed. The Park Service had received several threats from various hunters, and considered that there was a high potential for risk of injury. The operation took place without any injuries.[74]

The following month, on February 7, 1997, Francis Gherini made a last ditch effort to block the legislation by filing a federal lawsuit to enjoin the Park Service from seizing possession.[75] Francis contended that the government could not take his property without first depositing sufficient funds to pay for it. He also

---

[72]*San Francisco Chronicle,* October 4, 1996, A-1.

[73]*Los Angeles Times,* January 16, 1997.

[74]*Los Angeles Times,* February 15, 1997. After several days of testimony, the Santa Barbara County Grand Jury returned one felony and five misdemeanor indictments against one of the guides for Island Adventures.

[75]*Francis Gherini v. United States et al,* CV97-0819, United States District Court, Central District of California.

claimed a reservation of right of use similar to the one granted his brother's heirs, notwithstanding the fact he had previously questioned the legality of such a reservation.[76] After hearing arguments that day, United States District Judge George H. King denied Francis Gherini's request for a temporary injunction. Judge King also denied any right of use and occupancy for Francis Gherini since he had not negotiated a sale to the Park Service under the original legislation enacted in 1980.[77]

Over the weekend prior to February 10th, hordes of hunters from Island Adventures swarmed upon the Gherini Ranch for the final hunt. Hundreds of sheep fell victim to the weekend onslaught. After taking possession on February 10th, the Park Service imposed an immediate ceasefire and opened the park to the general public.[78]

As a result of the passage of H.R. 4059 and nearly seventeen years after the original Channel Island Legislation was enacted, the National Park Service can, in the words of the late local historian Walker Tompkins, raise its flag over the east end of the island. Even this event will leave the island divided between the National Park Service and The Nature Conservancy. Because of the burdens of managing such a large tract of land on a long-term basis, it is not unreasonable to speculate that perhaps the Conservancy may at some point in the future transfer its 90 percent of the island to the National Park Service. Such a transfer would complete the acquisition of all privately held lands in the Channel Islands National Park. The entire Santa Cruz Island would then become part of the public domain for the first time since 1848 when Mexico and the United States signed the Treaty of Guadalupe Hidalgo.

As for the future of the park, C. Mack Shaver, Channel Islands superintendent from 1989 to 1996, asserts that the original intent of Congress will be carried out. This includes the restoration of the natural ecosystems, protection and interpretation of natural and cultural resources, and low intensity and low volume visitor

---

[76]Letter from Francis Gherini to Mack Shaver, December 12, 1995.
[77]*Ventura Star,* February 8, 1997.
[78]*Los Angeles Times,* February 9, 1997

236 use. When this is accomplished, Superintendent Shaver observes that the "fascinating history and feeling, of Santa Cruz Island can, for the first time, be made available to the general public, not just a select few, on the island."[79]

CONCLUSION

Santa Cruz, the Island of the Holy Cross, is symbolic in many ways. It symbolizes death and resurrection; it symbolizes the burdens which were carried by those who owned it. The island survived the very volcanic eruption which gave it birth; for millions of years, its only conflict was the natural process which changed its appearance as the island gradually evolved. Then came human existence. People wanted to own it; use it; fight over it; and protect it. The island has endured it all. As its name implies, the island will always be remembered as something sacred; it is one of nature's true wonders, with a storied history, teeming with diversity, and of course, conflict.

---

[79]Letter from C. Mack Shaver to John Gherini, June 30, 1993. Shaver retired in March 1996.

PERSONAL PROPERTY INVENTORY OF SANTA CRUZ ISLAND COMPANY ON NOVEMBER 30, 1911.

1 schooner (power) called Santa Cruz 44 gross tons
10 wagons
7 dump carts
2 village carts
2 breaking plows
3 double gang plows
3 horse rakes, double
1 hay press—power
1 " " "
5 mowers
1 barley crusher
2 cultivators—1 horse
15 " 2 horse
3 barley seeders—geared
4 hand
2 gas engines
1 steam boiler
2 hot air pumps
2 power pumps
4 windmills
1 grape crusher & stemmer
2 grape presses
2 blacksmith forges & bellows
3 portable forges
4 anvils
4 bench vises—blks.
2 " " ordinary

3 drills blks.
2 fanning mills
3 platform scales
3 corn shellers
6 grindstones
35 saddles
18 sets harness
2 ranges—French
4 stoves
Goods in store for sale value $240.00
7 bulls—pure bred
7 " graded
4 " " yearling
27 cows—old
13 cows—milk
567 " range
128 " yearling
75 " heifer calves
16 side hill and other plows
11 vineyard plows
7 harrows
4 disc harrows
3 horse rakes—singles
229,600 wine gals. merchantable
26,000 " " distilling
3 oak tanks 9x6
3 oak tanks 10x10

238

4	14 x 12	1	stallion—pure bred
17	oval oak casks	1	" graded
6	redwood tanks 5x5	3	gelding old
21	7x7	56	" working
2	redwood tanks 8x6	6	mares sold
15	" 9x6	51	" working
15	" 10x10	6	colts under 1 year
116	puncheons oak 148/180 gals.	16	fillies "
		178	sheep—pure bred
200	barrels	257	rams—range (estimated)
25	half barrels	19,745	ewes " "
26	kegs—10 gals.	6,600	wethers " "
12	" 5 gals.	4,000	lambs " "
358	demijohns 5 gals.	79	hogs
5	cows, pure bred	43	turkeys
323	steers—2 yrs. old	203	hens and roosters
152	" yearling	150	pigeons
101	" calves	12	redwood tanks 11x4½

Source: Transcript on Appeal in *Rossi v. Caire,* S.F. 7101 (174 Cal. 74), pp. 110-112

Bibliography

PRIMARY SOURCES

Agreement between Jaret Owens and Marie Ringrose et al., December 31, 1984.

Agreement between William C. Peterson and Marie Ringrose et al., January 10, 1979.

Agreement between André Castillero and William Forbes and Isidoro de la Torre, February 18, 1850; the original Spanish document, located in the Bancroft Library, University of California, Berkeley, was translated by Geraldine Sahyun, a member of the Board of Trustees of the Santa Barbara Mission Archive Library. The English translation of Guillermo is William and of Ysidoro is Isidoro.

Ambrose Gherini register of cases, 1911-1930.

Articles of Incorporation of the Buena Ventura Company, April 27, 1863, located in the offices of the California Historical Society in San Francisco.

Articles of Incorporation Santa Cruz Island Company, February 20, 1869, July 13, 1964, April 8,1988. The original 1869 incorporation document is located in the California State Archives, Sacramento.

Articles of Re-Incorporation and amendments of Santa Cruz Island Company, March 31, 1873, December 8, 1964, July 30, 1976, March 31,1978, July 24, 1978.

Articles of Incorporation of Justinian Caire Company, November 15, 1895, located in the California State Archives in Sacramento.

Articles of Incorporation of the National Trading Company filed in the office of the Secretary of State, California, on October 4, 1916.

Articles of Incorporation of Santa Cruz Island Foundation filed in the office of the Secretary of State, California, on September 22, 1986 and restated in 1990.

Certificate of Diminution of the Capital Stock of the Santa Cruz Island Company, December 26, 1879.

Certificate of Winding Up and Dissolution of Justinian Caire Company was filed with the office of the California Secretary of State on November 13, 1945.

Certificates of Election of The Santa Cruz Island Company to Wind Up and Dissolve, filed in the office of the Secretary of State, December 30, 1946, November 12, 1992.

Certificates of Winding Up and Dissolution of National Trading Company, Ltd. filed in the office of the Secretary of State on March 15, 1963.

House Bills: H.R.7264 (May 18,1977), H.R.2975 (March 4, 1979), H.R. 3737 (1979), H.R. 4059 (September 11, 1996), H.R. 4236 (September 27, 1996), House Joint Resolution 50.

House Congressional Record, 31 Congress., lst session, January 29, 1850.

240

House Congressional Record, 96 Cong., lst session, April 30, 1979 and May 7, 1979.

Island Adventures financial statements, 1984-1990.

Lux, Fred. "Report of Scorpion Valley," December 9, 1895.

Marriage Record of Guistiniano Caire and Maria Molfino, December 16, 1854.

National Trading Company minute book, 1916–1953.

National Trading Company financial reports 1927-1959.

National Trading Company Payroll Journal, 1943-1960.

Original Maps of Santa Cruz Island, 1876-1891.

Pier Gherini radio logs, January 29, 1951 to March 21, 1984.

Pier Gherini, personal papers and file, 1940–1989.

Santa Barbara County Assessment Tax Rolls, for years, 1853, 1855-1858; 1860, 1863-1869, located in the Library of the Santa Barbara Historical Society.

Santa Barbara County Board of Supervisors Resolution 66-108, March 8, 1966.

Santa Barbara County Planning Department file on Santa Cruz Island.

Santa Barbara Harbor development file located in the Library of the Santa Barbara Historical Society.

Santa Cruz Island diaries of foremen from years 1885-1898.

Santa Cruz Island Company payroll records (1885-1890), employee records (1889-1892) invoices (1885-1890), correspondence (1904-1921) and maps (1884-1892), located at Santa Cruz Island Foundation.

Santa Cruz Island Company, *Sale of stock and Assets to The Nature Conservancy,* two volumes, 1977 and 1978, located at the Santa Cruz Island Foundation.

Santa Cruz Island Company minute books from September 1964 through 1986. The books are located at the Santa Barbara field office of The Nature Conservancy.

Santa Cruz Island Company files located at the Santa Barbara field office of The Nature Conservancy.

Senate Bills: S.B.543 (January, 1961), S.B.1303 (April, 1963), S.B.1906 (1977) and S.B.1104 (May 9, 1979).

The Nature Conservancy agreement with Santa Cruz Island Company (feral sheep), June 26, 1984.

Toll, R.W., "Report on the Channel Island Survey," January 1933 to Horace Albright. Original report located in the Archive Library of the Channel Islands Headquarters, Ventura, California.

Transcripts of County of Santa Barbara Planning Commission hearing of October 20, 1965, December 1, 1965, January 5, 1966, January 12, 1966. Original transcripts in author's files.

BOOKS

Albright, Horace M, Russell E. Dickenson, and William Penn Mott, Jr. edited by Mary Lu Moore. *The National Park Service, The Story Behind The Scenery.* Las Vegas: KC Publications, 1987.

Bancroft, Hubert Howe. *History of California.* 7 vols. San Francisco: A.L. Bancroft Publishers, 1884–1890.

Bean, Lowell J. and Thomas C. Blackburn. *Native Californians, A Theoretical Retrospective.* Ramona:Bellena Press, 1976.

Bean, Walton and James J. Rawls. *California, An Interpretive History.* 5th ed. New York: McGraw Hill, Inc., 1988.

Benoist, H., and Sr. M. C. Flores. *The Spanish Missionary Heritage of the United States.* U.S. National Park Service, 1993.

Bookspan, Rochelle, ed. *Santa Barbara by The Sea.* Santa Barbara: McNally & Loftin, West, 1982.

Bremner, Carl St. J. *Geology of Santa Cruz Island, Santa Barbara County.* Santa Barbara: Santa Barbara Museum of Natural History. Occasional Papers No. 1, November 1, 1932.

Bunnell, David. *Sea Caves of Santa Cruz Island.* Santa Barbara: McNally & Loftin, 1988.

Caire, Helen. *Santa Cruz Island, A History and Recollections of an Old California Rancho.* Spokane: The Arthur H. Clark Company, 1993.

Child, Ernest. *Tools of a Chemist.* New York: Reinhold Publishing Co., 1940.

Cleland, Robert Glass. *The Cattle on a Thousand Hills.* San Marino: The Huntington Library, 1951.

Cowan, Robert G. *Ranchos of California, a List of Spanish Concessions, 1775-1822 and Mexican Grants, 1822-1846.* Fresno: Academy Library Guild, 1956.

Daily, Marla. *California's Channel Islands--1001 Questions Answered.* Santa Barbara: McNally & Loftin, 1987.

_____. ed. *Santa Cruz Island Anthology.* Santa Barbara: Santa Cruz Island Foundation, 1989. Occasional Paper No. 1.

_____. ed. *Northern Channel Islands Anthology.* Santa Barbara: Santa Cruz Island Foundation, 1989. Occasional Paper No.2.

_____. ed. *Chapel of the Holy Cross, 1891-1991 Santa Cruz Island.* Santa Barbara: Santa Cruz Island Foundation, 1991. Occasional Paper No. 5.

Dana, Richard Henry. *Two Years Before The Mast.* New York: Modern Library, 1936.

Dana, Samuel Trask, and Myron Krueger. *California Lands, Ownership, Use and Management.* Narberth: The Livingston Publishing Company, 1958.

Delgado, James P. *To California by Sea.* Columbia: University of South Carolina Press, 1990.

Doran, Adelaide LeMert. *Pieces of Eight Channel Island.* Glendale: The Arthur H. Clark Company, 1980.

Eaton, Margaret. *Diary of a Sea Captain's Wife: The Tales of Santa Cruz Island.* Edited by Janice Timbrook. Santa Barbara: McNally & Loftin, 1980.

Englehardt, Zephyrin, O.F.M. *Santa Barbara Mission.* San Francisco: The James H. Barry Company, 1923.

_____. *The California Missions and Missionaries of California.* 4 vols. San Francisco: The James H. Barry Company, 1912.

Forbes, Alexander. *California: A History of Upper and Lower California.* London: Smith, Elder and Co., 1839.

Geiger, Maynard J. and Clement W. Meighan. *As the Padres Saw Them. California Indian Life and Customs as reported by the Franciscan Missionaries 1813-1815.* Edited by Doyce B. Nunis, Jr. Santa Barbara: Santa Barbara Mission Archive Library, 1970.

Glassow, Michael A., with contributions by Larry R. Wilcoxon. *The Status of Archaeological Research on Eastern Santa Cruz Island, California.* Santa Barbara: University of California at Santa Barbara Social Process Research, 1983.

_____. ed. *Archaeology on the Northern Channel Islands of California, studies of subsistence, economics and social organization.* Salinas: Coyote Press, 1993.

242

Gleason, Duncan. *Islands of California, Their History, Romance and Physical Characteristics.* Los Angeles: Sea Publications, Inc., 1950.

Graburn, Nelson, Michael Jochim, Marc Swartz and B.J. Williams, eds. *University of California Publications in Anthropology,* 18. Berkeley: University of California Press, 1987.

Gudde, Erwin G. *California Place Names, The Origin and Etymology of Current Geographical Names.* Berkeley and Los Angeles: University of California Press, 1969.

Gulick, Howard E. *Nayarit, Mexico, A Traveler's Guide.* Glendale: The Arthur H. Clark Company, 1965.

Halvorson, William L. and Gloria J. Maender, editors. *The Fourth California Islands Symposium: Update on the Status of Resources.* Santa Barbara: Santa Barbara Museum of Natural History, 1994.

Hamilton, Edith. *Mythology, Timeless Tales of Gods and Heroes.* New York: The New American Library of World Literature, 1953.

Hillinger, Charles. *The California Islands.* Los Angeles: Academy Publishers, 1958.

Hittell, Theodore H. *History of California.* 4 vols. San Francisco: Pacific Press Publishing House and Occidental Publishing Co., 1885.

Hochberg, F.G., ed. *Third California Islands Symposium.* Santa Barbara: Santa Barbara Museum of Natural History, 1993.

Hoffman, Ogden. *Reports of Land Cases Determined in the United States District Court for the Northern District of California.* San Francisco: 1862, Appendix.

Holder, Charles F. *The Channel Islands of California.* Chicago: A.C. McClurg & Co., 1910.

Holdredge, Helen. *Mammy Pleasant's Partner.* New York: G.P. Putnam's Sons, 1954.
_____. *Mammy Pleasant.* New York: G.P.Putnam's Sons, 1953.

Hudson, Travis and Ernest Underhay. *Crystals in the Sky: An Intellectual Odyssey Involving Chumash Astronomy, Cosmology and Rock Art.* Santa Barbara: A Ballena Press, Santa Barbara Museum of Natural History Cooperative Publication, 1978.

Johnson, Kenneth M. *The New Almaden Quicksilver Mine, with an account of the land claims involving the mine and its role in California History.* Georgetown: The Talisman Press, 1963.

Junak, Steve, Tina Ayers, Randy Scott, Dieter Wilken, and David Young. *A Flora of Santa Cruz Island.* Santa Barbara: Santa Barbara Botanic Garden, 1995.

Kelsey, Harry. *Juan Rodríguez Cabrillo.* San Marino: Huntington Library, 1986.

King, Chester. *Evolution of Chumash Society.* New York: Garland Publishing, Inc., 1990.

Kitsepawit, Fernando. *The Eye of the Flute, Chumash Traditional History and Ritual.* Edited by Travis Hudson, Thomas Blackburn, Rosario Curletti, and Janice Timbrook. Santa Barbara: Santa Barbara Museum of Natural History, 1977.

Kroeber, A. L. *Handbook of the Indians of California.* Berkeley: California Book Company, Ltd., 1953.

Mason, Jesse D. *History of Santa Barbara County.* Oakland: Thompson & West, 1883.

McElrath, Clifford. *On Santa Cruz Island.* Los Angeles: Dawson's Book Shop, 1967, reprinted in 1993 by the Santa Barbara Historical Society.

Meyer, Jean. *De Canton de Tepíc a Estado De Nayarit, 1810-1940.* Mexico City: Centre d'Etudes Mexicaines et Centramericaines, 1990.

Miller, Bruce W. *Chumash, A Picture of Their World.* Los Osos: Sand River Press, 1988.

BIBLIOGRAPHY

Morris, Don P. and James Lima. *Channel Islands National Park and Channel Islands National Marine Sanctuary Submerged Cultural Resources Assessment.* Santa Fe: National Park Service, 1996.

Ogden, Adele. *The California Sea Otter Trade, 1782-1848.* Berkeley: University of California Press, 1941.

O'Neill, Owen H., and Harold McLean Meier. *History of Santa Barbara County, Its People and Its Resources.* Santa Barbara: The Union Printing Company, 1939.

Ord, Angustias de la Guerra. *Occurrences in Hispanic California.* Washington: Academy of American Franciscan History, 1956.

Orr, Phil C. *Archaeology of Mescalitan Island and Customs of the Canalino.* Santa Barbara: Santa Barbara Museum of Natural History, Occasional Papers No. 5, 1943.

_____. *Prehistory of Santa Rosa Island.* Santa Barbara: Santa Barbara Museum of Natural History, 1968.

Palóu, Fray Francisco. *Historical Memoirs of New California.* 4 vols. Edited by Eugene Bolton. New York: Russell and Russell, 1966.

Pavlik, Bruce M., Pamela C. Muick, Sharon Johnson, and Marjorie Popper. *Oaks of California.* Los Olivos: Cachuma Press, 1990.

Pinney, Thomas. *The Wine of Santa Cruz Island.* Santa Barbara and Los Angeles: The Santa Cruz Island Foundation and The Zamorano Club, 1994.

Power, Dennis M. ed. *The California Islands: Proceedings of a Multidisciplinary Symposium.* Santa Barbara: Santa Barbara Museum of Natural History, 1980.

Rasmussen, Louis J. *San Francisco Passenger Lists.* 4 vols. Colma: San Francisco Historic Records, 1966-1970.

Roberts, Lois J. *San Miguel Island, Santa Barbara's Fourth Island West.* Carmel: Cal Rim Books, 1991.

Rogers, Cameron. *A County Judge in Arcady, Selected Papers of Charles Fernald, Pioneer Jurist.* Glendale: The Arthur H. Clark Company, 1951.

Rogers, David Banks. *Prehistoric Man of the Santa Barbara Coast.* Santa Barbara: Santa Barbara Museum of Natural History, 1929.

Rolle, Andrew. *California, A History.* Arlington Heights: Harlan Davidson, Inc., 1987 fourth ed.

Stanton, Carey. *An Island Memoir.* Los Angeles: The Santa Cruz Island Company, 1984.

Stork, Yda Addis. *A Memorial and Biographical History of the Counties of Santa Barbara, San Luis Obispo and Ventura.* Chicago: Lewis, 1891.

Sturtevant, William C. general editor, *Handbook of North American Indians.* Washington: Smithsonian Institution, 1978.

Tompkins, Walker A. *A Centennial History of Stearns Wharf.* Santa Barbara: The Santa Barbara Wharf Company, 1972.

_____. *Santa Barbara History Makers.* Santa Barbara: McNally & Loftin, 1983.

Towne, Charles Wayland, and Edward Norris Wentworth. *Shepard's Empire.* Norman: University of Oklahoma Press, 1945.

Udall, Stewart L. *The Quiet Crisis.* New York: Holt, Rinehart and Winston, 1963.

Wagner, Henry R. *The Cartography of the Northwest Coast of America to the Year 1800.* 2 vols. Berkeley: University of California Press, 1937.

_____. *Juan Rodríguez Cabrillo, Discoverer of the Coast of California.* San Francisco: California Historical Society, 1941.

Watkins, T.H. *California, An Illustrated History.* New York: Weathervane Books, 1973.

244

Weaver, Donald W. *Geology of the Northern Channel Islands.* Special Publication, Pacific Section of The American Association of Petroleum Geologists and The Society of Economic Paleontologists and Mineralogists, 1969.

Wentworth, Edward Norris. *America's Sheep Trails.* Ames: The Iowa State College Press, 1948.

Woodward, Arthur, translator. *The Sea Diary of Fr. Juan Vizcaino to Alta California, 1769.* Los Angeles: Glen Dawson, 1959.

Writer's Program, California. *Santa Barbara, A Guide to the Channel City and its Environs.* New York: Hastings House, 1941.

ARTICLES AND PERIODICALS

Arnold, Jeanne E. "Craft Specialization in the Prehistoric Channel Islands, California," *University of California Publications in Anthropology,* 18 (Berkeley: University of California Press, 1987):1-136.

Ascher, Leonard. "Lincoln's Administration and the New Almaden Scandal," *Pacific Historical Review,* 5 (December 1936):38-51.

Atwood, Jonathan L. "Breeding Biology of the Santa Cruz Island Scrub Jay," *The California Island: Proceedings of a Multidisciplinary Symposium,* edited by Dennis M. Power (Santa Barbara, CA: Santa Barbara Museum of Natural History, 1980): 675-688.

Baccari, Alessandro and Andrew M. Canepa, with translation by Olga Richardson. "The Italians of San Francisco in 1865: G.B. Cerruti's Report to the Ministry of Foreign Affairs," *California History,* 60 (Winter 1981/82):350-369.

Bastian, Beverly E. "I Heartily Regret That I Ever Touched a Title in California"— Henry Wagner Halleck, "The *Californios,* and the Clash of Legal Cultures," *California History,* 72 (Winter 1993/94): 311-323.

Bowman, J.N. "The Question of Sovereignty over California's Off-shore Islands," *Pacific Historical Review,* 31 (August, 1962): 291-300.

Caire, Delphine. "The History of the Holy Chapel," *Chapel of the Holy Cross, 1891-1991 Santa Cruz Island,* Occasional Paper No. 5, ed. by Marla Daily (Santa Cruz Island Foundation: 1991):15-24.

Caire, Helen. "A Brief History of Santa Cruz Island from 1869 to 1991," *Anthology,* Occasional Paper No. 1, ed. by Marla Daily (Santa Cruz Island Foundation: 1991): 29-61.

_____, "The Last Vacquero," *Anthology,* Occasional Paper No. 1, ed. by Marla Daily (Santa Cruz Island Foundation: 1991): 107-120.

_____, "Hunting Wild Hogs," *Anthology,* Occasional Paper No. 1, ed. by Marla Daily (Santa Cruz Island Foundation: 1991): 121-132.

Caire, Jean. "Delphine A. Caire, in Memoriam," *California Historical Society,* 29 (March, 1950):81-83.

Chinard, Gilbert. "When the French Came to California," *California Historical Society Quarterly,* 22 (December, 1943):289-314.

Daily, Marla. "Cemetery of the Holy Cross," *Chapel of the Holy Cross, 1891-1991 Santa Cruz Island,* Occasional Paper No. 5, ed. by Marla Daily (Santa Cruz Island Foundation: 1991):29-56.

_____, "Deaths on Santa Cruz Island," *Chapel of the Holy Cross, 1891-1991 Santa Cruz Island,* Occasional Paper No. 5, ed. by Marla Daily (Santa Cruz Island Foundation: 1991):61-70.

Dane, George Ezra. "The French Consûlate in California 1843-1856," *California Historical Society,* 13 (March, 1934):56-62.

Davenport, Demorest, John R. Johnson and Jan Timbrook. "The Chumash and the Swordfish," *Antiquity.* 67 (June, 1993):257-272.

Douglas, John A. "The Santa Barbara Harbor: Nature Confronts the Breakwater," in *Santa Barbara By The Sea,* edited by Rochelle Bookspan. Santa Barbara: McNally & Loftin, 1982:68-87.

Ellison, William Henry. "History of the Santa Cruz Island Grant," *Pacific Historical Review,* 6 (September, 1937):270-283.

Engstrand, Iris H. W. "The Legal Heritage of Spanish California," *Southern California Quarterly.* 75 no. 3-4 (Fall/Winter 1993):205-236.

Field, Alston G. "Attorney-General Black and the California Land Claims." *Pacific Historical Review,* 4 (December, 1935):235-245.

Garrett, Lula May. "San Francisco in 1851 As Described by Eyewitnesses," *California Historical Society Quarterly,* 22 (September, 1943):253-275.

Gherini, John. "Santa Cruz Island: Conflict in the Courts." *The Fourth California Islands Symposium: Update on the Status of Resources,* edited by William L. Halvorson, and Gloria J. Maender. (Santa Barbara, CA: Santa Barbara Museum of Natural History, 1994):165-170.

Gherini, Mrs. Ambrose. (Marie Rossi Gherini), "Santa Cruz Island," interview by Edward Selden Spaulding, *Noticias,* Santa Barbara Historical Society, 5 (Fall 1959):1-11, and reprinted in *Santa Cruz Island Anthology,* Occasional Paper No. 1, edited by Marla Daily (Santa Barbara: Santa Cruz Island Foundation, 1991): 63-70.

Gherini, Pier. "Island Rancho," *Noticias,* Santa Barbara Historical Society, 12 (Winter 1966):14-20, and reprinted in *Santa Cruz Island Anthology,* Occasional Paper No. 1, edited by Marla Daily (Santa Barbara: Santa Cruz Island Foundation, 1989) :71-78.

Giovinco, Joseph. "Democracy in Banking: The Bank of Italy and California's Italians," *California Historical Society Quarterly,* 47 (September, 1968):195-204.

Glassow, Michael A. "Recent Developments in the Archaeology of the Channel Islands," *The California Island: Proceedings of a Multidisciplinary Symposium,* edited by Dennis M. Power (Santa Barbara, CA: Santa Barbara Museum of Natural History, 1980): 79-99.

Goeden, Richard D., Charles A. Fleschner and Donald W. Ricker. "Biological Control of Prickly Pear Cacti on Santa Cruz Island, California," *Hilgardia,* 38 (1967): 579-606.

Graffy, Erin. "The Italian Renaissance in Santa Barbara," *Noticias,* Santa Barbara Historical Society, 41 (Winter 1995): 69-92.

Grant, Campbell. "Chumash: Introduction," and "Eastern Coastal Chumash," *California, Handbook of North American Indians* (Washington D.C.: Smithsonian Institution, 1978), vol., 8: 505-519.

Jackson, Sheldon G. "Two Pro-British Plots in Alta California," *Southern California Quarterly* 55 (Summer 1973): 251-270.

———. "The British and the California Dream Rumors: Myths and Legends," *Southern California Quarterly,* 57(Fall 1975):105-139.

Johnson, John R. "Cruzeño Chumash Social Geography," *Archaeology on the Northern Channel Islands of California, studies of subsistence, economics and social organization:* Glassow, Michael A., editor (Salinas: Coyote Press, 1993):19-46.

———. "The Chumash Indians After Secularization," *The Spanish Missionary Heritage of the United States.* H. Benoist and Sr. M. C. Flores, editors (United States National Park Service, 1993): 143-164.

———. "The Trail to Fernando." *Journal of California and Great Basis Anthropology.* 4:132-138.

246

_____. "A Geographic Analysis of Island Chumash Marriage Networks," *Archaeology on the Northern Channel Islands of California, studies of subsistence, economics and social organization:* 19-46.

Johnson, Kenneth M. "The Judges Colton," *Southern California Quarterly,* 57 (Winter 1975):349-360.

Karasik, Gary. "Islanders, Francis Gherini: Clouds over Santa Cruz," *Islands, an International Magazine* (April, 1985): 16.

King, Chester. "Chumash Inter-village Economic Exchange," *Native Californians, A Theoretical Retrospective,* edited by Lowell J. Bean and Thomas C. Blackburn, (Ramona: Ballena Press, 1976): 288-318.

Kinsell, Martinette. "The Santa Barbara Islands," *Overland Monthly,* 18 (December, 1891):617-631.

Laughrin, Lyndal. "Populations and Status of the Island Fox," *The California Island: Proceedings of a Multidisciplinary Symposium,* edited by Dennis M. Power, (Santa Barbara, CA: Santa Barbara Museum of Natural History, 1980):745-756.

Lima, James. "Historic Study Prisoners' Harbor Landing Site Santa Cruz Island," California, February 16, 1994, unpublished report prepared by the Channel Islands National Park: 1-52.

Meighan, Clement W. "Indians and California Missions," *Southern California Quarterly,* 49 (Fall 1987):187-201.

Menzies, Jean Storke. "The Staff of the Holy Cross," *Chapel of the Holy Cross, 1891-1991, Santa Cruz Island,* Occasional Paper No. 5, edited by Marla Daily (Santa Barbara, CA: Santa Cruz Island Foundation, 1991): 9-14.

Neuerburg, Norman. "Important Mission Paintings in the Archive Library," *La Gazeta Del Archivo,* (Fall/Winter 1995), Newsletter of the Santa Barbara Mission Archive-Library:4-10.

Nunis, Doyce B., Jr. "Medicine in Hispanic California," *Southern California Quarterly,* 76 (Spring 1994):31-57.

Ogden, Adele. "Russian Sea-Otter and Seal Hunting on the California Coast," *California Historical Society Quarterly,* 12 (September, 1933):217-218.

Reichlen, Henry and Robert F. Heizer. "The Scientific Expedition of Leon de Cessac to California, 1877-1879," *Reports of the University of California Archaeological Survey,* No. 61 (Berkeley: University of California Archaeological Research Facility, 1964):9-23.

Ryder, Judith Anne. "Santa Barbara's Best Kept Secret: Industry and Commerce in the Harbor Area," *Santa Barbara By The Sea,* edited by Rochelle Bookspan (Santa Barbara: McNally & Loftin, 1982):144-161.

St. Clair, David J. "New Almaden and California Quicksilver in the Pacific Rim Economy," *California History,* 73 (Winter 1994/95):279-294.

Schuyler, Peter. "Control of Feral Sheep (*Ovis aries*) on Santa Cruz Island, California," *Third California Islands Symposium,* ed. by F.G. Hochberg (Santa Barbara Museum of Natural History, 1993):443-462.

Tays, George. "Captain Andres Castillero, Diplomat, an account from unpublished sources of his services to Mexico in the Alvarado Revolution of 1836-1838," *California Historical Society Quarterly,* 14 (September, 1935): 230-268.

Timbrook, Jan. "Island Chumash Ethnobotany," *Archaeology on the Northern Channel Islands of California, studies of subsistence, economics and social organization.* Michael A. Glassow, editor (Salinas: Coyote Press, 1993):47-62.

BIBLIOGRAPHY

Tompkins, Walker A. "Channel Islands Nomenclature," *Noticias, Santa Barbara Historical Society,* 4 (October, 1958): 9.

Vail, Al and Marla Daily. "Santa Rosa Island: Past, Present and Future," *Northern Channel Islands Anthology, Occasional Paper No. 2,* edited by Marla Daily (Santa Barbara, CA: Santa Cruz Island Foundation, 1989):97-104.

Vedder, J.G. and D.G. Howell. "Topographic Evolution of the Southern California Borderland During Late Cenozoic Time," *California Island Proceedings of a Mutidisciplinary Symposium,* edited by Dennis M. Power (Santa Barbara, CA: Santa Barbara Museum of Natural History, 1980):7-31.

Wagner, Henry R. "George Davidson, Geographer of the Northwest Coast of America," *California Historical Society Quarterly,* 11 (December, 1932): 299-301.

_____. "The Voyage to California of Sebastian Cermeño in 1895," *California Historical Society Quarterly,* 3 (April, 1924):3-24.

Warren, Earl, Jr. "California's Ranches in the Sea," *The National Geographic Magazine,* 114, (August, 1958):267-270.

Weigand, Peter W. "Geochemistry and Origin of Middle Miocene Volcanic Rocks from Santa Cruz and Anacapa Islands, Southern California Borderland," *Third California Islands Symposium* edited by F.G.Hochberg (Santa Barbara: Santa Barbara Museum of Natural History, 1993):21-37.

Wenner, Adrian M. and Donald L. Johnson. "Land Vertebrates on the California Channel Islands: Sweepstakes or Bridges?" *The California Island: Proceedings of a Multidisciplinary Symposium,* edited by Dennis M. Power (Santa Barbara, CA: Santa Barbara Museum of Natural History, 1980):497-530.

THESES AND DISSERTATIONS

Johnson, John Richard. "An Ethnohistoric Study of the Island Chumash." Unpublished Masters Thesis, University of California at Santa Barbara, December 1982.

_____. "Chumash Social Organization: An Ethnohistoric Perspective." Unpublished Doctoral Dissertation, University of California at Santa Barbara, December 1988.

Warren, Earl, Jr. "The Agriculture of Santa Cruz Island." Unpublished Masters Thesis, University of California, 1953.

COURT CASES

Andrés Castillero v. United States, 1852, District Court of the United States for the Southern District, Case No. 340.

Barker v. Harvey, (1901) 181 U.S. 481, 21 S.Ct. 690, 45 L.Ed. 963.

Capuccio v. Caire, (1922) 189 Cal. 514.

Capuccio v. Caire, (1929) 207 Cal. 200.

Capuccio v. Caire, (1932) 215 Cal. 518.

Capuccio v. Caire, Los Angeles Superior Court No. 7709.

Capuccio v. Caire, City and County San Francisco Superior Court No. 48031.

Capuccio v. Caire, Santa Barbara Superior Court No. 10812.

David Freidenrich Jr. v. Ambrose Gherini and Aglae S. Capuccio, 1929, Santa Barbara Superior Court No. 20397.

David Freidenrich Jr. v. Ambrose Gherini and Edmund Rossi et al., 1929, Santa Barbara Superior Court No. 20129.

248

Edmund A. Rossi v. Arthur Caire, et al, 1912, City and County Superior Court of San Francisco, No. 43295.

Edwin L. Stanton III v. Carey Stanton et al, 1976, Los Angeles Superior Court No. C 152947.

Edwin L. Stanton III v. Santa Cruz Island Company, et al, 1976, Los Angeles Superior Court No. C180228.

Francis Gherini v. Thomas Gherini as executor of the Will of Pier Gherini, 1990, Santa Barbara Superior Court No. 181262.

Francis Gherini v. United States et al, CV97-0819, United States District Court, Central District of California.

In the Matter of the Estate of Albina Caire, 1924, County of Alameda Superior Court No. 35871.

In the Matter of the Estate of Ambrose Gherini, 1952, County of San Mateo Superior Court No. 19005.

In the Matter of the Estate of Amelie A. Rossi, 1917, San Francisco Superior Court No. 22514.

In the Matter of the Estate of Arthur J. Caire, 1942, Alameda Superior Court No. 81414.

In the Matter of the Estate of Fred F. Caire, 1950, Alameda Superior Court No. 114091.

In the Matter of the Estate of Helene Caire, 1929, Alameda Superior Court No. 45581.

In the Matter of the Estate of Maria Gherini, 1960, County of San Mateo Superior Court No. 29153.

In the Matter of the Estate of Justinian Caire, 1898, Alameda Superior Court No. 5540.

In the Matter of the Estate of Pier Gherini, 1989, Santa Barbara Superior Court No. 177668.

In the Matter of the Estate Edwin L. Stanton, 1963, Los Angeles Superior Court No. 470036.

Jones v. H. F. Ahmanson & Co. (1969) 1 Cal.3rd 93.

Pier Gherini et al. v. California Coastal Comm, (1988) 204 Cal.App.3d 699.

Peralta v. United States, 70 U.S. (3 Wall.) 434, 18 L.Ed. 221 (1866).

Rossi v. Caire, (1916) 174 Cal. 74.

Rossi v. Caire, (1919) 39 Cal. App. 776.

Rossi v. Caire, (1921) 186 Cal. 544.

Rossi v. Caire, (1922) 189 Cal. 507.

Sierra Club et al. v. Beattie et al., 1969, Santa Barbara Superior Court No. 86643.

Thomas Wallace More v. M. J. Box, Santa Barbara County District Court, 2nd Judicial District (1857).

United States v. Bolton, 64 U.S. (23 How.) 341; 17 Law Ed. 569. (1860).

United States v. Castillero, 64 U.S. (23 How.) 464; 16 Law Ed. 498 (1860).

United States v. Castillero, 67 U.S. (2 Black) 17; 17 Law Ed. 360 (1863).

United States of America ex rel. Chunie v. Ringrose et al. (9th Cir. 1986) 788 F.2d 638.

United States v. Title Insurance and Trust Co., (1924) 265 U.S. 472, 44 S.Ct. 621, 68 L.Ed. 1110 .

COURT DOCUMENTS

Affidavit of Arthur J. Caire, filed in *Capuccio v. Caire,* Santa Barbara Superior Court No. 10812.

Castillero transcript No. 176 in *Andrés Castillero v. United States,* 340 S.D., 1864.
Order in Nicholas Larco bankruptcy action, December 13, 1872.
Referee's Report in Partition of Santa Cruz Island prepared by F. F. Flournoy, George W. McComber, and H. J. Doulton, 1923-1924. County of Santa Barbara Superior Court, *Capuccio v. Caire,* No. 10812.
Reporter's Transcript in *Capuccio v. Caire,* Santa Barbara Superior Court No. 10812.
Transcript on Appeal in *Capuccio v. Caire,* Los Angeles Supreme Court No. 9165 (207 Cal. 200).
Transcript on Appeal in *Rossi v. Caire,* S.F. 7101 (174 Cal. 74). The original transcript is in the California State Archives.
Transcript of oral arguments of Frank P. Deering and Orrin K. McMurray in *Rossi v. Caire,* S.F. No. 9402, the original transcript is in the California State Archives.
Transcript of Proceedings in *Estate of Pier Gherini,* Santa Barbara Superior Court No. 177668, April 30, 1990.

STATUTES

California Penal Code Section 622½.
California Public Resources Code Section 5097.991.
Public Resource Section 21000, et seq.
Public Resources section 27000.
Public Law 96-199; Public Law 104-333.
United States Code: 16 U.S.C. 410ff-1.

RECORDED DOCUMENTS

Albina C.S. Caire et al. indenture to Santa Cruz Island Company, dated January 30, 1917, and recorded in Book 162, p. 491 in the Official Records of Santa Barbara County.
Albina C.S. Caire transfer of 45 shares of Santa Cruz Island Company was recorded on April 28, 1913, in Book of Deeds 139, p. 417 of the Official Records of Santa Barbara County.
Andrés Castillero indenture to William E. Barron was recorded on June 23, 1857 at Book B, p. 527 of the Official Records of Santa Barbara County.
Antonio Maria de la Guerra, as treasurer, indenture to Francisco de la Guerra (tax sale) was recorded on November 23, 1850, in Book B, p. 10 of Official Records of Santa Barbara County.
Augustus Hinchman and Maria Hinchman indenture to James B. Shaw was recorded on September 23, 1858, in Book C of Deeds, p. 83.
Capuccio memorandum of agreement with Freidenrich et al, January 28, 1921, recorded on June 14, 1929, in Book 181, page 579 of the Official Records of Santa Barbara County.
David Freidenrich, Jr.'s Indenture relinquishing any and all interest in the island to Ambrose Gherini was dated December 11, 1929, and was recorded on December 13, 1929, in Book 203, p. 203 of the Official Records of Santa Barbara County, California.
Decree entered on November 16, 1928, in *Rossi v. Caire,* San Francisco Superior Court No. 84070 and recorded on November 19, 1928, in volume 290, p. 54 of the Official Records of the City and County of San Francisco.

Eaton Quitclaim Deed was recorded on May 28, 1937, in book 398, p. 392 of the Official Records of Santa Barbara County.

Final Decree of Partition in *Capuccio v. Caire,* Santa Barbara Superior Court No. 10812 was recorded on December 4, 1925, in Book 81, p. 376 of the Official Records of Santa Barbara County.

Francis Gherini Gift Deed to Santa Cruz Island Foundation, recorded in the Official Records of Santa Barbara County on December 3, 1996.

Francisco de la Guerra and Concepcion de la Guerra indenture to James R. Bolton was recorded on December 31, 1851, in Book B, p. 43 of the Official Records of Santa Barbara County.

Gustave Mahé et al. indenture to Santa Cruz Island Company, recorded on March 29, 1869, in Book Y, p. 170 in the Official Records of Santa Barbara County.

Interlocutory Judgment filed in *Rossi v. Caire,* San Francisco Superior Court No. 84070 was recorded December 9, 1921, in vol. 173, p. 6 of the Official Records of the City and County of San Francisco.

James Barron Shaw indenture to Santa Cruz Island Company recorded on April 9, 1869, in Book of Deeds, pp. 80-81 of the Official Records of Santa Barbara County.

Judgment of Final Distribution filed on February 14, 1956, *In the Matter of the Estate of Ambrose Gherini,* County of San Mateo Superior Court No. 19005 and recorded as instrument number 3829 on February 28, 1956, Book 1364, p. 287 of the Official Records of Santa Barbara County.

Judgment of Final Distribution filed on July 23, 1962, *In the Matter of the Estate of Maria Gherini,* County of San Mateo Superior Court No. 29153 and recorded as document No. 44246, Book 1958, p. 116 in the Official Records of Santa Barbara County on October 22, 1962.

La Societé Francaise d'Epargnes et de Prévoyance Mutuelle, mortgage to William E. Barron was recorded in the Official Records of Santa Barbara County on September 14, 1869, in Book G, p. 732.

Lis Pendens recorded on June 9, 1923, in Book F (notice of actions), p. 56 in the Official Records of Santa Barbara County.

Memorandum of Agreements, dated January 28, 1921, between Aglae Capuccio and David Freidenrich and Ambrose Gherini recorded on June 14, 1929, in book 181, p. 579 of the Official Records of Santa Barbara County, and between Edmund Rossi and David Freidenrich and Ambrose Gherini recorded in book 181, p. 581 of the Official Records of Santa Barbara County.

Order authorizing Carey Q. Stanton as executor of the *Estate of Edwin L. Stanton, deceased,* Los Angeles Superior Court No. 470036. to exchange assets was entered on December 14, 1964, and recorded as instrument number 53510 at Book 2084, p. 291 of the Official Records of Santa Barbara County.

Order Authorizing Preliminary Distribution in the *Estate of Edwin L. Stanton* was entered December 14, 1964, and recorded as instrument number 53511 in Book 2084, p. 293 of the Official Records of Santa Barbara County.

Rossi and Capuccio deeds to David Freidenrich and Ambrose Gherini conveying fractional interest in the island were recorded on December 13, 1929, in Book 155, p. 332 and Book 202, p. 179 of the Official Records of Santa Barbara County.

Rossi and Capuccio indentures establishing the fractional interests of Ambrose Gherini were executed on October 26, 1926, and recorded on December 13, 1929 in Book 155, p. 332 and Book 202, p. 179 of the Official Records of Santa Barbara County.

Rossi deed to Maria Gherini, dated March 18, 1930, was recorded on September 13, 1932, in Book 269 p. 365 of the Official Records of Santa Barbara County.

Rossi memorandum of agreement with Freidenrich et al, January 28, 1921, recorded on June 14, 1929, in Book 181, page 581 of the Official Records of Santa Barbara County.

Santa Cruz Island Company indenture of May 21, 1900, to Edward R. Spaulding was recorded on June 6, 1900, in Book of Deeds, pp. 10-11 of the Official Records of Santa Barbara County.

Santa Cruz Island Company Deed of Trust securing the note ($65,000) was recorded on February 19, 1930, in Book 160, p. 1 of the Official Records of Santa Barbara County.

Santa Cruz Island Company Deed of Reconveyance was recorded on January 30, 1935, in Book 325, p. 96 of the Official Records of Santa Barbara County.

Santa Cruz Island Company Chattel Mortgage ($25,000) securing the loan was recorded on June 30, 1933, in Book 286, p. 109 in the Official Records of Santa Barbara County. The Discharge of the Chattel Mortgage was recorded on June 30, 1934, in book 313, p. 56 of the Official Records of Santa Barbara County.

Santa Cruz Island Company Deed of Trust securing the note ($30,000) was recorded on June 30, 1934, in book 314, p. 46 of the Official Records of Santa Barbara County.

Santa Cruz Island Deed of Trust securing the note ($110,000) was recorded on January 30, 1935, in book 327, p. 33 of the Official Records of Santa Barbara County.

Santa Cruz Island Company corporation grant deed to Edwin Stanton was recorded on April 22, 1937, in the Official Records of Santa Barbara in volume 396, p. 36.

Santa Cruz Island Company Mortgage securing the promissory note to Stanton was recorded in Book 391, p. 450 in the Official Records of Santa Barbara County.

Santa Cruz Island Company lease with Standard Oil Company of California was recorded on January 9, 1930, in Book 203, p. 358 of the Official Records of Santa Barbara County.

Thomas Gherini, as executor of *Estate of Pier Gherini,* warranty deed to United States of America was recorded on April 25, 1990, as instrument number 90-027494 in the Official Records of Santa Barbara County.

Thomas Jeffreys quitclaim of frame house at Prisoners' Harbor to Charles Fernald was recorded on November 12, 1852, in Deed Book A, p. 72 of the Official Records of Santa Barbara County.

United States of America patent to Andrés Castillero was recorded in the Official Records of Santa Barbara County on February 2, 1869, in Book A, p. 34 of Patents.

William E. Barron indenture of February 16, 1869, to Gustave Mahé et al., recorded on February 22, 1869, in Deed Book F of the Official Records of Santa Barbara County, p. 792.

UNPUBLISHED ARTICLES (COPIES IN AUTHOR'S POSSESSION)

Caire, Delphine Adelaide. "First Visit to Santa Cruz Island, 1880," excerpts from the 1933 Memoirs of Delphine Adelaide Caire.

Daily, Marla and Carey Stanton. "Santa Cruz Island, A Brief History of its Buildings, 1981."

Ehorn, William H. "The Establishment of Channel Islands National Park," April 1994.

Lima, James. "Historic Study Prisoners' Harbor Landing Site, Santa Cruz Island," February 16, 1994, unpublished report prepared for Channel Islands National Park.

Neuerburg, Norman. "The Painted Cross of Santa Cruz," July 1987.

UNPUBLISHED MEMORANDA (COPIES IN AUTHOR'S POSSESSION)

Capuccio, Goffredo Sr. 1912-1915.

Gherini, Ambrose. 1922 Deering Settlement memo; 1925 memo; 1937 memo

Gherini, Maria. unedited notes to Edward S. Spaulding, 1959.

Gherini, Pier. memos and notes.

NEWSPAPERS

Daily Alta California, April 27, 1857, May 25, 1858, October 26, 1871.

Goleta Gazette Citizen, December 2, 1965, December 16, 1965.

Golden Coast News, Oct. 22, 1964.

Lompoc Record, January 13, 1966.

Los Angeles Herald-Examiner, March 25, 1970.

Los Angeles Times, April 23, 1937, June 19, 1950, June 25, 1950, May 24, 1990, February 21, 1995, October 4, 1996, January 16, 1997, February 8, 1997, February 9, 1997, February 15, 1997.

New York Times, November, 1964.

Oakland Enquirer, December 11, 1897.

Oakland Tribune, April 4, 1965.

Sacramento Daily Union, June, 2, 1860.

San Francisco Bulletin, July 23, 1863.

San Francisco Call, December 10, 1897.

San Francisco Chronicle, October 8, 1911, February 21, 1995, October 4, 1996, December 11, 1996.

San Francisco Examiner, December 11, 1897, October 12, 1911.

Santa Barbara Daily, February 24, March 4, 1880.

Santa Barbara Daily Independent, March 21, 1885, May 11, 1894, June 26, 1885, June 26, 1893, June 21, 1990.

Santa Barbara Daily Press, March 29, March 30, 1880.

Santa Barbara Morning Press, March 26, 1893, May 5, May 7, May 18, 1893, May 23, June 28, 1893, February 9, 1902, April, 18, 1928.

Santa Barbara News-Press, April 23, 1937, August 28, 1945, January 16, 1949, March 26, 1961, April 17, April 20, 1963, October 14, October 29, 1964, November 1, 1964, June 20, 1965, January 9, 1966, January 13, 1966, March 9, 1966, March 10, 1966, January 10, January 11, 1976, September 1, 1984, August 19, 1986, July, 8, 1989, October 24, November 14, 1993, December 9, 1994, February 24, 1995, November 19, 1995, January 21, July 6, 1996, October 4, 1996.

Santa Barbara Post, February 17, 1869, March 3, 1869, May 5, 1869.
Ventura Star Free Press, July 7, 1989.
Ventura Star, June 19, 1996, October 4, 8, 1996, February 8, 1997.

PERSONAL INTERVIEWS/ORAL HISTORIES

Bergen, Richard. Interview by Marla Daily, March 11, 1992, transcribed by the Santa Cruz Island Foundation.

Caire, Justinian II. Interview by Marla Daily on November 14, 1981, transcribed by the Santa Cruz Island Foundation.

Craine, Red. Interview by John Gherini on September 13, 1983.

Daily, Marla. Interview by John Gherini, September 2, 1993, at Santa Cruz Island Foundation.

Devine, Diane Elfstrom. Interview by John Gherini on January 18, 1995.

Ehorn, William. Telephone interview by John Gherini on April 7, 1994.

Green, Ted. Telephone interview by John Gherini on January 4 and October 18, 1995.

Hansen, Robert. Telephone interview by John Gherini on September 13, 1994.

Huffman, Bill. Telephone interview by John Gherini on January 6, 1995.

Johnson, John. Field trip to Santa Cruz Island August 2-5, 1994.

Lagomarsino, Rick. Telephone interview by John Gherini on January 6, 1995.

Langel, Noel. Telephone interview by John Gherini, March 5, 1996.

Lea, Donna. Interview by John Gherini, March 15, 1996.

McComb, Francis. Interview by Marla Daily, September 1993, transcribed by the Santa Cruz Island Foundation.

McGinness, Ilda. Telephone interview by John Gherini, June 27, 1996, July 23, 1996.
_____. Interview by Marla Daily, July 3, 1995.

Owens, Jaret. Telephone interview by John Gherini on January 4, 1995.

Peterson, William C. Interview by John Gherini on February 22, 1996.

Peterson, Michel. Interview by John Gherini on March 15, 1996.

Pinney, Thomas. Interview by John Gherini and Marla Daily on April 23, 1993 at the Santa Cruz Island Foundation.

Ringrose, Marie Gherini. Unpublished interview by John Gherini, June 24, 1983.

Rossi, Edmund. Interview conducted by Ruth Teiser of the "Italian Swiss Colony and the Wine Industry," University of California, Bancroft Library, Berkeley, Regional Oral History, 1971, p.6.

Setnicka, Tim. Telephone interview, November 27, 1995, February 13, 1996.

Vail, Al. Interview by John Gherini on Santa Rosa Island on June 30, 1993.

Welborn, Dave. Field trip to Santa Cruz Island, September 1, 1994.

MISCELLANEOUS

Affidavit of Ambrose Gherini, April 7, 1938.

"Channel Islands, legislative background," October 1978 (National Monument, California).

Checklist of Vascular Plants of Channel Islands National Park (Tucson, AZ: Southwest Parks and Monument Association, 1987).

Coldwell Banker & Company listing , March 6, 1950.

Gherini, John, personal files regarding Santa Cruz Island acquisition by the National Park Service.

254

Hanson, Robert, "Sequence of events regarding elimination of feral sheep."

History of Italian Swiss Colony, published by the company, circa, 1915.

Peterson, Michel, "Once upon an Island." Unpublished manuscript.

Russell, George Vernon & Associates, "A Master Plan for the Gherini Ranch Development Santa Cruz Island," (June 1965). John A. Blum and Associates were consulting engineers.

Shaw, James Barron, dictated oral history, 1886. The transcript is located in Bancroft Library, University of California, Berkeley.

Staff Report of California Coastal Commission for application No 4-90-32, September 20, 1990.

Symmes, Leslie. "Santa Cruz Island, estimated operating cost and returns," 1922.

Symmes & Associates, "Report on Santa Cruz Island, Santa Barbara Co., California, 1922."

The New Encyclopaedia Britannica, 15th ed., "United States of America," vol. 29, p.177.

Witken, *Summary of California Law.* Ninth edition. vol. 4: San Francisco: Bancroft-Whitney Co, 1987.

DIRECTORIES

A.W. Morgan and Company. *San Francisco City Directory,* 1852. Pioneer Society of San Francisco has directories for years prior to 1859.

Bagget, Joseph and Company. *San Francisco Directory,* 1856.

Bishop, D.M. *San Francisco Directory, 1875.* (San Francisco, B.C. Vandall, 1875), p. 24A.

Colville, Samuel. *Colvilles's San Francisco Directory,* 1856-1857,

Crocker-Langley. San Francisco Directories for years 1898-1943, *San Francisco Directory,* 1897.

Langley, Henry. *San Francisco Directory.* 1863-1864, California Historical Society, San Francisco.

Lecount and Strong. *San Francisco Directory,* 1854.

River, Frank. *San Francisco Directory for 1854.* (San Francisco, CA: Lecount and Strong, 1854).

Santa Barbara City Directory, 1918-1938, Santa Barbara Directory Co., Santa Barbara Public Library.

LETTERS AND TELEGRAMS

Justinian Caire to Santa Barbara Tax Collector, November 14, 1892.

Justinian Caire to Maria Rossi Gherini, May 26, 1893.

P.C. Rossi to Goffredo Capuccio, August 30, 1906.

Aglae Capuccio to Ambrose Gherini, June 1, 1916.

Chicago Flexible Shaft Co. from Superintendent Swain, December 14, 1917.

Swain to Congressman E.A.Hayes, April 17, 1918.

Deputy Commissioner of Internal Revenue Service J. Hagerman to Ambrose Gherini, June 28, 1919.

Clifford McElrath to Ira Eaton, September 13, 1920.

Clifford McElrath to Santa Barbara County Sheriff James Ross, September 20, 1920.

Earle Ovington to Ambrose Gherini, April 17, 1928.

BIBLIOGRAPHY

Ambrose Gherini to Henry E. Monroe, December 7, 1929.
Ambrose Gherini to Oakland Title Insurance & Guaranty Co., April 21, 1930.
Edwin Stanton to Ambrose Gherini, December 5, 1938.
Ambrose Gherini to Paul F. Clark, President of John Hancock Mutual Life Insurance Co., April 16, 1947.
Ambrose Gherini to Lucius T. Hill of John Hancock Mutual Life Insurance Company, April 21, 1947.
Ambrose Gherini to Pier Gherini, April 29, 1947.
Ambrose Gherini to Pier Gherini, May 19, 1947
Ambrose Gherini to Pier Gherini, May 27, 1947.
Ambrose Gherini to Pier Gherini, April 7, 1948.
Joe Griggs to Ambrose Gherini, December 12, 1948.
Ambrose Gherini to Joe Griggs, December 15, 1948.
Ambrose Gherini to Malcolm Smith of Hughes Tool Company, June 22, 1949.
Ambrose Gherini to Robert Sudden, January 4, 1950.
Ambrose Gherini to Pier Gherini, January 9, 1950.
Ambrose Gherini to Pier Gherini, January 20, 1950.
Ambrose Gherini to Pier Gherini, February 17, 1950.
Ambrose Gherini to Pier Gherini, April 28, 1950.
Edwin L. Stanton to Ambrose Gherini, June 22, 1950.
Ambrose Gherini to Pier Gherini, October 24, 1951.
Ambrose Gherini to Pier Gherini, January 21, 1952.
Robert I. Hoyt to Edward S. Spaulding, July 21, 1959.
Julius Bergen of the Max C. Fleischmann Foundation of Nevada to Edward S. Spaulding, June 1, 1961.
Pier Gherini to Senator Thomas H. Kuchel, June 7, 1961.
Edwin Stanton, Pier Gherini and Edward Vail to State Senator John J. Hollister, Jr., telegram dated May 30, 1961.
Pier Gherini to Senator Claire Engle, January 22,1963.
Senator Claire Engle to Pier Gherini, April 10, 1963.
Pier Gherini to Secretary Stuart Udall, December 10, 1964.
William P. Clark, Jr., to County of Santa Barbara, January 5, 1966.
Dr. Carey Stanton to Congressman Charles M. Teague, June 9, 1966.
Captain G.F. Swanson, Marine Surveyor to Wm. H. McGee & Co., April 1, 1976.
Francis Gherini to Pier Gherini, January 10, 1978.
Frederick A. Richman to Santa Barbara County Assessor, July 24, 1978.
David D. Watts to Walter Alves, August 4, 1978.
Francis Gherini to Pier Gherini, February 1. 1979.
Francis Gherini to Pier Gherini, March 27, 1979.
J. Brian Atwood, acting Assistant Secretary for Congressional Relations, State Department to Honorable Robert J. Lagomarsino, July 26, 1979.
F.R. Breen of the Max C. Fleischmann Foundation to Thomas T. Macy of The Nature Conservancy, February 13, 1980.
Thomas T. Macy to F.R. Breen, February 29, 1980.
Pier Gherini to Graydon B. Hall, February 14, 1980.
Pier Gherini to Graydon B. Hall, February 18, 1981
Francis Gherini to Pier Gherini, May 13, 1981.

Francis Gherini to William H. Ehorn, July 1, 1982.

Pier Gherini to Graydon B. Hall, December 21, 1982.

Carey Stanton to David D. Watts, September 27, 1983.

Carey Stanton to Frank Boren, April 16, 1983.

Francis Gherini to Marie (Dini) Ringrose, January 1, 1984.

Francis Gherini to William Clark, Jr., Secretary of Interior, June 18, 1984.

Douglas L. Thorpe to David D. Watts, June 29, 1984.

M.L. Grier, Acting Director of the Park Service, to Francis Gherini, July 13, 1984.

Francis Gherini to Pier Gherini, July 23, 1984

Carey Stanton to David D. Watts, July 27, 1984.

Francis Gherini to Thomas Gherini, August 1, 1984.

David D. Watts to Frank D. Boren, January 10, 1986.

Francis Gherini to John Gherini, July 29, 1986.

Douglas L. Thorpe to Quin Denvir, November 26, 1986.

Francis Gherini to Stanley Albright, Regional Director of Western Region of National Park Service, August 14, 1989.

Roger M. Sullivan to Stanley T. Albright, August 16, 1989.

Lewis M. Baylor, Chief of Title Unit, Department of Justice to David A. Watts, Assistant Solicitor of Parks and Recreation, March 12, 1990.

Ralph Regula (R.Oh.) and Sidney Yates (D.Ill.) to Secretary of Interior Manuel Lujan, Jr., March 30, 1990.

Senator Robert C. Byrd to Lou Gallegos, April 20, 1990.

John Patton to Harvey Carlson of The Nature Conservancy, June 26, 1990.

Veronica L. Lanz to C. Mack Shaver, July 10, 1991.

Veronica L. Lanz to Jaret Owens, January 28, 1992.

Francis Gherini to Veronica L. Lanz, March 12, 1992.

C. Mack Shaver to Veronica L. Lanz, July 18, 1991.

Noel Langle to C. Mack Shaver, July 15, 1992.

C. Mack Shaver to John Gherini, June 30, 1993.

Francis Gherini to Mack Shaver, December 12, 1995.

Index

John Gherini. *Photo courtesy of Anne Marie Gherini.*

About the Author

John Gherini, born and raised in Santa Barbara, California, received his undergraduate and law degrees from the University of San Francisco. In 1972, he joined his father in private practice doing civil trial and appellate litigation and estate planning. Since his father's death in 1989, he works as a sole practitioner in the field of estate planning, probate and trust administration.

He served on the Marymount Academy Board of Directors for ten years. Currently, he is a member of the Board of Trustees of Santa Barbara Mission Archive Library and Bishop Garcia Diego High School. He has been on a number of advisory committees and presently is on the Advisory Council of the Santa Cruz Island Foundation.

Like his father, Santa Cruz Island has been a large part of his life. While growing up, he often traveled to the island on various boats and was on the *Hodge* when it sank in 1976. He spent time, particularly during summers, building and repairing fences, herding sheep, sacking wool, and doing other ranch work. After law school, he became involved in management of the Gherini Ranch and its many legal issues.

He and his wife, Mary Ann, and their three children: John (19), Anne (16) and Paul (6), continue to enjoy time spent on the island.

Santa Cruz Island: A History of Conflict and Diversity,
has been issued in an edition of 750 copies.
The text type is ITC New Baskerville;
display type is Sanvito.
Typesetting by Barbara Soles,
design by Robert A. Clark.
Printing and binding by Braun-Brumfield,
Ann Arbor, Michigan.